American Indian Warrior Chiefs

TECUMSEH · CRAZY HORSE · CHIEF JOSEPH · GERONIMO

JASON HOOK
Plates by RICHARD HOOK

Firebird Books

Acknowledgements

Many thanks to Badger and Dawn Kirby; and Mike Johnson. Also to Ellen Jamieson at the Heye Foundation's Museum of the American Indian and to Marty Miller at the Nebraska State Historical Society. Additional thanks too to all other individuals and organisations who assisted in providing references and illustrations.

First published in the UK 1989 by Firebird Books
P.O. Box 327, Poole, Dorset BH15 2RG
Reprinted 1990
Paperback edition 1990

Copyright © 1989 and 1990 Firebird Books Ltd.
Text copyright © 1989 Jason Hook

Distributed in the United States by
Sterling Publishing Co. Inc
387 Park Avenue South, New York, N.Y. 10016 8810

Distributed in Australia by
Capricorn Link (Australia) Pty Ltd
P.O. Box 665, Lane Cove, NSW 2066

British Library Cataloguing in Publication Data

Hook, Jason
   American Indian warrior chiefs : Tecumseh, Crazy Horse, Chief Joseph, Geronimo.
   1.   North American Indians.   Biographies.   Collections
   I.   Title
   920009297

ISBN 1 85314 103 8 (HARDBACK)
    1 85314 114 3 (PAPERBACK)

Series editor Stuart Booth
Designed by Kathryn S.A. Booth
Typeset by Inforum Typesetting, Portsmouth
Monochrome origination by Castle Graphics, Frome
Colour separations by Kingfisher Facsimile
Colour printed by Barwell Colour Print Ltd (Midsomer Norton)
Printed and bound in Great Britain by The Bath Press

Contents

Tecumseh

VISIONARY CHIEF OF THE SHAWNEE

Portrait of Tecumseh by Benjamin J. Lossing from about 1875. Lossing based the head upon a pencil sketch made from life at Vincennes in 1808 by a young French fur trader named Pierre Le Dru. Of Tecumseh's dress in the sketch, Lossing noted, 'he appears as a brigadier-general of the British army, and is from a rough drawing, which I saw in Montreal in the summer of 1858, made at Malden soon after the surrender of Detroit . . . When in full dress he wore a cocked hat and plume, but would not give up his blue breech-cloth, red leggings fringed with buckskin, and buckskin moccasins.' Note also the three small crosses suspended from the cartilage of Tecumseh's nose, and his George III peace medal, apparently inherited from an ancestor.

TECUMSEH'S 'OLD NORTHWEST'

But hear me: a single twig breaks, but the bundle of sticks is strong. Someday I will embrace our brother tribes and draw them into a bundle and together we will win our country back from the whites.

(Tecumseh speaking of the Greenville Treaty of 1795)

Uncommon Genius

As the fledgling European settlements in the North-east of North America grew in size, friendly contact with the native Americans inevitably dissolved into a bitter dispute for land. Among the tribes of the eastern Woodlands, and of the Old Northwest of settled America, there were a succession of Indian leaders with the vision and influence to unite the scattered tribes in concerted defence. Metacom of the Wampanoags, known to the whites as King Philip, forged the first great Indian alliance in 1675. Almost a century later, the Ottawa leader Pontiac again welded a number of Woodlands tribes together in a brief repulsion of the white man's burgeoning civilisation.

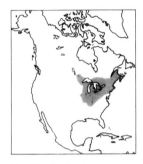

The Woodlands culture region.

No Indian, though, attempted to unite the tribes on the scale visualized by Tecumseh, the Shawnee chief and visionary. Repudiating tribal rivalries, Tecumseh conceived the Indians as a distinct people, not as a succession of divided nations. He attempted to unite not merely a few select tribes, but all the eastern Indians from Canada to the deep south. He denied any right of the whites to purchase land from whichever tribe would sell it, and insisted upon common ownership by all the Indians. By pursuing passionately his grand vision – that of a single Indian confederacy and even an American Indian state – Tecumseh embodied the eastern Indians' last hope of saving their culture.

His breadth of vision, the eloquence with which he recruited tribes to his cause, and his constant humanity towards his enemies earned him great respect from the Indians and whites alike. He is often spoken of as the greatest of all the remarkable chiefs to have emerged during the long struggle of the Indian Wars. One of his fiercest adversaries said of him:

The implicit obedience and respect which followers of Tecumseh pay him is really astonishing and more than any other circumstance bespeaks him one of those uncommon geniuses which spring up occasionally to produce revolutions and overturn the established order of things. If it were not for the vicinity of the United States, he would perhaps be the founder of an Empire that would rival in glory Mexico or Peru.

(General William Harrison)

The Shawnee

It is impossible to assign a specific location to the Shawnee, since they were among the most fragmented of tribes and moved to new areas with great frequency. Their name means 'southerners' and they demonstrated aspects of both Eastern and South-eastern Indian cultures.

Migration and Conflict

The Shawnee were first documented living in the Ohio Valley. Between 1662 and 1673, they were ousted from their homeland by frequent attacks from the powerful Iroquois tribes. In order to survive, the Shawnee split into a number of fragments, probably based on their five hinterland divisions; and scattered in various directions.

The history of Shawnee migrations in the 1600s is complex and obscure, but becomes clearer by the eighteenth century. A number of groups settled among the Delaware and Susquehannock tribes in Pennsylvania which became the major Shawnee territory in the early 1700s. They continued to live in the shadow of the powerful and dominant Iroquois. A second group established a permanent town among the Creek, first on the Chattahoochee River and later on the Tallapoosa River.

Iroquois intimidation and French promise of protection urged the Pennsylvania Shawnee westward; by 1731 some twelve hundred tribesmen occupied the Ohio headwaters. In 1735, the Hathawekela division precipitated a new series of complex migrations by taking flight after the killing of an Iroquois chief. Lower Shawnee Town was established on the Scioto before 1739, and by 1752 had become the tribal centre. The Shawnee were subsequently caught up in the French and British dispute for the Ohio Valley. The British treated them with contempt, and following General Braddock's defeat in 1755, they joined the victorious French. The Shawnee attacked frontier settlements in Pennsylvania and Virginia until the fall of Fort Duquesne restored the British presence in 1758. They then fought as allies of the British in the later years of the French and Indian Wars (1754–1763).

As the war drew to a close, the removal of the French threat opened the floodgates for settlers to invade the Kentucky and Ohio hunting grounds of the Shawnee. Also resentful of their mistreatment at the hands of the British, they joined the Indian uprising inspired by Pontiac in 1763. Following Pontiac's defeat, and the subsequent decline of the stabilising power of the Iroquois, the Shawnee faced open conflict with the settlers.

Tribe and Season

The Shawnee were divided into five patrilineal divisions, each traditionally having distinct political and ritual responsibilities. The Chillicothe (First Men) and Hathawekela (Eagle), each considered superior in power to the other divisions, were responsible for political affairs and

The cheaply-constructed, light but sturdy, smooth-bore, Northwest Guns enjoyed great popularity among the Indians, and were traded in vast quantities by the Hudson's Bay Company after 1750. With a large trigger guard to facilitate use by a mittened hand, and a distinctive serpent side-plate opposite the lock, the Northwest Gun was an impressive shock weapon at close range.

8

Beaded bag, typical of the Woodlands culture, attributed to Chief Tuskina of the Creek.

were expected to provide the tribal chief. The Mequachake (Red Earth) were responsible for medicine and health, and provided the priesthood. Tribal council and ritual were governed by the Piqua (Rising from Ashes) people. The Kishpokotha, a name of uncertain derivation, were Tecumseh's people; they were the war division of the Shawnee. The tribe was also divided into sub-groups according to the geographic location of its towns. These were related to the five divisions, since a town's chief was usually drawn from the division with the largest representation.

Each division had a peace chief and a war chief who made decisions, affecting all the Shawnee people, in a council that was advised by elders and presided over by the tribal chief. Chieftainship was often hereditary, though powerful men would naturally rise to influence regardless of their birthright.

Shawnee economy combined hunting, gathering and the raising of crops, and became strongly orientated towards the fur trade after the

Ojibwa-type Woodlands gunstock-club of about 1800. The steel blade is fixed in a flat-sided, wooden handle engraved with designs, including the panther, to invoke supernatural guidance from the warrior's guardian spirit.

early 1700s. A Shawnee town was built around a large council house, which was surrounded by bark-covered lodges resembling the longhouses of the Iroquois. To the south lay the town's fields, which were planted with corn and beans in April. This was accomplished by the women, who also gathered wild plants, while the men occasionally fished or hunted for deer. After the final harvest in August, all but the elderly and infirm left the town and made their way slowly towards their winter camp, situated in a sheltered valley. There, the men undertook the vital winter hunt, securing deer, buffalo, bears, wild turkeys and other game. From December to February they turned their attention to trapping small animals, particularly the racoon. Then, in March, the Shawnee returned to their summer towns, and the cycle began again.

Warfare and Weapons

When the civil and war chiefs councilled for war against a certain tribe, a tomahawk painted with red clay was circulated through the towns of the Shawnee and their allies. The war medicine of the Kishpokotha traditionally accompanied a war party, whose departure was preceded by a war dance. The killing of twelve deer was ceremonially undertaken immediately prior to the warriors attacking their enemy.

If the warriors returned triumphant, they recited their honours at the War Dance, before undergoing a four-day period of purification in the council lodge. Prisoners, painted black, were condemned to death, unless first claimed by the principal female peace chief. Captives were forced to 'run the gauntlet' between two lines of armed men and women; they suffered torture and were often burned to death. Seemingly, there existed a religiously motivated cannibal society, headed by four old hags, and whose members burned and devoured the warriors' prisoners. More fortunate captives were adopted into the tribe.

Traditional Woodland weapons were the bow and stone-tipped arrow, used silently at long range from the forest's excellent concealment. The stone tomahawk and war club were used for hand-to-hand fighting.

Wood was very plentiful and most warriors were adept at fashioning it into ferocious war clubs. The most typical form was the ball-headed club, carved from ironwood to resemble a human hand or animal claw clasping a round ball. Some two feet in length with protective medicine symbols carved into the handles, these smoothly finished clubs made formidable weapons.

By 1763, the French trading posts, and more increasingly those of the British, had radically altered the Woodland Indians' armoury. Bows were largely replaced by guns, available from Montreal traders in exchange for twenty beaver skins. Iron knives facilitated the carving of wooden clubs, but these were rapidly replaced by gun-stock clubs mounted with vicious metal blades, and by iron-headed tomahawks.

Gun-stock war-club of the Winnebago tribe before 1835, with iron blade and decoration of red, gold, green and mauve woollen tape. The eagle feather might also be a symbol of the Woodlands warrior's medicine.

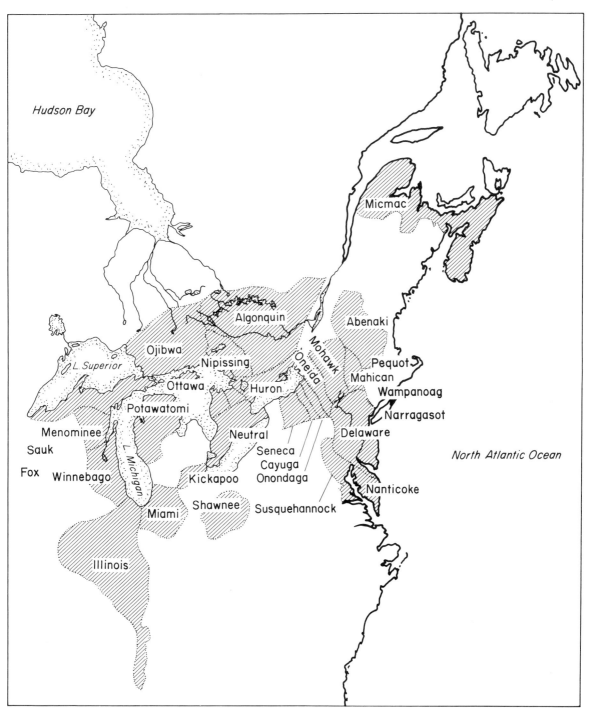

Major tribes of the North-east culture area – Tecumseh's 'Old Northwest'.

An early French trade gun, shipped to Canada in the eighteenth century. According to one story, early traders demanded beaver skins piled as high as the muzzle in exchange for a gun; and so they enjoyed high prices for long-barrelled pieces.

Shawnee warriors often carried special sashes, with which to secure captive prisoners about their necks. These ties were also decorated with medicine symbols, and were believed to give supernatural assistance in taking captives. Armour, used by some Woodland tribes, was not typically worn by Shawnee warriors. Instead, the Shawnee relied upon medicines and amulets such as herbs, animal skins and the feathers of birds to invoke supernatural protection.

Woodlands Welfare

The Shawnee believed that their welfare and indeed their universe was wrapped up in the 'sacred packs'. Each of the five divisions originally possessed one of these tribal bundles; buckskin cases containing various amulets and medicine symbols. Their sanctity was such that they were kept in separate lodges, treated like humans, and regularly shifted to ensure their comfort. Few spoke of them, to avoid desecrating their medicine.

The bundles were given to the Shawnee by Our Grandmother, the most prominent Shawnee deity. She created the Earth, and taught the Shawnee how to live. Through the bundles, She continued to control her children; and the bundles also provided the most sacred path to Her. Both the sacred packs and Our Grandmother were aspects of the ceremonial dances through which communal worship was made. The most important of these were the Spring and Fall Bread Dances. In these, twelve women (twelve being considered the sacred number) cooked meat, secured by twelve hunters, for a ceremonial feast; prayers and ceremonies were offered in a plea for plentiful game.

Shooting Star

Tecumseh was born in March 1768, at the Shawnee village of Piqua, on Mad River, about six miles south-west of present day Springfield, Ohio. His father was a Shawnee warrior named Puckeshinwa, which meant 'I alight from flying' or 'One who drops down'. Puckeshinwa's first wife had been a Creek Indian, but Tecumseh's mother was a Shawnee woman from among the Creeks. Called Methoataske, her name signified 'Turtle laying eggs in the sand.'

Puckeshinwa and Methoataske's first child, a son named Cheesekau,

Typical ball-headed club of about 1800, made from a single piece of wood, with iron blade and decoration of clipped feathers and red-dyed horsehair. Originally it would have been painted red, the colour of war.

had been born while the couple were living with a Shawnee group among the Creeks of eastern Alabama. Then, as these Shawnee migrated north, they had a daughter, Menewaulaakoosee, and another son, Sauawaseekau.

There are two versions of the circumstances of Tecumseh's birth. The first states that Tecumseh was born one of triplets. One of the three was deformed and died young. The other was called Laulewasika, and was destined to gain great fame under the name of 'the Prophet'. The second and more likely version states that Tecumseh alone was born in 1768, while the Prophet, possibly one of twins, was born three years later. A fifth son, Nehaaseemo, was born in the intervening years, and a seventh, Kumskaukau some time later.

Methoataske gave birth to Tecumseh in a hut specially erected near to the family's lodge. Mother and son stayed in the hut for ten days before the child's naming ceremony was held. At a feast given for the parents'

An early depiction of Tecumseh from an unidentified relief cut – thought to be after an original by Trenchard, after Bortram.

relatives, an old man named the boy Tecumseh (or Tekumthe) meaning 'Flying or Springing Across'. This, like his father's name, signified membership of the Great Lynx Clan, one of the patrilineal clans of the Shawnee. The name Tecumseh was consequently translated as 'Crouching Lynx', or 'Panther', or 'Shooting Star', the Shawnee equating a meteor with a springing lynx. Members of the Great Lynx clan were responsible for guarding the rear of a returning war-party, the most dangerous position.

From his father, Tecumseh also inherited a place in the Kishpokotha division of the Shawnee. Responsible for warfare, this group were 'always inclined to war and gave much trouble to the nation'. The war chief of the tribe was expected to be a member of both the Great Lynx Clan and the Kishpokotha division. Clearly, Tecumseh's very lineage directed his life towards war.

Cornstalk's Example

Though the Royal Proclamation of 1763 had prohibited white settlement west of the Appalachians, the Iroquois ceded Kentucky to settlers in the year of Tecumseh's birth. Virginia's colonial governor, the Earl of Dunmore, granted Shawnee land to veterans of the French and Indian Wars, and there were growing clashes as the Shawnee defended their hunting grounds. In 1774, frontiersmen brutally murdered thirteen Shawnee and Mingo (displaced Iroquois tribesmen) in a series of unprovoked attacks. The victims' relatives formed a war-party which killed an equivalent number of settlers, though the Shawnee, unable to secure allies, refrained from formally going to war.

This attack, though, precipitated Lord Dunmore's War. A militia of 1500 men marched from Virginia and destroyed a Shawnee town in the Muskingum Valley. The Shawnee appealed to the Iroquois League for help but only the Seneca chief Logan rallied to their cause. While

A conical lodge, covered with bark, used alongside the domed wigwam and substantial long-house as a home in the Eastern Woodlands.

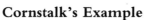

Iroquois pipe-tomahawk, symbol of both peace and war.

Dunmore led another force from Fort Pitt, Pittsburgh, Andrew Lewis led a column through the Kanawha Valley. In an attempt to defend the Scioto Valley, the Shawnee, led by the chief Cornstalk, made a surprise dawn attack on Lewis' force at Point Pleasant on 6th October 1774. The battle raged throughout the day, and the Virginians lost 50 dead and 100 wounded before the Shawnee succumbed. Tecumseh's father Puckeshinwa and eldest brother Cheesekau, fought courageously and survived the battle of Point Pleasant.

In November, Cornstalk met Lord Dunmore at Chillicothe, and signed a treaty of peace. He recognised the Ohio River as the southern boundary of Shawnee territory, leaving Kentucky open to settlement. Cornstalk received great recognition for his generalship at the Battle of Point Pleasant. He also demonstrated his outstanding ability as an orator when appeasing those tribal factions that opposed the treaty. The young Tecumseh regarded Cornstalk with awe, and would himself demonstrate the same qualities in later life.

While Cornstalk diligently enforced the treaty, the white settlers disregarded it and continued to invade the Shawnee lands in Ohio. That year, a party of frontiersmen surprised Puckeshinwa in the woodlands near the Piqua settlement, and shot Tecumseh's father dead. His body was apparently found by Tecumseh and his mother, Methoataske, who instructed her young son to become a warrior like his father: 'a fire spreading over the hill and valley, consuming the race of dark souls.'

Such incidents drove the Shawnee towards war, and in 1777, Cornstalk took his son to Point Pleasant, to warn the settlers of the unrest. The chief and his son were taken prisoner, and shortly afterwards were murdered by soldiers in retaliation for the killing of a white settler. The Shawnee would seek vengeance for this outrage in a war that lasted nearly twenty years.

Tecumseh was adopted by Blackfish, leading chief of the main Shawnee settlement, Chillicothe. Having seen the white men cut down his father and Cornstalk, Tecumseh travelled between the Chillicothe and Piqua settlements, learning the lore of his people.

An Eastern Woodlands pipe-tomahawk, with engraving commemorating the killing of a European.

Cowardice and Courage

The Shawnee were inevitably drawn into the border wars of the American Revolution (1775–83). Even the peace faction joined the war against the settlers after the murder of Cornstalk; and alliance with the British simply furnished them with arms. American settlements came under frequent attacks from the start of the Revolution, and in 1776 the Shawnee joined a delegation of Delaware and Mohawks in recruiting Cherokee, Creek, Choctaw and Chickasaw to the British side. Tecumseh was to turn to these southern tribes when he sought support for his own wars some years later.

In 1778, the American general Edward Hand led a force from Fort Pitt

Typical Shawnee bead necklace. Like all such artefacts, its function was religious and decorative.

which destroyed Shawnee villages as far north as the Sandusky River. Major George Roger Clark's army of Kentuckians and Virginians also seized a number of Indian villages on the Ohio, and in 1780 destroyed the Chillicothe and Piqua settlements. The legendary frontiersman Daniel Boone had been captured with twenty-six other whites when Blackfish attacked Kentucky settlements in 1778. He was imprisoned at Chillicothe but later escaped his Shawnee captors. Also in 1780, a large number of Shawnee warriors joined loyalist Colonel William Byrd's 1000-strong Indian army in destroying the Kentucky settlements of Ruddle's and Martin's Stations, inflicting a heavy defeat on a force of Kentucky militia.

The destruction of their villages caused further migrations among the Shawnee. One group, the Hathawekela, travelled south to avoid conflict with the Americans, settling among the Creek possibly as early as 1774. Another group, primarily made up of the Kishpokotha and Piqua, migrated westward to escape the hostilities in 1780. Eventually, they settled in Missouri between the Mississippi and Whitewater Rivers, in Spanish territory. Tecumseh's mother, Methoataske, is believed to have travelled with this group. Tecumseh was left in the care of his brother Cheesekau, and remained with the Ohio Shawnee who rebuilt the Piqua settlement on the Miami River. Even this slight migration reflected the way in which American settlement was pushing the tribes ever westward.

Before he was thirteen, Tecumseh was probably sent out into the woodlands to seek a vision of supernatural assistance from some sacred helper. A Shawnee boy undertook this vision quest at an unusually early age compared with the other central Algonquin tribes, sometimes as young as seven years old. With his face blackened by charcoal, the vision-seeker fasted alone for up to four days, watching for some indication of his sacred power or 'medicine'. It is known that Tecumseh received a vision of the Buffalo, which procured him a powerful war medicine.

As a boy, Tecumseh distinguished himself in his early training as a warrior, and took responsibility for arranging his comrades into sides for sham battles. His courage and vigilance are said to have been keenly developed at an early age. When he was first tested in real warfare, though, Tecumseh was found severely wanting. At the age of fifteen, in 1783, he joined Cheesekau in a skirmish on the banks of the Mad River. When the engagement began, and blood started flowing, Tecumseh turned tail and ran. That night he lay in his lodge thoroughly ashamed of his cowardice. The momentary weakness, though, steeled rather than broke him, and Tecumseh would never again run from an enemy.

The Treaty of Paris in 1783 made no provision for the Indian population. As the British withdrew from along the Ohio, the Shawnee continued to clash with the settlers in the Old Northwest. The numerous

Tecumseh, wearing Kishpokotha war-bundle split feather plumes, with his face blackened for war, harangues 5000 Indians at the Creek town of Tukabatchi, October 1811, seeking to weld together his confederacy.

tribes of the Ohio country held a great council on the Sandusky in 1783, and formed an Indian confederacy to 'defend their country against all invaders'. They took up arms to protect their boundary on the Ohio River, attacking the supply boats that navigated its waters and the wagon trains moving west from Fort Pitt.

Tecumseh overcame his earlier indiscretion and participated boldly in the Shawnee attacks which imperilled every flatboat that carried settlers down the Ohio from Pennsylvania. When aged about seventeen, he showed great prowess in one such attack, which took place above present day Maysville. All the settlers were killed except one, who was taken prisoner. The captive of Tecumseh's war-party was painted black and detained in the village for one night. The following day, he was tied by a vine to a white oak sapling, and the warriors tortured him to death with burning brands. Tecumseh, a silent spectator, was horrified by the inhumanity of the act; he considered it dishonourable to the name of a warrior and simply barbaric in content. Rather than brooding on the matter, Tecumseh expressed his views to the other warriors with such eloquence and passion that they resolved to abandon the practice. The fact that the Shawnee adhered to this promise, refraining thereafter from burning captives, bears testimony to the prodigious powers of oration possessed already by the seventeen-year-old Tecumseh. He continued to display the same humanity and compassion throughout his life, his standing among the whites being greatly enhanced when he saved a number of white prisoners from torture and death.

Shawnee tomahawk with pierced design and decoration of trade tacks and blue cloth.

Little Turtle's War

By the age of twenty, Tecumseh had risen to a position of prominence among his people, leading many war-parties against the Americans. He continued to show great bravery in battle, and on one occasion escaped a seemingly impossible situation with a masterly charge, cutting his way through the ranks of Americans that surrounded him.

One autumn, possibly in 1788, Tecumseh participated in a buffalo hunt, and was thrown from his horse. He suffered a severely broken thigh, which left him with a shortened, disfigured leg, and a limp when walking. Slowly recovering the following spring, but finding himself unable to keep pace with a war-party, Tecumseh apparently despaired of becoming a successful warrior and hunter to the extent of once trying to kill himself.

About 1789, Tecumseh made the first of the many journeys that were to elevate him above the tribal and clanship rivalries and that so distinguished his life. Still recovering from his leg injury, he joined Cheesekau in riding to his mother's Shawnee village in Missouri. He also visited the

Tenskwatawa, clutching his 'medicine-fire', urges on Tecumseh's alliance of Woodlands warriors in the ill-fated assault upon General Harrison's militia at Tippecanoe, 3.45 a.m., 7th November 1811.

Shawnee of southern Illinois and the Miami tribe in Indiana. Later in the year, together with Cheesekau and their mother, Tecumseh joined a party of Kickapoo Indians travelling south to join the Creek and Cherokee. Having fully recovered from his fall, Tecumseh joined the Creek in fighting American settlers, before returning north.

Cheesekau was killed by white men in a skirmish on the Tennessee frontier in 1789, and Tecumseh bitterly answered the call of the Miami chief Michikinikwa – Little Turtle – to unite against the Americans. President George Washington had ordered General Josiah Harmar to lead an expedition to pacify the Old Northwest, and Little Turtle raised a force of Miami, Shawnee, Potawatomi, and Chippewa to meet him. Little Turtle was supported by Blue Jacket of the Shawnee and Buckongahelas, a Delaware chief. In 1790, Harmar, a heavy-drinking, ill-disciplined general, led 1400 men – 1100 of them being militia – north from Fort Washington, Cincinnati. Little Turtle, an astute commander, retreated slowly up the Maumee valley, burning the occasional village to feign a desperate rout. In September, with Harmar drawn deep into the woodlands, the Indians turned and outflanked the disorganised Americans. Tecumseh joined the two ambushes which saw 183 soldiers killed and 31 wounded. Harmar retreated, claiming a victory, while Little Turtle watched him go.

Routing the Militia

A new American expedition was organised in March 1791, comprising about 2000 men, again largely militia purchased 'from prisons, wheelbarrows and brothels at two dollars a month.' It was led by General Arthur St. Clair, Governor of the North-West Territory and a hero of the American Revolution. Like Harmar, St. Clair had no experience of fighting Indians. As he led his men towards the Miami and Wabash Rivers, Tecumseh's scouts harried his flanks and reported his movements. St. Clair was suffering so severely from gout that he had to be borne on a litter. His 600 regular soldiers had to guard the supply train from the ill-fed militia; by November, some 600 men had deserted.

Reaching high ground on the upper Wabash on 3rd November, St. Clair relaxed his defences – and the following dawn, Little Turtle struck. Emerging silently and suddenly from the forest with Tecumseh at their head, the Indians routed the outlying militia men, and attacked St. Clair's artillery. With smoke choking the air, St. Clair mounted several bayonet charges; but the Indians simply melted back into the woodlands and picked off the greenhorn troops.

Completely surrounded, and with half his men dead, St. Clair ordered the retreat, battling through the Indian lines to effect it. The Indians pursued the army for four miles, but the rout continued clear to Fort Jefferson, twenty-nine miles away, with many men discarding their guns. Tecumseh had been a prominent figure in this, the worst ever

Powder-horn of white manufacture, with brass and wood fittings, attached by leather thong to a finger-woven woollen sash; from the Great Lakes region around 1780. The Great Lakes Indians had woven sashes of hemp and animal hair since prehistoric times and readily adapted the technique to the white man's coloured yarns.

disaster suffered by the Americans in the Indian Wars; 630 soldiers were killed and a further three hundred wounded. Not surprisingly, settlement of the Old Northwest slowed to a cautious trickle.

Tecumseh continued to harass any who dared to settle on his lands. In May, 1792, he led an attack against the family of John Waggoner. Waggoner outran the limping chief, but his wife was killed and their children captured and adopted into the Shawnee tribe. Shortly afterwards, a party of twenty-eight whites led by renowned frontiersman Simon Kenton assailed a group of Shawnees led by Tecumseh. Though accompanied by only ten warriors, Tecumseh drove off the Americans after a ferocious fight.

Later in the year, Tecumseh again journeyed south, replacing his brother in the southern Shawnees, and leading their allies, the Creeks and Cherokee, against the settlements near Nashville. His reputation grew quickly among the tribes of the south-eastern states, and he formed many friendships upon which he could call in later life.

Fallen Timbers and the Greenville Treaty

Between the autumns of 1792 and 1793, the U.S. Army General-in-Chief 'Mad Anthony' Wayne drilled and disciplined a select force of over 3000 troops at Legionville and Washington. The Government made peace overtures to the Indians at the 1793 Sandusky Conference, but after the chiefs insisted upon recognition of the Ohio as their eastern boundary, Wayne took to the field.

Following St. Clair's route, Wayne first established Fort Recovery near Greenville, Ohio, and then Fort Adams at the mouth of the Auglaize in the summer of 1794. Little Turtle and Tecumseh led an attack against Fort Recovery, but it was repelled. Little Turtle shrewdly recognised the calibre of his new adversary and advised the Indians to seek peace with this 'chief who never sleeps'. Unheedingly, the warriors ousted him in favour of the less able Turkey Foot.

Wayne, whom the Indians called 'Black Snake', pursued the Indians north to the British post of Fort Miami, where the Indians rejected a new offer of peace. On 20th August 1794, Wayne led a surprise attack against the Indians at Fallen Timbers, on the Maumee River. Tecumseh's party of scouts met the initial charge of the infantry, and bore the brunt of the fiercest fighting. Tecumseh's courage was again outstanding and he continued to rally the Indians the width of the battlefield even after his rifle jammed. When the Indians were overwhelmed and thrown into retreat, Tecumseh led a small party in capturing a field-piece. They cut free the horses harnessed to the gun, and rode them to safety.

The Indians, most of whom carried British weapons, fled to Fort Miami; but the soldiers there, in fear of Wayne, refused to open the gates. Only 38 Americans fell in the fighting, while several hundred Indians including another of Tecumseh's brothers, were killed. Wayne laid

Knife and knife-sheath of the Eastern Great Lakes region, before 1800. The iron-bladed knife, a trade item, has a brass handle inlaid with tortoiseshell. Its elaborate leather sheath illustrates the intricacy of Woodland quillwork – dyed porcupine quills sewn with sinew – before the increased use of trade beads. The strap is also decorated with quills wrapped around leather thongs.

waste to the Indian villages before establishing Fort Wayne in Indiana at the confluence of the St. Joseph and St. Mary Rivers.

Wayne wintered at Greenville, where he called the tribes to council in the spring of 1795. A thousand Indians, with chiefs representing twelve different tribes, attended, and conferred for two months. On 3rd August, they signed the Greenville Treaty, ceding most of Ohio, a portion of Indiana, and more distant enclaves including Detroit, to the United States in exchange for annuities of $10,000. The treaty concluded the last throes of the Revolution and a Wyandot chief reflected that, 'we . . . acknowledge the fifteen United States . . . to be our father . . . (and) must call them brother no more.'

Blue Jacket signed for the Shawnee, and the Miami also accepted American rule as Little Turtle touched the pen. He declared: 'I am the last to sign it, and I will be the last to break it.' True to his word he remained a proponent of peace, and became a celebrity among the white settlers.

Tecumseh was furious with the chiefs, recognising that the treaty would simply open up the Northwest to ever greater settlement. He did not attend the council, and refused to accept its conclusions. Splitting with Blue Jacket, Tecumseh led a faction of warriors west to the Wabash drainage, and became the leading hostile chief in the region. He declared the Greenville Treaty worthless:

My heart is a stone: heavy with sadness for my people; cold with the knowledge that no treaty will keep the whites out of our lands; hard with the determination to resist as long as I live and breathe. Now we are weak and many of our people are afraid. But hear me: a single twig breaks, but the bundle of twigs is strong. Someday I will embrace our brother tribes and draw them into a bundle and together we will win our country back from the whites.

Rebecca Galloway

Finding support among the Delaware, Tecumseh resided in Indiana until about 1805. In 1796, he married a half-breed woman named Manete who bore him a son shortly before their quarrels caused her to leave. The boy was called Puchethei, meaning 'crouching or watching his prey', again signifying membership of the Great Medicine Lynx clan.

Just before the end of the eighteenth century, Tecumseh met and formed a close friendship with Rebecca Galloway, the beautiful blonde daughter of an Ohio farmer. They met frequently, and Rebecca taught her eager student to speak English fluently, and to read the Bible and great literary works such as Shakespeare. Tecumseh also learned World history, and Rebecca told him of the great white leaders of the past like Alexander the Great and Julius Caesar. Possibly in light of this new knowledge, he considered the attempts of Pontiac to unite the Indian tribes, and his plans for building an Indian confederacy matured. Rebecca's teaching also confirmed in Tecumseh's mind the belief that all Indians held common ownership of the land, and that no one tribe had the right to sell it.

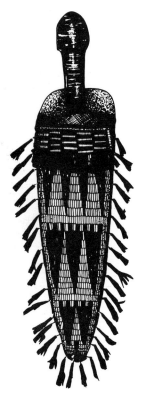

This Northern Ojibwa-type knife and sheath of about 1800 demonstrates the Indians' fusion of European culture with their own. The horn-handled iron blade is held in a leather sheath lined with birch-bark, which is decorated with typical quillwork, horsehair fringes, glass beads, green wool, and brass cones.

The compassion for which Tecumseh was already famous, was enhanced by his relationships with the Galloway family. Rebecca was also naturally fascinated by Tecumseh's way of life, and, according to one tale, pressed the Shawnee chief on the medicinal effects of a certain flowering tree. Tecumseh purportedly told her:

The red man takes the powder of the flowers and leaves . . . into battle with him. If the bullet bites or the arrow pierces, the potion quiets the pain. If the warrior falls in battle, it eases him. What you had in your hand, the fruit, is best. With it, the pain of the fire at the stake is little. If wounded the warrior can be removed to a place of safety without pain. The powder is as powerful to quiet pain as your opium is, but does not do the harm it has done. No paleface knows its power. It is our secret.

(W.A. Galloway)

Tecumseh eventually proposed marriage to Rebecca, who, with her father's permission, consented on condition that Tecumseh abandoned his Indian ways and lived like a white man. For a month Tecumseh deliberated, before sadly leaving Rebecca, telling her that he could never abandon his people.

Buffalo and Bundle

A new threat to the Shawnee lands was meanwhile engendered by the formation in 1800 of Indiana Territory, creating political machinery for administering the land west of Ohio. General William Henry Harrison became Governor of Indiana, and was also given the rôle of Superintendent of Indian Affairs. As such, Harrison, an ambitious and capable administrator as well as a notable soldier, became a life-long adversary of Tecumseh.

About this time, Tecumseh received a new vision from his guardian spirit, the Buffalo, in which he was taught a sacred war dance. This Buffalo Dance is still performed by the Shawnee, and by the Delaware, among whom Tecumseh was living at this time. Participants invoke the Buffalo's power by painting a buffalo-head design on their chests, and a red line from the corner of each eye, and performing a simple dance imitating the buffalo's movements. The power of the dance was such that it was quickly adopted by the Shawnee and introduced to other tribes by Tecumseh during his later travels.

Tecumseh also became responsible for the sacred pack of the Kishpokotha Shawnee division, one of the five treasured, esoteric tribal bundles. The 'Tecumseh bundle' as it has become known, contained four plumes of hawk feathers; a wooden image of a man in Shawnee costume, with tiny bow and arrows; two turkey feather roach headdresses; and, according to myth, the flesh and bones of the Giant Horned Snake, a Shawnee deity. The bundle was opened for the tribal war ceremonies, and Tecumseh's possession of it reflects his standing in the tribe. He even added his own talisman to the pack, an ancient trefoil-

A Woodlands badger-skin medicine bag adorned with eagle talons, quills, beads, ribbons and bells, probably Ojibwa of about 1800. The badger was a protective spirit to the Midewiwin or Medicine Lodge Society. This was an esoteric priesthood, found among many of the Woodlands tribes, including Tecumseh's Shawnee, who possessed an occult knowledge of killing and curing. It was demonstrated at annual ceremonies, with the use of herbs, medicine bundles and the magical 'shooting' of a cowrie shell into the patient's body. The badger has been spiritually resurrected by the eagle talon 'horns'.

shaped steel tomahawk, which became an integral part of the bundle's ceremonies.

Tecumseh's medicine attained great renown, and one Winnebago informant remembered him as 'a powerful man. Bullets could not penetrate him, and indeed it was impossible to kill him in any way.'

The Prophet

During this period, contact with white civilisation had a further detrimental effect upon the Shawnee and other tribes of the region. Traders opened negotiations and bidded for trade by offering liberal quantities of whiskey, to which many Indians became wretchedly addicted. Tecumseh shrewdly preached abstinence, and Colonel John Johnston described him at the time:

Sober and abstencious; never indulging in the use of liquors, nor catering to excess; fluent in conversation, and a great public speaker. He despised dress, and all effeminacy of manners; he was disinterested, hospitable, generous and humane – the resolute indefatigable advocate of the rights and independence of the Indians.

The carved otter – running across the top of this ball-headed club – was a frequent addition to such weapons invoking the Woodlands' warrior's supernatural guardian in battle.

One of the worst drunkards, though, was Tecumseh's brother, Laulewasika, a powerful man whose loss of one eye gave him a gruesome appearance. His name meant 'Rattle', and he was said to possess a belt which he could transform into a rattlesnake. Laulewasika was unpopular and feared as a young man, and Thomas Forsyth recalled of him: 'When a boy he was a perfect vagabond and as he grew up he would not hunt and became a great drunkard.'

In 1805, Laulewasika fell into a trance, and awoke claiming to have spoken with the supreme deity, the Master of Life. He changed his name to Tenskwatawa, meaning 'The Open Door'; and in November, at a tribal council at the ancient capital of Wapakoneta, Ohio, he pronounced himself the Prophet.

Tenskwatawa preached against the adoption of the white man's way of life, his tools, clothes and weapons. In particular he condemned the use of alcohol that had so corrupted his own early life. Tenskwatawa promised the return of divine favour if the Shawnees returned to their traditional way of life. He also, rather curiously, proscribed use of the medicine bundles, songs and dances that were such a prominent feature of Shawnee culture. While intended to combat evil witchcraft, this rule also encompassed the traditional medicines and ceremonies of the Indians, and therefore met with strong opposition. It did, though, provide a medium through which Tenskwatawa could challenge those who opposed the rest of his doctrines.

Amongst a people whose way of life was severely threatened by the encroaching white civilisation – and delivered by such a wily preacher –

Tenskwatawa's religion quickly became popular among the Shawnee and their neighbouring tribes. Like the Delaware Prophet of Pontiac's time, Tenskwatawa created a religious movement which could be harnessed by Tecumseh for his own needs. Tenskwatawa inspired the fanaticism and became the figurehead of a movement of which Tecumseh gradually assumed control.

After Wayne's victory, the Indians had been divided into small groups who fought sporadically and individually to halt the continued invasion of their lands. In 1805, Tecumseh took his followers to Greenville, Ohio. There, he attempted to use the revitalization movement of his brother to re-unify the tribes, on the very site of the treaty signing that had divided them.

Tenskwatawa, Open Door, the Shawnee 'Prophet', painted in Washington by Henry Inman around 1830. The costume and likeness are accurate, corresponding to George Catlin's portrait of the Prophet, and the ear-rings and nose ornament are typical Shawnee.

Medicine of Prophecy

Tenskwatawa inevitably accompanied his preaching with claims to be

23

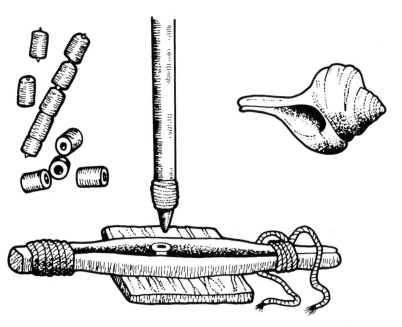

able to perform prophecy, healing and other supernatural feats. He travelled to distant tribes proclaiming his abilities, and teaching a ceremony closely related to the War Dance of Tecumseh. Amongst the Creek and Cherokee, followers of the Prophet anticipated a terrible hailstorm engulfing the whites and Indian unbelievers, from which Tenskwatawa would lead the faithful to safety. The Prophet also predicted that after four years, a blanket of darkness would cover the land, and the people's dead would be restored to them. He also foresaw the reappearance of plentiful game, in a doctrine with notable similarities to the Ghost Dance that would sweep the Plains in 1890.

As Tenskwatawa's popularity grew, and word of his abilities spread as far as the central Canadian Plains, Harrison attempted to quell the religious fervour. He told one tribe:

If he is really a prophet ask him to cause the sun to stand still, the moon to alter its course, the rivers to cease to flow, or the dead to rise from their graves. If he does these things you may then believe he has been sent from God.

The Prophet answered any doubts raised by Harrison, by calling a large assembly at Greenville and proclaiming that he would darken the face of the Sun. Shortly before noon, 16th June 1806, Tenskwatawa gestured triumphantly at the sky, as the sun was slowly eclipsed by the moon. 'Did I not speak the truth? See, the sun is dark!' he cried, as the Indians stared in terror at the sky and knew in their hearts that the Prophet must be holy.

The miracle of the eclipse spread Tenskwatawa's fame to the remotest tribes, from the Ottawa and Ojibwa, south to the Creek and Cherokee, and west as far as the Ponca, Mandan, Blackfoot and Sioux. Tenskwatawa and his agents travelled extensively to secure new disciples for his religion, and warriors for Tecumseh's wars. The Prophet carried sacred slabs, pictographic slats depicting his deities, which he presented to the war chiefs of the tribes. He also possessed a 'medicine fire' of feathers and beads to symbolise the 'eternal fire', an ancient Shawnee symbol. He called upon the Indians he visited to resurrect the tradition of maintaining an eternal fire in their lodge, and warned that should it die, they would die with it. Sacred strings of discoloured beans were also a prominent symbol of Tenskwatawa's medicine, and were said to contain the Prophet's own flesh. Tenskwatawa instructed his followers to swear their allegiance to him by running these beans through their hands, in a ceremony known as 'shaking hands with the prophet.'

Tenskwatawa's most striking medicine, though, was a life-size representation of a corpse, described in 1830 by George Catlin:

He carried with him into every wig-wam that he visited, the image of a dead person of the size of life; which was made ingeniously of some light material, and always kept concealed under bandages of thin white muslin cloths and not to be opened; of this he made great mystery, and got his recruits to swear by touching a sacred string of white beans, which he had attached to his neck or some other way secreted about him. In this way, by his extraordinary cunning, he had carried terror into the country as far as he went; and had actually enlisted some eight or ten thousand men, who were sworn to follow him home . . .

Tenskwatawa also supervised a more practical terrorising of the Indians, when his followers purged those who opposed the Prophet's teachings. In the spring of 1809, a Kickapoo man was denounced as a witch and burned to death for refusing to surrender his medicine bundle. Several Delaware suffered the same fate, as did Leatherlips, the Syandot *sachem* or chief. The bloodshed was eventually halted by the intervention of Tecumseh, who also encouraged the Indians to abandon those chiefs who were too friendly towards the Americans; but through peaceful methods.

Prophet's Town

Tecumseh now conceived the idea of welding the divided tribes into a mighty alliance, though which to defend their lands. Tenskwatawa later told Catlin that:

Tecumseh's plans were to embody all the Indian tribes in a grand confederacy, from the province of Mexico, to the Great Lakes, to unite their forces in an army that would be able to meet and drive back the white people, who were continually advancing on the Indian tribes, and forcing them from their lands towards the Rocky Mountains.

Tecumseh insisted that the land was held in common by all the Indians, and that no single tribe had the right to independently sell its hunting grounds. His brother's creed held practical value to Tecumseh, for he knew that only by abandoning trade for the Americans' guns, tools,

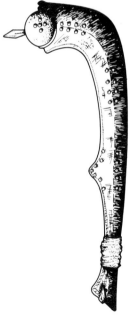

Ball-headed club, adorned with brass tacks and wood spikes. This example from the Great Lakes, 1800–50.

25

cloths and whiskey could the Indians hope to protect their independence. As early as 1806, he formed a powerful alliance with Roundhead, the leader of the most war-like Wyandot warriors.

In 1808, Tecumseh and Tenskwatawa established a settlement called Prophet's Town at the confluence of the Wabash and Tippecanoe Rivers. Apparently, the Miami tribe resented this intrusion into their hunting grounds; many of their chiefs were killed by Tenskwatawa's followers. This reduced the Prophet's popularity, so that while the Americans regarded him as the leader of the movement, Tecumseh was gradually assuming control.

That same year, Tecumseh made the first of his epic journeys to address tribes throughout the Old Northwest and the South, from the head of the Missouri down to Florida. Many of the old chiefs resisted his call to arms, preferring to preserve the Greenville Treaty, but most of the young warriors were excited by his plans for an Indian confederacy. Tecumseh cajoled great crowds with his exceptional oratory, and spoke privately with those chiefs of greatest influence. To the west he gained support from the Sauk and Winnebago tribes. To the south Creeks, Cherokees and Seminoles found new heart in his flowing speeches. Returning north, Tecumseh tried in vain to gain the support of the powerful Iroquois. By 1810, a thousand warriors were gathered at Prophet's Town, drawn from the Shawnee, Kickapoo, Delaware, Potawatomi, Ottawa and Chippewa tribes.

Vincennes

Tecumseh returned to Prophet's Town to discover that Harrison, in his bid to secure Indiana's statehood, had persuaded a number of chiefs to sell more of the Indian land. Harrison had met the older representatives of the Delaware, Miami and Potawatomi tribes at Fort Wayne, in the summer of 1809. Plying them with alcohol and sweet words, he persuaded the chiefs to sign the Treaty of Fort Wayne. This ceded three million acres of land, extending in a sixty-mile strip up the Wabash from Vincennes, in exchange for $7000 and an annuity of $1750. Tenskwatawa had failed to oppose the treaty; but Tecumseh, on his return, was outraged. His claim that the land was the Indians' common property was justified in this case; the three signatory tribes had sold land to which they had no claim. He refused to recognise the treaty, and, in his fury, even threatened to kill the chiefs that had touched the pen.

When Harrison learned of the displeasure at Prophet's Town, he dispatched a messenger to Tenskwatawa, who he still believed to be the leader of the Indians there. It invited him to Vincennes, assuring him 'that any claims he might have to the lands which had been ceded, were

not affected by the treaty; that he might come to Vincennes and exhibit his pretensions, and if they were found to be valid, the land would be either given up, or an ample compensation made for it.'

Opening Speeches

In August of 1810, Tecumseh arrived at Vincennes at the head of four hundred warriors, much to the alarm of the Americans. One officer present described Tecumseh as, 'one of the finest men I have ever met – about six feet high, straight with large, fine features and altogether a daring, bold-looking fellow.'

On 12th August, Tecumseh and some forty warriors met Harrison in a large portico erected before the governor's house. Harrison approached Tecumseh, and told him, 'Your father requests you to take a chair.'

With great indignation, Tecumseh walked away and sat on the ground in the shade of some trees, declaring, 'My father? The Sun is my father, and the earth is my mother, and on her bosom I will repose.'

Then the Shawnee chief addressed the council in his native language, which was translated with difficulty by the interpreter:

It is true that I am a Shawnee. My forefathers were warriors. Their son is a warrior. From them I only take my existence; from my tribe I take nothing. I am the maker of my own fortune: and, oh, that I could make that of my red people, and of my country, as great as the conceptions of my mind, when I think of the Spirit that rules the Universe! I would not then come to Governor Harrison, to ask him to tear up the treaty, and to obliterate the landmark; but I would say to him, 'Sir, you have liberty to return to your own country.'

The being within, communing with past ages, tells me, that once, nor until lately, there was no white man on this continent. That it then all belonged to red men, children of the same parents, placed on it by the Great Spirit that made them, to keep it, to traverse it, to enjoy its productions, and to fill it with the same race. Once a happy race. Since made miserable by the white race, who are never contented but always encroaching.

The way, and the only way, to check and stop this evil, is for all the red men to unite in

A pipe, with sandstone bowl. Although this example is from the Naskapi tribe of the sub-Arctic, smoking the pipe was a ritual practice among most of the tribes including Tecumseh's confederation – the smoke carrying a prayer up to the spirits. It was an activity which often preceeded councils and medicine ceremonies.

claiming a common and equal right in the land, as it was at first, and should be yet; for it was never divided, but belongs to all, for the use of each. That no part has a right to sell, even to each other, much less to strangers; those who want all, and will not do with less. The white people have no right to take the land from the Indians, because they had it first; it is theirs. They may sell, but all must join. Any sale not made by all is not valid. The late sale is bad. It was made by a part only. Part do not know how to sell. It requires all to make a bargain for all. All red men have equal rights to the unoccupied land. The right of occupancy is as good in one place as in another. There cannot be two occupations in the same place. The first excludes all others. It is not so in hunting or travelling; for there the same ground will serve many; as they may follow each other all day; but the camp is stationary, and that is occupancy. It belongs to the first who sits down on his blanket or skins, which he has thrown upon the ground, and till he leaves it no other has a right.

As Tecumseh seated himself upon the ground once more, Harrison stood up and replied:

The white people when they arrived upon the continent, had found the Miamies in the occupation of all the country on the Wabash, and at that time the Shawanese were residents of Georgia from which they were driven by the Creeks. That the land had been purchased from the Miamies, who were the true and original owners of it. That it was ridiculous to assert that all the Indians were one nation, for if such had been the intention of the Great Spirit he would not have put six different tongues into their heads, but have taught them all to speak a language all could understand. That the Miamies found it for their interest to sell a part of their lands, and receive for them a further annuity, the benefit of which they had long experienced, from the punctuality with which the seventeen fires (U.S. states) complied with their engagements; and that the Shawanese had no right to come from a distant country and control the Miamies in the disposal of their own property.

(Harrison's *Memoirs*)

As the interpreter explained this, Tecumseh replied furiously: 'Sell a country! Why not sell the air, the clouds and the great sea as well as the earth? Did not the Great Spirit make them all for the use of his children?'

Harrison attempted to placate the Shawnee chief by referring to the 'uniform regard to justice' demonstrated towards the Indians by the Americans. At this Tecumseh leapt to his feet, his eyes blazing with anger, crying: 'It is all false! Tell him he lies!'

An official ordered a lieutenant to summon reinforcements, muttering, 'This fellow means mischief, you'd better bring up the guard.'

Tecumseh's warriors now picked up their war-clubs and gathered around their chief. Harrison, upon learning that he was being called a liar, drew his sword to defend his honour. He calmly told the Shawnee leader, 'that he was a bad man – that he would have no further talk with him – that he must now return to his camp, and take his departure from the settlements immediately'. Tecumseh led his warriors away, and bloodshed was avoided.

Lesson on a Bench

The following day, Tecumseh sent apologies for any affront, and asked that the council be reconvened. Harrison consented, but guarded the

subsequent meeting with two companies of militia. At this council Tecumseh seated himself beside Harrison on a bench. He denied ever having intended to attack the governor, and excused his conduct by explaining, according to Harrison's memoirs, that he had been ill-advised by two white men; possibly British representatives or political opponents of the Governor.

As he explained all this, Tecumseh shuffled along the bench, forcing Harrison to do the same. When the Governor asked Tecumseh whether he would prevent a survey of the land, the chief declared his intention to 'adhere to the old boundary.'

Chiefs from the Wyandot, Kickapoo, Potawatomi, Ottawa, and Winnebago tribes all stood up to voice their support; while Tecumseh forced Harrison further along the bench. The Governor informed the Indians that their words would be conveyed to the President, but that the treaty lands would be defended by the sword. Now Tecumseh pushed along the council bench until Harrison protested that he was about to be shoved off. Thus, Tecumseh explained, laughing, the American settlers were forcing the Indians from their lands.

The following day, Harrison attempted to conciliate Tecumseh by meeting him in his own camp. He explained that the President would probably not comply with the chief's wishes, and Tecumseh replied:

Well, as the great chief is to determine the matter, I hope the Great Spirit will put sense

Nineteenth century Shawnee moccasins decorated with green, beige and red silk ribbon.

29

enough into his head to induce him to direct you to give up this land. It is true, he is so far off, he will not be injured by the war. He may sit still in his town and drink his wine, while you and I will have to fight it out.

Before leaving Vincennes, Tecumseh insisted that he would wage war to defend his land, saying, 'nor will I give rest to my feet until I have united all the red men in the like resolution.'

Harrison addressed to the War Department Tecumseh's complaint 'that the Americans had driven them from the sea-coasts, and that they would shortly push them into the lakes, and that they were determined to make a stand where they were.' Harrison himself found Tecumseh's grievances 'sufficiently insolent and his pretensions arrogant.' He further illustrated his attitude six weeks later when he spoke of the Indian land of the Old Northwest:

Is one of the fairest portions of the globe to remain in a state of nature, the haunt of a few wretched savages, when it seems destined, by the Creator, to give support to a large population and to be the sea of civilisation, of science, and true religion?

Forging the Alliance

Tecumseh once more travelled the eastern Woodlands of America to reaffirm the unity of his confederacy. In November of 1810, he ventured into Canada and pleaded for support from the Ottawa, Sauk, Fox, Potawatomi, Winnebago and Menominee tribes.

Then, in July of 1811, some settlers were killed by Potawatomi Indians in Illinois. Harrison, seizing his chance to take the offensive, summoned Tecumseh to Vincennes once more. Harrison insisted that the Indians responsible for the murders were followers of Tenskwatawa, and demanded that they be turned over at once. Tecumseh refused, and set out with twenty-four warriors the next day, to summon the Southern tribes to the war he knew now to be imminent. Tenskwatawa was dispatched back to Prophet's Town with instructions to avoid premature conflict with the Americans.

Tecumseh now made an epic six-month tour of the eastern and south-eastern tribes, visiting the tribes living in Mississippi, Georgia, the Carolinas, Alabama, Florida and Arkansas. He found growing support among the young warriors, but faced vociferous opposition from the older chiefs, grown fat on their government annuities. Generally, he found his dream of confederacy ill-prepared for war. Nevertheless, he persisted, with magnificent displays of oratory, beseeching the tribes to support him.

In Florida, Tecumseh found great support among the Seminole, and gave their chiefs bundles of red-painted sticks. He directed that after he sent word to them, they should cast away one stick each day. When they had disposed of all the markers, they would know that the time was right for a simultaneous attack against the Americans by all the tribes supporting Tecumseh. From this practice, the tribe gained the nick-name of Red Sticks in the Seminole Wars.

Converting the Creek

Travelling up to Alabama, Tecumseh urged the Creek to join his confederacy and take up arms with the Seminole. His visit had a lasting effect upon Creek culture; he introduced one of his sacred war dances to the tribe, which was eagerly adopted and renamed the 'Dance of the Lakes'. At a large Creek council, Tecumseh addressed the Indians with his customary passion and eloquence:

Where today are the Pequot? Where are the Narragansett, the Mohican, the Pokanoket, and many other once powerful tribes of our people? They have vanished before the avarice and oppression of the White Man, as snow before a summer sun.

Will we let ourselves be destroyed in our turn without a struggle, give up our homes, our country bequeathed to us by the Great Spirit, the graves of our dead and everything that is dear and sacred to us? I know you will cry with me, 'Never! Never!'

In October 1811, at Tukabatchi, a Creek town on the west bank of the

Shawnee water drum and drum-stick, used to accompany ceremonial and social dances. The drum's adornments identify it as belonging to the Hathawekela (Eagle) division of the Shawnee.

31

Tallapoosa River, a council of 5000 Indians heard Tecumseh's war-like rhetoric:

Accursed be the race that has seized on our country and made women of our warriors. Our fathers from their tombs reproach us as slaves and cowards. I hear them now on the wailing winds . . . the spirits of the mighty dead complain. Their tears drop from the wailing skies. Let the white race perish. They seize your land, they corrupt your women, they trample on the ashes of your dead. Back whence they came upon a trail of blood, they must be driven.

At the lodge of the influential Tukabatchi chief Menawa or Big Warrior, Tecumseh made another speech designed to fan the flames of Creek hatred towards the whites. Menawa feigned approval and Tecumseh presented him with a bundle of red sticks, a piece of wampum, and a tomahawk, to symbolise the Creek chief's allegiance to the Shawnee. Then, looking into Big Warrior's eyes, and reading his actual intentions, Tecumseh declared:

Your blood is white. You have taken my talk, and the sticks, and the wampum, and the hatchet, but you do not mean to fight. I know the reason. You do not believe the Great Spirit has sent me. You shall know. I leave Tukabatchi directly – and shall go straight to Detroit. When I arrive there, I will stamp on the ground with my foot, and shake down every house in Tukabatchi.

As Tecumseh departed, the followers of Big Warrior began to count with dread the days until they estimated the Shawnee chief would arrive in Detroit. On that fateful day, the famous earthquake of Madrid shook every house in Tukabatchi to the ground, and the Creek murmured in terror, 'Tecumseh has got to Detroit.' This extraordinary miracle, which was testified to by Big Warrior's followers, was tangible proof of Tecumseh's great powers of prophecy; and the Creeks hurriedly took up their rifles to support him.

Tecumseh continued north, trying to piece together his visionary union. One of his orations was witnessed by Captain Sam Dale, a Mississippi Indian fighter:

'His eyes burned with supernatural lustre, and his whole frame trembled with emotion. His voice resounded over the multitude – now sinking in low and musical whispers, now rising to the highest key, hurling out his words like a succession of thunderbolts . . . I have heard many great orators, but I never saw one with the vocal powers of Tecumseh.'

Ashes of Prophet's Town

In the fall of 1811, some Indians stole the horses of an army dispatch rider. Harrison saw this as an opportunity to assail Prophet's Town, and break the power of the Indians, which had been growing alarmingly. Encouraged by Tecumseh's absence, Harrison determined, 'that that part of the fabric which he considered complete will be demolished and even its foundations rooted up.' Raising a militia of some 1000 men, Harrison marched up the Wabash towards Prophet's Town. Tenskwata-wa's emissaries met him on 6th November, and asked to council the

At General Brock's side, Tecumseh leads the British forces into the captured city of Detroit, wearing a brigadier-general's scarlet overcoat and with Brock's own pistols in his sash.

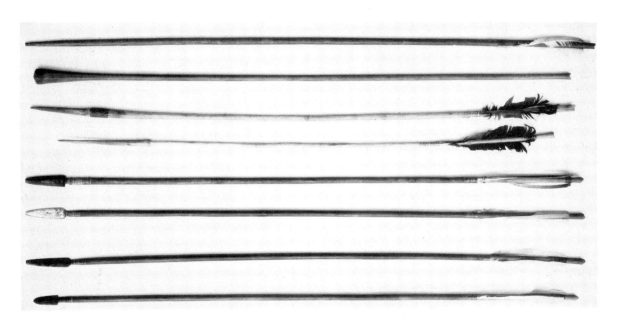

A collection of arrows from the Oklahoma Shawnee. The top one measures 31 inches.

following day. Harrison agreed and camped on Burnet's Creek, three miles from the village. Fearing treachery, though, he wisely ordered his men to sleep in a circular formation, their guns beside them.

Tenskwatawa was distracted from his brother's warnings by the urging of a militant group of Winnebago warriors. He ordered an immediate attack, telling his followers that his medicine would make the white men as harmless as sand, and their bullets as soft as rain. Indeed, he proclaimed, many of the Americans were already dead. Crawling on their bellies, nearly 1000 Indian warriors advanced upon Harrison's camp before dawn.

At 3.45 a.m. on 7th November, 1811, a sentry spotted the warriors and discharged a shot before he was cut to the ground. The soldiers awoke to find bullets whistling amongst them, the Indians having broken their line in two places. Harrison master-minded a desperate defence until the Indians were driven off. The warriors mounted a series of furious charges throughout the night, but the inexperienced militia held firm, behaving, according to Harrison, 'in a manner that can never be too much applauded.' Harrison's commanding voice resounded above the noise of battle; meanwhile Tenskwatawa apparently skulked on a hill beyond the range of fire.

By dawn, the attacks had ceased. Sporadic fire continued throughout the day, but by nightfall the warriors had drifted silently away. Sixty-one soldiers had been killed, and twice as many wounded; Indian casualties were slightly lighter. On 8th November, Harrison found Prophet's Town abandoned, and burned it to the ground; along with Tecumseh's precious stores.

Tecumseh returned to Prophet's Town early in 1812, to find his

In his native deerskins, Tecumseh is shot down by Colonel Johnson's Kentuckian Cavalry while leading his Indians and faltering British troops in a last desperate charge at the Battle of the Thames, 5th October 1813.

brother and a diminished band of followers living among the ashes. Since Tenskwatawa had predicted that his medicine would assure an easy victory at the Battle of Tippecanoe, his credibility was now destroyed. Tecumseh was furious with him for having launched a premature attack. After shaking him by the hair and threatening to kill him, Tecumseh cast his brother into exile. With his religion discredited and without his brother's guidance, Tenskwatawa's influence quickly dwindled.

As Tecumseh had feared, the Indian tribes now sought vengeance independently, raiding the American settlements without Tecumseh to unify them. In despair, Tecumseh himself later recalled:

I stood upon the ashes of my own home . . . and there I summoned the spirits of the braves who had fallen in their vain attempt to protect their homes from the grasping invader, and as I snuffed up the smell of their blood from the ground I swore once more eternal hatred – the hatred of an avenger.

The War of 1812

As the Indian attacks spread panic among the settlements, American anger was directed increasingly at the British in Canada, whom the Americans believed to be fermenting Indian unrest. Border disputes and arguments over shipping rights also developed, and on 18th June 1812, the United States declared war on Great Britain.

Agents from both powers now sought the help of the Indians, and Tecumseh was unquestionably the most influential chief at this time. Quickly, he seized this last opportunity to unite the Indians, announcing to a large tribal council:

Here is a chance . . . a chance such as will never occur again: for us Indians of North America to form ourselves into one great combination and cast our lot with the British in this war. And should they conquer and again get the mastery of all North America, our rights to at least a portion of the land of our fathers would be respected by the King. If they should not win and the whole country should pass into the hands of the Long Knives – we see this plainly – it will not be many years before our last place of abode and our last hunting ground will be taken from us, and the remnants of the different tribes between the Mississippi, the Lakes, and the Ohio River will all be driven toward the setting sun.

Travelling to Fort Malden, Tecumseh pledged his support to the British. Attracted by his great name, and by the additional strength of his British allies, the Indian tribes at last came together into the confederacy he had conceived so many years before. Some tribes continued to attack the American settlements independently, but many rallied to Tecumseh's side. At Brownstown alone, American intelligence reported 1630 warriors drawn from the Shawnee, Winnebago, Kickapoo, Sauk, Potawatomi, Ottawa, Delaware, Seneca, and Ojibwa tribes. William Jones of the Indian Department recalled that 'as nearly as I can recollect there were about 10,000 souls, exclusive of children at the breast,' gathered in

The wool bunting British flag said to have been given to Tecumseh when he was made a brigadier. The gift, from Sawa Banashe (Yellow Hawk), was then handed down as an heirloom.

scattered bands about the British posts. Many camped on Grosse Isle on the Detroit River, following Tecumseh.

'We are indebted . . . much more to the Chief Tecumthe for our Indian arm,' said Britain's Colonel Proctor. 'He convinced the Indians that our cause was theirs and his influence and example determined and fixed the Wyandots whose selection determined every tribe.' Later he remarked 'Tecumseh's example and talents governed the councils of his brethren.'

In recognition of those talents, the British gave Tecumseh independent command of the Indian forces, with the Indian Department providing advisers to the 2000 warriors. Tecumseh was given a regular commission as a brigadier general, an extraordinary rank to be attained by a tribal leader.

Capture of Detroit

In July 1812, American General William Hull led 2200 men from Detroit to invade Canada. Hull had been a daring officer in the Revolution, but had grown nervous and, some said, senile. His ponderous advance was harried on both flanks by Tecumseh's Indians; slowly, he was forced to a halt.

Then on 4th August, Hull dispatched 200 men southward under Major Vanhorn. Their task was to meet and escort a supply convoy travelling under Captain Brush from the River Raisin. Tecumseh intercepted Vanhorn near Brownstown and his Indian warriors killed twenty soldiers. The rest were sent scurrying back to Hull but not before Tecumseh captured the American general's dispatches. Hull, alarmed at this break in his supply line, hurried back across the border to Detroit. This action only served to increase the troops' contempt for him. On 8th August, a new relief column of 600 men under Colonel Miller ventured south. In a bloody engagement at Monguaga, south of Detroit, they clashed with a large body of Indians led by Tecumseh and the famous Sauk chief Black Hawk. Tecumseh fought bravely, receiving a wound in the leg, but the Americans forced the Indians and their British allies to cross over into Canada once more.

On 13th August, 300 British reinforcements arrived at Fort Malden, Amherstburg, under Major General Isaac Brock. Brock was a pleasant but powerful officer, and Tecumseh and he quickly developed a close friendship and a mutual admiration. When Tecumseh suggested an immediate attack on Detroit, Brock, perceiving Hull's nervousness, agreed, overruling his own officers in the decision. Tecumseh demonstrated his detailed knowledge of the area by furnishing Brock with a hastily drawn map, etched on a piece of bark.

Brock said of Tecumseh, 'A more gallant warrior does not . . . exist,' and presented the Shawnee chief with an engraved compass, his pistols, and his officer's sash. When Brock saw Tecumseh the next day without the sash, he asked if he had displeased him. Tecumseh replied that, not wishing to wear such a mark of distinction when an older, more accomplished warrior was present, he had passed the sash on to his lieutenant the Wyandot chief Roundhead.

When Hull refused Brock's call for surrender, Tecumseh led his warriors across the river under the cover of the British guns. Hull had sent a new relief force south towards Brush's convoy, and Tecumseh quickly cut them off from Detroit. Brock meanwhile allowed a courier to be captured, who told Hull that 5000 Chippewa would shortly arrive to support the British. As Brock led 700 troops across the river, Tecumseh marched his 600 Indian warriors three times through a clearing, to convince the Americans that the Chippewa had arrived.

Hull was fooled. On 16th August, without consulting his officers, and with his men planning to mutiny in order to continue the fight, the frightened old commander raised the white flag. He surrendered to a force half the size of his own.

Tecumseh marched proudly into Detroit, wearing a red cap topped with a single white-tipped eagle-feather, blue breechcloth, red leggings fringed with buckskin, and buckskin moccasins. About his shoulders was the British dress-coat of his rank, and around his neck a silver medal.

Hindrance of Proctor
After the capture of Detroit, Tecumseh's followers ravaged the Old

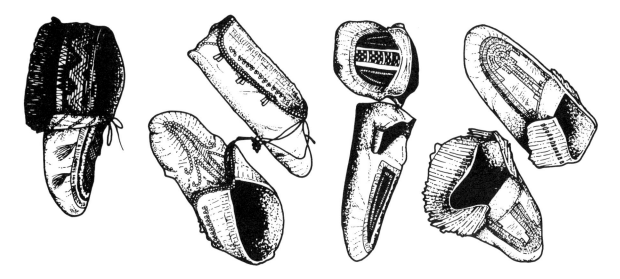

Northwest, capturing a number of American outposts. In the fall of 1812, Tecumseh found time to travel south again, and may have played some part in inciting the Creek War of 1813.

Brock had been killed in October 1812 and replaced by the far less able Colonel Henry Proctor, who would hinder Tecumseh's efforts constantly. General Harrison meanwhile took charge of the Second Northwestern Army, and led 1100 men north. On the Maumee River he built Fort Meigs, near the site of the Battle of Fallen Timbers. Tecumseh returned to Fort Malden in April, having instigated the mustering of some 4000 warriors, from the Shawnee, Sauk, Fox, Kickapoo, Winnebago, Menominee, Ojibwa, Wyandot, Delaware, Ottawa, Potawatomi, Miami and even the Sioux.

In April 1813, a British force of 2500 approached and besieged Fort Meigs under the command of Proctor and Tecumseh. When the fort held firm, Proctor chose to invest rather than storm it. His hesitancy, reminiscent of Hull, infuriated Tecumseh, and allowed the Americans to send for vital reinforcements.

On 5th May, some 1100 Kentuckians under General Greenclay emerged from the forests, taking the British completely by surprise. The militiamen in their eagerness broke ranks and charged into the British. The redcoats and Tecumseh's Indians made an incisive counter-attack, and surrounded the entire force. Nearly 500 of the Kentuckians were killed, and 150 captured.

While Tecumseh remained at the siege lines, the Kentuckian prisoners were marched down-river to Proctor's headquarters at Fort Miami. Here, twenty of them were tomahawked to death and scalped by the Indians in two hours of savage butchery. Proctor turned a blind eye, until Tecumseh suddenly arrived, his horse coated in sweat. Drawing his knife and tomahawk, Tecumseh plunged in to the Indian ranks and

Typical, highly-decorated, Woodlands skin moccasins, adorned with quillwork, beadwork, animal hair and metal cones. The Cree, who made moccasins from caribou and moose skin, estimated that each man used ten pairs a year.

37

Wampum was woven into belts (top) *to signify tribal authority and to represent treaty signings, both between tribes and with the whites. A predominantly dark purple belt symbolised sadness and death, and therefore probably a declaration of war. The ringed 'pouch' designs* (lower) *are less typical.*

brought the carnage to an immediate halt. Tearfully, he admonished, 'Oh, What will become of my Indians!'

Seeking out the Colonel, Tecumseh demanded to know why he had not prevented the slaughter. 'Sir,' Proctor replied, 'Your Indians cannot be commanded.'

With utter disdain, Tecumseh replied, 'Be gone! You are unfit to command; go and put on petticoats!'

Following an unsuccessful attempt to destroy Harrison's stores at nearby Fort Stephenson, Proctor grew weary of the campaining. In late July, he withdrew to Fort Malden on the Canadian side of the Detroit River, much to Tecumseh's disgust. Harrison was delighted, however, for it gave him precious time in which to build up a stronger army, which numbered 4500 men by September.

On 10th September 1813, the British Fleet on Lake Erie under Lieutenant Barclay was defeated by the American Navy led by Captain Perry. This cut the British supply line to Fort Malden, and – as Harrison prepared to march from Fort Meigs – left Proctor with no alternative but to retreat. For the next thirteen days, Proctor prepared for a retreat which he knew would be very unpopular among his Indian allies. Unfortunately, the timid commander did not have the courage to inform Tecumseh of the situation, and slyly concealed all plans for the retreat from the Indians for as long as possible.

On 13th September, Proctor ordered the dismantling of Fort Malden, to be executed quietly so as not to alarm the Indians! Tecumseh, whose rank alone gave him every right to be informed of Proctor's secret orders, inevitably discovered the commander's duplicity, and demanded that a council be held. On 18th September, the Indian chiefs gathered in the centre of Amherstburg council room. Around its walls stood the British officers, who declared their intention to retreat. In response,

A nineteenth century painting believed to be of Tecumseh.

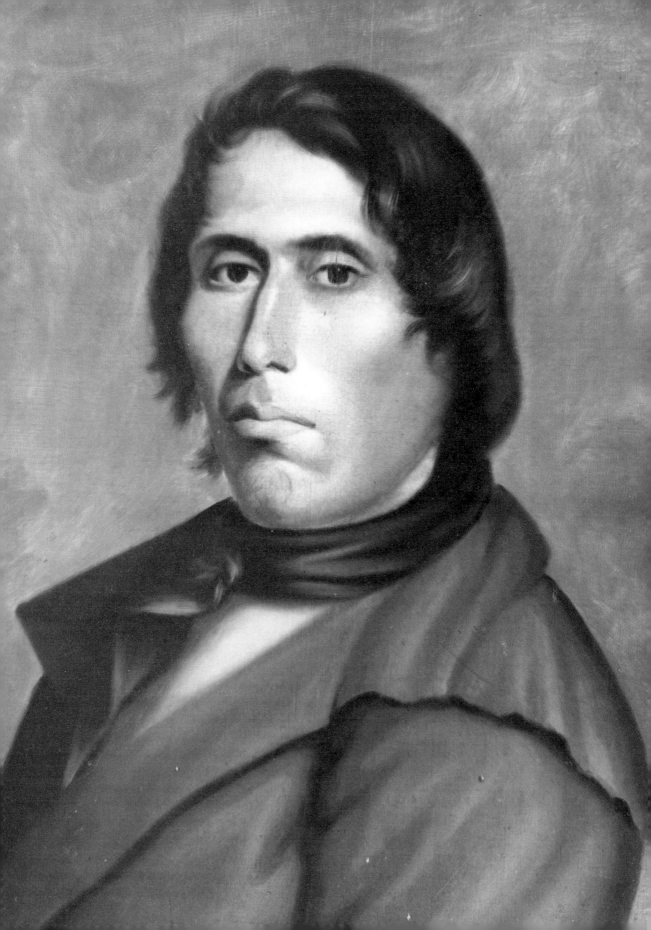

Tecumseh stood up clutching a belt of wampum; and delivered a devastating speech. He concluded:

Father, listen! Our fleet has gone out, we know they have fought; we have heard the great guns; but know nothing of what has happened to our Father with one arm (Barclay). Our ships have gone one way, and we are much astonished to see our father tying up everything and preparing to run the other; without letting his red children know what his intentions are. You always told us to remain here and take care of our lands; it made our hearts glad to hear that was your wish. Our Great Father, the King, is the head and you represent him. You always told us that you would never draw your foot off British ground; but now, Father, we see you are drawing back, and we are sorry to see our Father doing so, without seeing the enemy. We must compare our Father's conduct to a fat animal that carries its tall, bushy tail upon its back; but when affrighted, it drops it between its legs and runs off.

While Tecumseh delivered his speech, one witness recalled, 'the darkness of his complexion and the brilliancy of his black and piercing eye, gave a singularly wild and terrific expression to his features. It was evident that he could be terrible.' There was muffled laughter at Proctor's expense as the interpreter translated Tecumseh's last sentence, before he continued:

Listen Father! The Americans have not yet defeated us by land; neither are we sure that they have done so by water; we therefore wish to remain here, and fight our enemy should they make their appearance. If they defeat us we will then retreat with our Father. At the battle of the Rapids (1794) the Americans certainly defeated us; and when we retreated to our Father's fort at that place the gates were shut against us. We were afraid that it would now be the case; but instead of that we now see our British Father preparing to march out of his garrison.

Father! You have got the arms and ammunition which our Great Father sent for his red children. If you have an idea of going away, give them to us, and you may go, and welcome for us. Our lives are in the hands of the Great Spirit. We are determined to defend our lands, and if it is his will, we wish to leave our bones upon them.

As Tecumseh finished, his chiefs leaped to their feet, screaming their approval. Proctor quickly left the council room, promising to make his reply in a subsequent council.

The following day, rumours abounded that the Indians planned to tear in two a belt of wampum at the next council, an act to symbolise the fracture of their alliance with the British. Proctor now summoned Tecumseh, and at last explained his reasons for retreating. Upon receiving assurances that the British would make a stand on the Thames, Tecumseh agreed to placate the other chiefs. Proctor affirmed his resolution to fight on the Thames at a second council later that day. Sending their guns and stores north-east up the Thames, the British withdrew to Sandwich on 23rd September. Burning all the buildings, they commenced the retreat up the Thames on 27th September.

Proctor's duplicity had cost Tecumseh some 800 followers; the Potawatomi Indians, in particular, drifting back to their villages. Tecumseh led about 1200 warriors up the Thames, reflecting to one of his comrades; 'We are now going to follow the British, and I feel certain that we shall never return.'

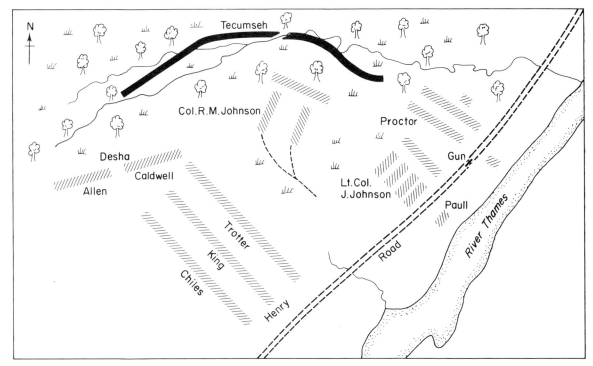

The deployment of the American, English and Indian troops at the Battle of the Thames, 5 October, 1813.

The Last Prophecy

Harrison led 2000 regulars and 3000 militia into Canada, and the smouldering remains of Fort Malden, on 27th September 1813. On 2nd October he proceeded with about 3500 men from Sandwich, in pursuit of the British. Tecumseh's Indians guarded Proctor's tail, and fought a furious rearguard action at MacGregor's Creek on 4th October. The battle lasted for two hours, but after being wounded in the arm, and losing thirteen warriors, Tecumseh was forced to retreat.

On the afternoon of 5th October 1813, the British and Indian army took up positions at Moraviantown, near present-day Chatham. Proctor seemingly remained reluctant to stand and fight, and Tecumseh was prominent in forcing the battle upon the British, and orchestrating their defences. The British arrayed their ranks on the north side of the Thames, with a swamp guarding their right flank. Tecumseh deployed his warriors in woodland to the north of the swamp; a larger marsh guarding their right flank.

Proctor's deficiencies had by now depleted the Indian forces, through disaffected desertion, to little more than 500 warriors. Tecumseh's choice of battlefield, though, was excellent. The forest would break up

41

any cavalry charge, while the extent of the Indian lines would allow them to rake the Americans' left flank with fire.

Prior to the battle, Tecumseh and some British officers heard the sound of a shot, though none had been fired. Tecumseh doubled up momentarily as if hit, and told the officers that a bad spirit was present. He subsequently made his last prophecy, telling the chiefs that had remained loyal to his cause: 'Brother warriors, we are now about to enter into an engagement from which I shall never come out – my body will remain on the field of battle.'

He then offered his sword to one of them, saying, 'When my son becomes a noted warrior and able to wield a sword, give this to him.'

He dressed for the battle not in the scarlet coat of the British but in the deerskin of his people.

As the British forces awaited the Americans, Tecumseh instructed Proctor to re-deploy his men more sparsely, to minimise their exposure to enemy fire. He then reassured the general: 'Father! Have a big heart! Tell your young men to be firm and all will be well.'

Having thus raised Proctor's spirits, Tecumseh reviewed the troops. John Richardson, a volunteer in the British Forty-first Regiment of Foot recalled the event:

Only a few minutes before the clang of the American bugles was heard ringing through the forest . . . the haughty chieftain had passed along our line, pleased with the manner in which his left was supported, and seemingly sanguine of success. He was dressed in his usual deer skin dress, which admirably displayed his light yet sinewy figure, and in his handkerchief, rolled as a turban over his brow, was placed a handsome white ostrich feather, which had been given to him by a near relation of the writer . . . and on which he was ever fond of decorating himself, either for the Hall of Council or the battle field. He pressed the hand of each officer as he passed, made some remark in Shawnee, appropriate to the occasion, which was sufficiently understood by the expressive signs accompanying them, and then passed away forever from our view.

Another account, by Captain Hall, also provides a significant insight into the inspection and the demeanour of Tecumseh in contrast to that of Proctor:

After the line was formed I first me[t] General Proctor riding down from the right of the line towards the left with Colonel Elliot and Tecumseth. After they had passed the line and returned again, Colonel Elliot interpreted some observations that had passed between him and Tecumseth intended for the general. The first was that our men were too thickly posted – that they would be exposed to the enemy's riflemen, and thrown away to no advantage. The second was to desire his young men to be stout hearted as the enemy would make a push at the gun; Tecumseth then left the general apparently in very high spirits.

The impression is certainly created that the British and Indians alike took their inspiration not from Proctor, but from Tecumseh.

The Fatal Charge
Harrison's force of approximately 3000 men attacked at 4 p.m. on 5th October 1813. They were met by perhaps as few as 450 regulars and 500

Indians under the British flag. Harrison chose to mount a full-blooded cavalry charge into the British ranks. It was a measure which he conceded later was 'not sanctioned by anything I had seen or heard of; but I was fully convinced it would succeed.' Colonel Richard Johnson's Kentuckian cavalry made the charge, sending about 500 troopers against the British lines, and a like number across the swamp towards the Indians.

The charge broke the British lines almost immediately. The redcoats wounded only three or four American troops with their first volley. They did not even pause to reload before making a retreat described by one British officer as 'shameful in the highest degree.' Proctor fled to his carriage and galloped to the safety of eastern Ontario.

The Indians, in stark contrast, fought magnificently under Tecumseh's brave example. They unleashed a volley of fire which stopped the American cavalry charge in its tracks. The troopers were thrown back, and forced to dismount before entering the mêlée once more. The Indians met them in furious hand-to-hand fighting, Tecumseh at their centre, blood streaming down his face from a head wound, his arm still bandaged.

The death of Tecumseh, at the Battle of the Thames, as shown in the painting by Alonzo Chappel, published in 1857.

'He yelled like a tiger, and urged his braves to attack,' one American later recalled. Defiantly, Tecumseh led a charge into the heart of the American ranks. A bullet struck him in the left breast, and he fell, mortally wounded. His dream of an Indian confederacy fell with him in the dust of Moraviantown.

There is strong evidence to suggest that it was Johnson himself who killed Tecumseh. Some time later, William Clark, Superintendent of Indian Affairs at St. Louis questioned a Potawatami chief as to his memory of the events:

Were you at the battle of the Thames? Yes. Did you know Tecumseh? Yes. Were you near him in the fight? Yes. Did you see him fall? Yes. Who shot him? Don't know. Did you see the man that shot him? Yes. What sort of looking man was he? Short, thick man. What color was the horse he rode? Most white. How do you know this man shot Tecumseh? I saw the man ride up – saw his horse get tangled in some bushes – when the horse was most still, I saw Tecumseh level his rifle at the man and shoot – the man shook on his horse – soon the horse got out of the bushes, and the man spurred him up – horse came slow – Tecumseh right before him – man's left hand hung down – just as he got near, Tecumseh lifted his tomahawk and was going to throw it, when the man shot him with a short gun – Tecumseh fell dead and we all ran.

Demoralized by the British rout, and disheartened by the fall of their great prophet and chief, the Indians slowly gave way. They retreated to Moraviantown, and the battle was over.

Legacy and Legend

'With deep concern I mention the death of the chief Tecumthée, who was shot on the 5th instant.' So read Proctor's despatch of 23rd October 1813, but the facts surrounding Tecumseh's demise were far less simple.

Native dress of a Shawnee man, and probably not unlike that of Tecumseh prior to his adoption of European uniform of around 1796. Note the roach haircut, (red) face paint, ear ornaments, bead necklace, cloth shirt and breechcloth, white blanket, cloth leggings, garters, silver armlet with feather pendants, and bow with fletched arrows.

After the battle, a number of Kentuckians viciously mutilated a body identified, by British officers amongst others, as being that of Tecumseh. They scalped the corpse, and tore long strips of skin from its back and thighs. The body subsequently disappeared, and was secretly interred by the Indians. Tecumseh's followers later claimed that this was not in fact the body of the Shawnee chief. Tecumseh's body, they insisted, had been carried away by his followers immediately after the battle, and buried in an unknown place.

For years, the Americans were plagued by rumours that Tecumseh was in fact still alive. These were unquestionably false, but reflected the fear and respect in which Tecumseh was held. Despite claims to various graves, the site of his resting place remains an intriguing mystery. One set of bones was preserved on St. Annes Island by the Indian chief Sha-wah-wan-noo, and found its way eventually to Walpole Island. Here, a monument to Tecumseh was raised over them, in 1941; despite the fact that the thigh-bones did not demonstrate the fractures suffered by Tecumseh as a young man.

The decline of the Indian alliance with the British was inevitably accelerated by Tecumseh's death. Without a leader of his strength, the British found those Indians that remained loyal, impossible to control. Naibush, the Ottawa chief, described the disunity:

Since our great chief Tecumtha has been killed, we do not listen to one another, we do not rise together, we hurt ourselves by it, it is our own fault . . . we do not when we go to war rise together, but we go one or two and the rest say they will go tomorrow.

Tecumseh's immediate followers turned to Tenskwatawa for leadership, and raised Tecumseh's son Puchethei, to the status of village chief, in honour of his father. They settled for a time at Fort Malden at the mouth of the Detroit River.

When the Americans signed the peace treaty at Ghent on 24th December 1814, they refused to concede British demands for a separate Indian state. Without a leader of Tecumseh's stature, the disordered Shawnee tribes, like all the fragmented tribes of the Old Northwest, were forced westward by American settlement. The various Shawnee divisions eventually settled in three distinct groups in Oklahoma.

Tecumseh's legend was powerful enough to enhance subsequent presidential elections. In 1837, Richard Johnson, the man most championed as the actual slayer of the Shawnee chief, ran for election with the slogan: 'Rumpsey, Dumpsey, Colonel Johnson killed Tecumseh.' Three years later, Harrison, with running mate John Tyler, succeeded to the White House using the nick-name he had acquired by destroying Prophet's Town: 'Tippecanoe and Tyler too.'

Though his dreams of an Indian state, and a grand confederacy of tribes, died at the Battle of the Thames, Tecumseh continued to be remembered as 'a saint' by the Shawnee. When Catlin met Tenskwatawa in 1830, the fallen Prophet said of his brother 'Tecumseh was a great general, and that nothing but his premature death defeated his grand plan'.

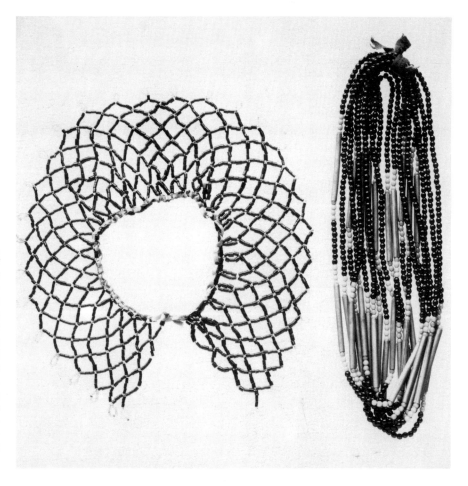

By the mid-nineteenth century, the Shawnee, like many of their former neighbours, ended up in Oklahoma as a result of government land cedes. This Shawnee man and small boy (opposite) were photographed there around 1900 – a long way in time and culture from the proud days of their ancestors in Tecumseh's Old Northwest. Nevertheless, traditional crafts still flourished among the Shawnee even after their relocation to Oklahoma as evidenced by this fine beadwork collar and necklace.

Chronology of Events

1675–76	War of King Philip (Metacom).
1754–63	French and Indian War.
1763	Royal Proclamation prohibits settlement west of Appalachians.
1763–4	Pontiac's Rebellion.
1768	MARCH Tecumseh born at Piqua, on Mad River.
1774	Thirteen Mingoes and Shawnee murdered by settlers.
1774	Lord Dunmore's War.
	6 October: Battle of Point Pleasant.
	NOVEMBER: Cornstalk signs treaty with Lord Dunmore at Chillicothe.
1775–83	American Revolution.
1777	Cornstalk murdered.
1778	General Edward Hand destroys Shawnee villages.
1778	Shawnee capture Daniel Boone.
1780	Major George Rogers Clark destroys Chillicothe and Piqua settlements.
1783	Tecumseh flees from Mad River battle.
	Treaty of Paris.
	Indian council on the Sandusky.
1788	Tecumseh breaks a leg, falling from his horse.
	Tecumseh travels among Missouri and Illinois Shawnee, Miami, Kickapoo, Creek and Cherokee.
	Cheesekau killed.
1790	SEPTEMBER: General Harmar defeated by Little Turtle.
1791	NOVEMBER: General St. Clair defeated by Little Turtle.
1793	Sandusky conference.
1794	AUGUST: Battle of Fallen Timbers.

1795	Greenville Treaty.
1796	Tecumseh marries half-breed Manete. His son Puchethei is born.
1799	Tecumseh meets Rebecca Galloway.
1800	Indiana Territory created.
1805	Laulewasika receives vision, and becomes Tenskwatawa, the Prophet.
	16 JUNE Tenskwatawa performs eclipse miracle.
	Tecumseh forms alliance with the Wyandot Roundhead.
1808	Prophet's Town established.
1808	Tecumseh travels among tribes from Missouri down to Florida.
1809	Treaty of Fort Wayne.
1810	AUGUST: Tecumseh meets Governor Harrison at Vincennes.
1811	JULY: Settlers killed by Potawatomi Indians.
	Tecumseh visits eastern and south-eastern tribes.
	OCTOBER: Tecumseh predicts earthquake.
	NOVEMBER: Battle of Tippecanoe. Harrison destroys Prophet's Town.
1812	Tecumseh exiles Tenskwatawa.
1812–15	War of 1812.
	AUGUST: Tecumseh and General Brock capture Detroit.
	AUTUMN: Tecumseh visits Creek.
	APRIL: Tecumseh and General Proctor besiege Fort Meigs.
1813	SEPTEMBER: British fleet defeated on Lake Erie. Proctor retreats.
	5 OCTOBER: Tecumseh killed in Battle of the Thames (Moraviantown).

Bibliography

Brandon, W. *American Heritage Book of Indians* American Heritage, 1982.

Catlin, G. *North American Indians* Dover, 1973.

Drake, B. *Life of Tecumseh and his brother the Prophet* Cincinnati, 1841.

Drake, S.G. *The Book of the Indians of North America* Boston, 1836.

Embleton, R. *Pioneers and Heroes of the Wild West* Parnell 1979.

Hodge, F.W. *Handbook of American Indians* Rowman and Littlefield, 1979.

Howard, J.H. *Shawnee!* Ohio University Press, 1981.

Josephy, A.M. *The Patriot Chiefs* Viking, 1961.

McKenney and Hall *History of the Indian Tribes of North America* Edinburgh, 1933.

Mcluhan, T.C. *Touch The Earth* Abacus, 1971.

Sturtevant, W.C. *Handbook of North American Indians – Northeast* Smithsonian Institution, 1978.

Sugden, J. *Tecumseh's Last Stand* Oklahoma University Press, 1985.

Swanton, J.R. *The Indian Tribes of North America* Oklahoma University Press, 1985.

Tucker, G. *Tecumseh, Vision of Glory* Indianapolis, 1956.

Utley, R.M. *The Indian Wars* Mitchell Beazley, 1977.

Waldman, C. *Atlas of the North American Indian* Facts on File, 1985.

Crazy Horse

SACRED WARRIOR OF THE SIOUX

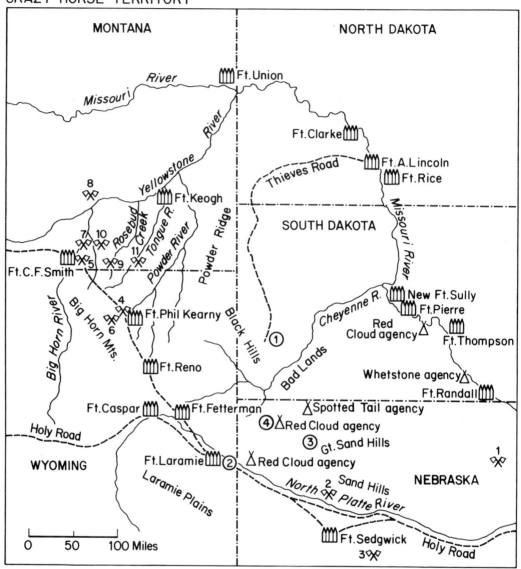

CRAZY HORSE TERRITORY

MONTANA

NORTH DAKOTA

Missouri River

Ft. Union

Yellowstone River

Ft. Clarke

Thieves Road

Ft. A. Lincoln
Ft. Rice

8

Ft. Keogh

SOUTH DAKOTA

Rosebud Creek
Tongue R.
Powder River

7 10
11
5   9

Ft. C. F. Smith

Powder Ridge

Cheyenne R.

New Ft. Sully
Ft. Pierre

Red
Cloud agency

Ft. Thompson

Big Horn River
Big Horn Mts.

4

Ft. Phil Kearny

Black Hills

6

Bad Lands

Whetstone agency

Ft. Randall

Ft. Reno

Ft. Caspar

Ft. Fetterman

④ Red Cloud agency

③ Gt. Sand Hills

Spotted Tail agency

Holy Road

Ft. Laramie ②

Red Cloud agency

1

WYOMING

Laramie Plains

② Sand Hills

North Platte River

NEBRASKA

Holy Road

0   50   100 Miles

Ft. Sedgwick

3

① Crazy Horse – Curly – born, Rapid Creek, 1841

② Great Lakota Council, 1857

③ Curly named Crazy Horse

④ Crazy Horse fatally wounded, 1877

Battles

1 Curly kills Omaha woman
2 Bluewater, 1855
3 Sumner's attack, 1857
4 Fetterman Massacre, 1866
5 Hayfield Fight, 1867
6 Wagon Box Fight, 1867

7 He Dog and Crazy Horse raid Crow, 1870
8 Fight with Custer and Stanley's troops 1873
9 Rosebud Creek 1876
10 Little Big Horn 1876
11 Miles' attack on Crazy Horse 1877

> One does not sell the earth upon which the people walk
> (Crazy Horse 1875)

The Greatest Leader

European settlement of North America met with its fiercest adversary in the shape of the Lakota or Western (Teton) Sioux, the powerful Indian nation that dominated the heart of the Great Plains. Central in the Lakota resistance to the white man's invasion were the people of the Oglala Sioux. The heart of the stubborn defence of their homeland was Crazy Horse. A peerless warrior and revered mystic, Crazy Horse fought for the traditions of his people, until those same people wearied of war and, in some cases, turned against him.

The Plains culture region.

Dr V.T. McGillycuddy, assistant post surgeon at Fort Robinson where Crazy Horse died, said of the ill-fated Oglala leader:

In him everything was made a second to patriotism and love of his people. Modest, fearless, a mystic, a believer in destiny, and much of a recluse, he was held in veneration and admiration by the younger warriors who would follow him anywhere . . . I could not but regard him as the greatest leader of his people in modern times.

The Sioux

Crazy Horse's people, known collectively as the Dakota nation, are popularly called the Sioux. Yet that word is a corruption, made by the early French settlers, of the name Nadouessioux. In turn, that was the Chippewa name for their 'adders' or 'enemies'. The Sioux nation had a complex structure, with a large number of tribal divisions and their own names.

The Sioux peoples' own name for themselves is Ocheti Shakowin, the 'Seven Council Fires', or seven tribes that originally formed their nation: the Mdewakanton, Wahpeton, Wahpekute, Sisseton, Yankton, Yankto-nai and Teton. In time, these groups became separated by dialect and geography into three distinct historical divisions.

The easternmost group, comprising the first four of the council fires, became the Dakota or Santee Sioux, retaining their agricultural tradition between the forks of the Missouri and Mississippi. By 1770, the second division, the Nakota, including and collectively referred to as the Yankton and Yanktonai, were living between the Missouri and James Rivers.

The Lakota or Teton Sioux, the westernmost spark from the council fires, were Crazy Horse's people. Just as their original nation comprised the seven fires, so the Lakota became divided into seven sub-tribes as they migrated in the 1700s from the Mississippi across the Missouri to the Great Plains. The Oglala (Those Who Scatter Their Own) and Brulé (Burnt Thighs) were the first Lakota west of the Missouri. They were followed by the Miniconjou (Those Who Plant By The Stream); Sans Arcs (Without Bows); Oohenonpa (Two Kettles); Sihasapa (Blackfoot) and Hunkpapa (Those Who Camp By The Entrance). Ideally, these seven tribes united each summer to renew the nation's unity; but in practice, each tribe was autonomous.

Crazy Horse was a member of the Hunkpatila band, one of seven bands that in theory made up the Oglala tribe. In reality, the name, number and size of the Oglala hunting bands fluctuated according to the prominence of different chiefs.

As early as the 1500s, the Sioux were established east of the Mississippi headwaters. There are historic records of their living in the Milles Lacs region of Minnesota in 1650, where they demonstrated a Woodlands culture. They hunted, raised corn and foraged for wild rice in the woodlands, travelling the lakes and rivers in bark canoes, and defending their lands aggressively. The formation of the Hudson's Bay trading company in 1670 made firearms available to the traditional eastern enemies of the Sioux, the Chippewa, through trade with their Indian allies. Hardpressed by the well-armed Chippewa and drawn by the rich buffalo herds that roamed the Great Plains, the Sioux migrated west-ward. This migration caused the division into Lakota, Nakota and Dakota, as the three groups settled into new territories, and led to the Lakotas' adoption of a Plains culture.

In 1680, Father Louis Hennepin identified some Sioux west of the Mississippi at the Sauk rapids. By 1700, French fur trader Pierre Charles le Sueur placed their territory on Blue Earth River, between the upper Mississippi and Missouri, with the westernmost vanguard hunting buffalo on the James River. In 1743, the La Vérendrye brothers placed the 'Prairie Sioux' fifty miles north of Pierre, South Dakota, on the eastern bank of the Missouri.

The acquisition of the horse, that came to dominate their culture, created a new boldness in the westward sweep of the Sioux after 1750. Their own calendar or 'winter count' records the discovery, in 1765, of Pa Sapa – the sacred Black Hills – that would become the beating heart of Lakota life and lands.

As the last major tribe on to the Plains, the Lakota had to fight for their new lands. In 1792, they defeated the Arikara tribe who were already

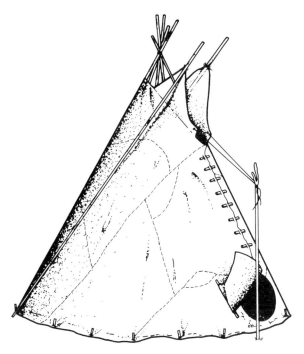

decimated by smallpox. By 1800, the Lakota had sufficient horses, warriors and spirit to possess the territory that they would defend against the white man. They claimed land south to the Platte River, east to the Missouri, north to the Yellowstone; and would dislodge tribes such as their greatest enemy, the Crow, west of the Black Hills to the Teton Mountains. The foremost of the Lakota tribes, the Brulé, lived in the White River, while the Oglala roamed west of the Bad River to Pa Sapa.

The Winter Count

The early history of the Sioux, aside from the accounts of the first trappers and traders, is recorded in their own historic calendars known as 'winter counts'. These pictographic records were painted on deerskins, often in spiral form, by the tribal historians. Each year was commemorated by its most significant event, and the winter counts were handed down through the generations.

The winter counts of White Man Stands in Sight of the Oglala, of Baptiste Good (Brown Hat) of the Brulé, and of Iron Shell of the Miniconjou record events as far back as the 1700s. A meteor shower made 1833 the Winter of Shooting Stars, while 1850 was the Winter of Smallpox and notated by a picture of a spotted face.

Pictographs were also made to narrate important events such as battles. The pictographic record of the Oglala historian Amos Bad Heart Bull illustrates many of the important events in the life of his cousin, Crazy Horse. The Lakota used to say: 'A people without history is like wind on the buffalo grass.'

The tipi or lodge was a tilted cone of three or four main poles interspersed with a number of strengthening poles, with a dressed buffalo skin cover. It could be dismantled very rapidly by two experienced women, and hauled by two or three horses. The tipi was equipped with smoke-flaps, permitting an interior fire, and a draught-excluding liner. It was warm and waterproof in the winter, and stream-lined and sturdy enough to resist the strongest winds. In summer, its sides could be rolled up for ventilation.

The Land and the People

The buffalo was the Lakota's staff of life, yielding food, shelter, clothing, fuel and numerous utensils. Thronging the Great Plains in vast numbers, these short-sighted, keen-scented beasts made a fearsome prey, whose capture was a spectacular, dangerous undertaking. The extinction of the buffalo at the white man's hands was one of the most important factors in the extinction of the Plains Indians' way of life.

The Great Plains of North America are a vast grassland covering some million square miles between the Mississippi and the Rockies, from Canada down to Texas. Limitless horizons are punctuated by occasional ranges of hills and cottonwood valleys, surrounding rivers that become mere dusty veins in summer. Constant winds sway deep-rooted 'buffalo-grass', forage for buffalo whose vast numbers once blackened the Plains.

The nineteenth century homeland of the Oglala spread outward from the Black Hills, to where now lie the states of Wyoming, Montana, South Dakota and Nebraska. Westward loomed the foreboding shadow of the Rockies; northwards lay a wasteland of buttes and crags, the Badlands; to the east were the White River hunting grounds of the Brulé.

Migration of the Lakota into the Black Hills dislodged several tribes from the region. The Kiowa were driven to the southern Plains, homeland of the Comanche. The Crow, pushed north to Montana, became the Lakota's most implacable foe. The Cheyenne were also swept aside by the Lakota, but formed a permanent alliance with them in 1843, when the Lakota people recovered one of the Cheyenne's Sacred Arrows, an ancient medicine item stolen by the Pawnee. The Plains tribes also included the Blackfoot, Assiniboin and Arapaho, all sharing with the Lakota a common culture that revolved around the buffalo and horse.

Buffalo and Sacred Dog

Buffalo used to roam the Plains in such numbers that Pedro de Castañeda, Coronado's chronicler, could only compare them to the fish in the sea. In 1830, George Catlin, the great western painter, wrote:

the buffalo congregate into such masses in some places as literally to blacken the prairies for miles together. It is no uncommon thing . . . to see several thousands in a mass, eddying and wheeling about under a cloud of dust.

56

Not only were the buffalo plentiful, they also provided for every conceivable need of the Plains Indians. Every part of their meat was eaten, boiled in water carried to camp in a container fashioned from the buffalo's belly, over a fire stoked by the dung. Buffalo hide was fashioned into clothes and shelter – for lodges or tipis – tanned with an agent made from the brains and liver. Boiled buffalo hooves glued the head on to an arrow, fired by a bow string made from the sinew. Even the buffalo's tail made a fly-brush.

When the Lakota were still poor in horses, they relied upon wolf-skin disguises in order to hunt the buffalo, or drove the heavy beasts into snow drifts in the winter. Large amounts of meat were secured by the communal drive or *piskun*; there a holy man with power to call the buffalo lured them to a high cliff. The entire band then surrounded and stampeded the herd over the cliff. Arrow-heads still litter the floors of cliffs favoured by tribes for the *piskun*.

The arrival of horses in great numbers created the golden age of the Plains Indians. After 1600, Pueblo Indians working on Spanish ranches in Texas and New Mexico passed on their knowledge, with stray and stolen horses, to the southern Plains tribes. Horses gradually filtered north and by 1750 were fully integrated into the culture of the Lakota so that General George Crook could one day describe them as the greatest light cavalry the World had ever known.

The nineteenth-century Lakota, a mounted, nomadic people, demonstrated the culture which is now considered typical of their people. The hunt was transformed into a glorious cavalry charge, on specially trained mounts – 'buffalo-runners' – and more meat could be carried back to camp. The horse's exceptional utility led to its name 'sacred dog'. Larger

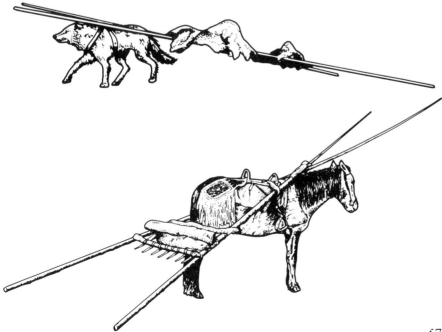

Before the arrival of the horse on the North American continent, the Indians used dogs to haul all their possessions and homes across the Plains on A-shaped frames called travois. The advent of the horse meant a great increase in material wealth for the Indians of the Plains. Longer lodge-poles could be hauled to fresh camp-sites, constructed into travois, so that the Indians' tipis became larger and their possessions more numerous.

Lakota eagle wingbone whistle, adorned with beaded ring, antelope skin, sweetgrass bundle, beaded thongs terminating in red-dyed skin bundles, and a rawhide necklace. Such whistles were blown by warriors during battle and when undertaking the Sun Dance ceremonies, to invoke the power of the eagle, messenger of the Sun.

lodges were now used, hauled along behind the horses in V-shaped travois.

The Lakota adopted a seasonal pattern which mirrored migrations and habits of the buffalo. From August (Moon of Ripe Plums) to November (Moon of Hairless Calves), the various hunting bands roamed independently, moving camp when buffalo were scarce. Meat and wild vegetables were stored for the winter, and new lodges made. Each band made its way gradually to its regular winter camp, often in a sheltered river valley. After December (Moon of Frost in the Tipi), camp was only moved when lack of resources so dictated.

When April (Moon of the Birth of Calves) brought the warm breath of spring, the Lakota began a new year. Leaving the winter sites in May (Moon of Thunderstorms), separate bands often camped together, as rich grazing drew the buffalo into larger herds. By July (Cherry Blackening Moon), all Oglala hunting bands would ideally be camped together, though a union of the entire Lakota tribe was rare. With many mouths to feed, warrior societies enforced hunting regulations in order to prevent individuals scaring away abundant herds. When the tribe was united, elders organised the greatest of the Lakota religious ceremonies, the Sun Dance. This complex ritual, the most striking aspect of which was the self-torture of supplicant dancers, renewed tribal unity and reaffirmed the People's relations with a world considered in all aspects to be sacred.

Before the arrival of the white man, the Lakota felt in control of, and in harmony with, an abundant world, bound only by the Earth below and the Sky above. The Oglala Luther Standing Bear recalled:

The old Lakota was wise. He knew that a man's heart away from nature becomes hard; he knew that lack of respect for growing, living things soon led to lack of respect for humans too. So he kept his youth close to its softening influence.

The Lakota's dispute with the white man was clearly not just a battle for land; it was a clash of cultures.

Warfare

Pipe tomahawks with pierced blade and brass tack decorations. The hatchet-type, shown here, was typical among the Lakota in the period 1860–80.

Of the Lakota, Francis Parkman, the great nineteenth-century historian, wrote:

War is the breath of their nostrils. Against most of the neighbouring tribes they cherish a rancorous hatred, transmitted from father to son, and inflamed by constant aggression and retaliation.

As newcomers to the Black Hills, the Lakota had to fight constantly to assert themselves. Ownership of Mother Earth was not conceived, but defending their hunting lands was a practical necessity. Survival was achieved through regular displays of aggression against the Crow, Pawnee and Shoshoni.

The importance of the horse was such that horse-raiding was the most popular form of war. Warriors made stealthy forays into the heart of enemy camps, stealing their finest ponies. Inevitably this led to bloody reprisal raids – not for horses but for scalps.

A warrior's record of his war deeds was vital to his standing in the tribe, and a system of exploits or 'coups' was recognised. The coup proper was to touch an enemy without harming him, so demonstrating superiority. Other coups, such as killing an enemy in hand-to-hand combat, were accorded varying credit. It is a measure of Lakota aggression that they rated the taking of a scalp more highly than most Plains tribes.

Both the tribe and the warrior fought constantly to assert themselves in a merciless world. A warrior recorded and displayed his coups in his costume and regalia, particularly through feather heraldry. Thus, the first man to strike an enemy boasted of his 'first coup' by wearing an eagle feather upright at the back of his head.

Warfare was a constant feature of Plains life; Indians slept with their weapons at their sides. Warriors vied with each other with shows of recklessness, and demonstrated a bravery emanating from a belief that death in battle was a glorious death.

Lakota war-bonnet with beaded brow-band. The double leather trailer of golden eagle tail feathers has cloth-wrapped stems and yellow horse-hair streamers; an eagle 'fluffy' is hung by a thong from the brow-band. The right to wear such magnificent bonnets, symbols of officership among the tribe and soldier societies, was earned only by the élite.

'Hairy Man From The East'

We did not think of the great open plains, the beautiful rolling hills, and winding streams with tangled growth, as 'wild'. Only to the white man was nature a 'wilderness', and only to him was the land 'infested' with 'wild' animals and savage people. To us it was tame. Earth was bountiful and we were surrounded with the blessings of the Great Mystery. Not until the hairy man from the east came and with brutal frenzy heaped injustices upon us and the families we loved was it 'wild' for us. When the very animals of the forest began fleeing from his approach, then it was that for us the 'Wild West' began.
(Luther Standing Bear)

After 1700, the migration of the Lakota was mirrored by the progress west of white trappers and traders. The French were the initial pathfinders, though they were supplanted by the English Hudson's Bay Company following the French and Indian Wars of 1754–63. Traders travelling the upper Missouri found the Sioux aggressive and with no desire to accumulate wealth, showing a lofty independence like 'the air they breathed or the wind that blew'.

By 1800, buffalo and Indian alike were being driven west of the

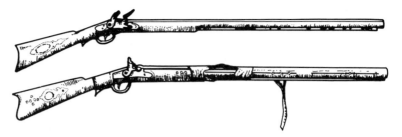

Lakota firearms: Henry Leman flintlock trade rifle and Leman percussion rifle with rawhide repairs and brass tack adornment, issued in government annuities 1850–70(top); Winchester Model 1866 carbine, a popular post-Civil War trade gun and Sitting Bull's Winchester Model 1866 carbine, surrendered in 1881(above); United States Springfield cavalry carbine, Model 1873, owned by Young Man Afraid of his Horses after its capture at the Little Bighorn, and a remarkable composite rifle, fashioned from an 1866 United States Army Model .50–70 barrel and receiver and .45–70 stock and lock, captured from the Lakota by Fort Robinson troops (opposite).

Mississippi by European settlement of north-east North America. The opening of the American West was founded by the Lewis and Clark expedition along the Missouri, and the subsequent settlement of hard-living white trappers, the mountain men. The American Fur Company, chartered in 1808, bidded against the Canadians for the Indian beaver trade with growing quantities of poor whiskey. The Lakota, who still travelled east to the Woodlands in spring, accepted the white man's guns, metal tools, tobacco, beads and cloth, and refrained from hostilities that might endanger their eastern relatives. The 1830 Indian Removal Act empowered President 'Sharp Knife' Jackson to drive the eastern tribes towards the hunting grounds of the Lakota.

Fort Pierre was built in the Dakotas in 1831 and three years later a crude stockade, Fort William, was built on the junction of the North Platte and Laramie Rivers. Later known as Fort Laramie, this stockade was constructed by William Sublette and Robert Campbell of the Rocky Mountain Fur Company, who invited Oglala chief Bull Bear to trade with them. Drawn by copious quantities of liquor and promises of fresh hunting grounds, the Oglala and Brulé migrated south. This brought them into close proximity with their bitter enemies, the Pawnee, and placed their camps directly in the path of what would become the Oregon Trail.

The wooden wheels of the first great wagon trains cut a swathe across the Plains in 1841. As the emigrants' axes chopped down the groves of trees, their cattle cropped the rich grasses, and their wagons scared the buffalo, the resentful Lakota demanded or exacted 'tributes'. However, at this time of crisis, the Oglala – already dismayed by whiskey – were cleft in two by tribal rivalries.

White traders had grown to favour a plump chief named Old Smoke, causing bitterness among the Bear people, aggressively led by Chief Bull Bear. Some years previously, Bull Bear had thrown down a challenge, by shooting Old Smoke's horse in the middle of that chief's camp circle. Old Smoke exacted his revenge in the fall of 1841, when Bull Bear rode into Smoke's camp on the Chugwater branch of Laramie fork. The Indians were drunk, and Bull Bear was shot dead; his assailant was rumoured to be an ambitious warrior of the Bad Face band, named Red Cloud. The killing created a split in the Oglala that was to pervade Crazy Horse's life.

The dead chief's Bear band drifted south-east between the Platte and Smoky Hill rivers, while the Bad Faces hunted north-west of the Platte to the Black Hills. By 1846, Old Smoke was chief of those Indians that persisted in begging idly at Fort Laramie, and disdainfully referred to by the free Oglala as the Loafers-Around-The-Fort. In 1841, as the Oglala unity was being shattered, Crazy Horse was born.

The Light-haired Boy

According to the testimony of his boyhood companion Chips, and of Dr McGillycuddy, Crazy Horse was born in the fall of 1841, the Winter of the Big Horse Steal. His birthplace was on Rapid Creek, east of the Black Hills, Pa Sapa. Before he earned his adult name, he was known as the Light-haired Boy, or just Curly. His father was called Crazy Horse, a humble but respected holy man of the Hunkpatila band of the Oglala. The Hunkpatila or 'End-of-Circle' band always camped at one point of the Oglala crescent when the tribe was together. Curly's mother was a Brulé, sister of Spotted Tail, who was now eighteen and killing a rival chief in his rise to prominence among his tribe. Curly's mother died when he was young, but her place in the lodge was taken by her younger

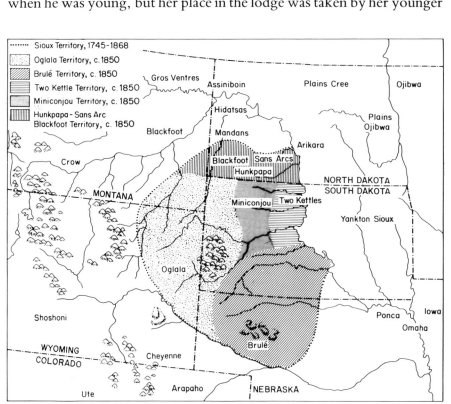

The homeland of the Lakota and Plains tribes in 1850.

Lakota umbilical cord protective amulets, of buckskin, beadwork and metal cones. Young children were called 'carry their navels', because they wore such amulets containing their own umbilical cords. The protection of the cord was considered, by extension, to grant sacred protection to the child. Thus amulets were fashioned after the protective symbols of the turtle (upper) which is difficult to kill, and the lizard (lower) which is difficult to catch.

sister. Curly had an older sister, and would have a younger brother who would take his uncle's name of Little Hawk.

Even as a child, Curly was set apart from other Lakota by his pale complexion and light wavy hair, characteristics that gave him his nickname and distinguished him throughout his life. Short Bull, an Oglala contemporary described Curly's adult appearance:

His hair was very light . . . he was a trifle under six feet tall. Crazy Horse had a very light complexion, much lighter than the other Indians. His features were not like the rest of us. His face was not broad and he had a sharp, high nose. He had black eyes that hardly ever looked straight at a man, but they didn't miss much that was going on all the same.

To the Lakota something unusual, such as an albino buffalo bull, was considered *wakan* or sacred. Curly, aware of his physical quirks, was a strangely quiet, thoughtful child; his father, a holy man, watched him with special interest.

When Curly was born, his umbilical cord was cut away and placed in a protective amulet fashioned after a turtle, to symbolise longevity. His ears were pierced during the first Sun Dance ceremony held after he could walk. Aged five, Curly received his own clothes and belongings to look after, and his umbilical amulet, and was known as a 'carry your navel' child. When the band moved camp, he rode on a horse travois.

Old Smoke, of the Loafers, liked whiskey, sugar and the 'black medicine', coffee; so Curly spent much of his early life around the trading posts on the Platte, where travellers on the Oregon Trail often mistook him for a captive white boy. Roaming north of the Platte, he learned the traditional ways of his people. When tall enough to ride, Curly received his first horse from his father, and by the age of ten had killed his first buffalo and held his seat on a wild horse. To celebrate these achievements, his father led Curly around the Hunkpatila camp calling that his son would now be called His Horse On Sight. The women of the camp, though, persisted in calling the light-haired boy Curly.

Though quieter than his comrades, Curly competed with the best of them in the rigorous training that prepared a Lakota youth for war. During the sham battles that they fought, Curly formed a special friendship with a comrade called High Back Bone or Hump. They were pledged to share their acquisitions and protect each other in battle, for High Back Bone was Curly's *kola* – his friend.

Horse Creek

'Since old Mahto-Tatonka (Bull Bear) died the People have been like children that do not know their own minds. They are no better than a body without a head.' So Eagle Feather spoke of the Oglala in 1846 to Francis Parkman. The old people were calling for peace, jealous of any threat to their supply of trade goods. The young warriors were buying their coffee in a different way, scaring the emigrants into parting with it, or stealing it from those foolish enough to wander off alone.

The stream of white-topped wagons had become a great river, and hostilities were increasing, when in the Moon of Making Fat, 15th June 1845, Colonel S.W. Kearney met the Oglala and Brulé at Laramie. He marched his five companies of dragoons up and down, fired his howitzers, and gave the Lakota beads and looking glasses, telling them that the travellers on the Oregon Trail were not to be harmed.

In 1849, the government bought and stationed troops at Fort Laramie. Further east at Grand Island, Fort Stephen Kearney was established. The Lakota and Cheyenne defiantly raised a war-party of five hundred warriors against the Pawnee, and raided the Fort Kearney supply train. Then, a new type of emigrant – 'forty-niners' bound for California to seek gold – thronged into their lands, bringing with them an epidemic of cholera. Curly's people fled north from the sickness, which left every lodge of one camp on the White River silently concealing its dead. One Cheyenne chief, Little Old Man, dressed for war and rode through his camp, singing: 'If I could see this thing; if I knew where it came from – then I would ride right into it and kill it.' Then he too fell with the stomach cramps.

The next year brought no relief, marked on the winter count of the Oglala as the Winter of Smallpox. Another 50,000 travellers passed Laramie that spring, and when the disease finally dissipated, the Indians were in an ugly mood. In response to pleas from alarmed agents and traders, the government sent messengers to the Plains tribes calling them to a great council at Laramie.

In July 1851, the Moon of Ripening Cherries, Curly's people joined a great gathering of Lakota and Cheyenne at Fort Laramie, there to meet Thomas 'Broken Hand' Fitzpatrick, Indian Agent on the Platte, and D.D. Mitchell, Superintendent of Indian Affairs. In September, the Moon of Yellow Leaves, the Shoshoni arrived; a Lakota warrior rushed out to kill their leader, Washakie, who had killed his father. Only the

Lakota dance shield of the Elk Dreamers Society. Constructed from painted muslin stretched over a willow hoop, it is decorated with a blue-painted elk head design, a sweetgrass bundle, hawk bells, orange-dyed horned-owl feathers and brown and white sage grouse tail-feathers. Lakota men who shared similar visions banded together in dreamer cults, each with distinctive songs, ceremony and regalia depicting their particular guardian spirit.

Oglala pipe and tobacco bag of tanned, white skin, decorated with typical Lakota beadwork, and quilled rawhide fringes. The smoking and giving of tobacco, with its associated utensils, were part of all major ceremonies.

physical intervention of a French interpreter saved the council from becoming a full-scale war.

The council moved thirty-six miles down the Platte to Horse Creek on 4th September, because the wagon-train of gifts promised to the Indians was late, and their ponies had cropped the grass. Two days later, 1,000 Lakota warriors singing their peace songs paraded before the commissioners and received gifts of tobacco. The next day, Curly stared wide-eyed as the Lakota feasted the Cheyenne, Arapaho and their enemies the Shoshoni; the pulse of the drum and shrill singing continuing until dawn.

On 8th September, a cannon's report opened the great Horse Creek council. Curly, aged ten, sat with the women and children behind the warriors, converged on the council lodge where the commissioners and the chiefs smoked the pipe. Then Mitchell outlined the purpose of the council. He said that the Great Father wished the Indians to stop molesting the emigrants and allow forts to be built on their lands. They should also refrain from attacking each other, and recognise boundaries to their lands. Each tribe was to select one chief to sign the treaty, and in return they would receive $50,000 of annuities for fifty years (reduced later by Congress to ten).

The Oglala held their eagle-wing fans to their faces when they heard these strange words. They did not understand this white man's ownership of Mother Earth that would prevent them from raiding for horses and prestige. When it came to selecting one chief for the entire Lakota nation, the chiefs shook their heads. Thus, Mitchell had to select his own 'paper chief', the Brulé Conquering Bear, who told Mitchell:

I am not afraid to die but to be chief of all the nation I must be a big chief, or in a few months I shall be dead on the prairie. I have a wife and children. I do not wish to leave. If I am not a powerful chief, my enemies will be on my trail all the time.

On 17th September, the various headmen 'touched the pen' to the treaty. The Oglala now called the Oregon Trail 'the Holy Road', for the treaty said that its people could not be touched. Conquering Bear, wearing the pantaloons and general's uniform presented to him, was the first chief to sign; but no Oglala or Cheyenne touched the pen:

You have split my land and I don't like it. These lands once belonged to the Kiowa and the Crow, but we whipped these nations out of them, and in this we did what the white men do when they want the lands of Indians.

(Black Hawk)

Then Curly's people 'removed from the plain with their families and lodges. They had heard the good news that the buffalo were numerous on the South Fork of the Platte.'

A Mormon's Cow
In the Moon of Making Fat, June of 1853, Curly's Hunkpatila band

Protected by the medicine items of his vision, Curly, at seventeen winters old, confronts two Arapaho warriors in the deed which earned him the name Crazy Horse, in Arapaho territory, Wyoming, summer 1858.

travelled with some Brulé to Laramie in order to collect their annuities. They were joined by some Miniconjou Lakota, who had not attended the Horse Creek Treaty, and felt even less bound by its rules than did the Oglala. On June 15th, a Miniconjou warrior loosed an arrow at a US sergeant as he crossed the Platte on the ferryboat. The commander at Fort Laramie, First Lieutenant Garnett, ordered the inexperienced brevet officer Lieutenant Fleming to arrest the warrior. Fleming promptly marched a detachment of infantry into the Lakota camp and shot dead three Miniconjou warriors. The Oglala and Brulé elders managed to pacify their guests, though the situation was not helped by Garnett's refusal to comply with the Lakota tradition of offering gifts as compensation for the killings.

The following summer of 1854, the Lakota once again gathered at Fort Laramie. Curly camped with some Brulé and with Man Afraid of His Horses, the Hunkpatila headman and leading chief of the Oglala, on the Platte six miles south of Fort Laramie. On 17th August, a small train of Mormon settlers passed the camp, one of them struggling behind, driving a worn out cow. The beast suddenly bolted into the Brulé camp circle where High Forehead, a Miniconjou warrior, shot an arrow through it. The frightened Mormon hurried away to demand compensation at Fort Laramie. The Lakota, awaiting the agent to distribute their overdue annuities, butchered the cow.

Conquering Bear was summoned to Fort Laramie by Fleming, who though only twenty-eight, was in command of the post. Conquering Bear offered to pay for the cow with ponies from his own herd, but Fleming demanded that the cow killer be turned over to him. He was urged on by Lieutenant John L. Grattan, a twenty-four year old fresh from West Point, who had boasted drunkenly that with thirty men he could whip the entire Sioux nation.

Conquering Bear told Fleming that the Miniconjou was a guest in his village, and that if Fleming wanted to arrest him he must do it himself. Fleming then ordered the hot-headed Grattan to arrest High Forehead 'if practicable and without unnecessary risks'.

Grattan, greatly excited, raised thirty volunteers for dangerous service, and set out on 19th August 1854, armed with a 12-pound field piece and a mountain howitzer, to 'conquer or die'.

The soldiers travelled east along the Oregon Trail to the trading post of James Bordeaux, three hundred yards from the Brulé camp. Here the Lakota chiefs Conquering Bear, Man Afraid of His Horses, Grand Partisan and Little Thunder urged him to turn back. Ignoring them, Grattan deployed his men in a line at the open end of Conquering Bear's camp circle. The white man's 'paper chief' tried to calm the situation, but Grattan aimed his howitzers at High Forehead's tipi, while the Miniconjou warrior sent word that he was ready to die.

Grattan's interpreter was Auguste Lucien who was married into the

Brought before his tribal headmen, the Big Bellies, in 1865, Crazy Horse receives the ceremonial shirt of big-horn skins, signifying his investiture as a Shirt Wearer of the Oglala.

Lakota but disliked by them. As Grattan lined up his guns, Lucien was meanwhile racing his horse to give it a second wind, as the Indians did before battle. He had drunk two bottles of whiskey, and was shouting wildly that the Lakota were all women; the soldiers would kill them all and he would cut out their hearts and eat them! He would give them new ears so that they understood his words! As Man Afraid of His Horses brought Bordeaux to replace the drunken interpreter, Grattan ordered his men to fire the howitzer.

A shot tore into the top of the lodges, and a Brulé warrior fell to the ground. Conquering Bear restrained his warriors, but Grattan's soldiers fired both cannons, and unleashed a volley from their Springfield rifles. Conquering Bear fell, mortally wounded, and the Horse Creek Treaty was torn in two.

Grattan fell under a hail of arrows. Spotted Tail's Brulé warriors rushed from the ravine behind the camp, Red Cloud's Oglala from the northern bluffs, and Grattan's men fell under blows from clubs and knives. Lucien's Lakota brother-in-law loosed an arrow into each of the fallen interpreter's ears, saying, 'Next time you will hear when we tell you not to live with the soldiers'. Grattan's body was later found, pierced by twenty-four arrows.

The excited Lakota warriors raided Bordeaux's trading post, and took their annuities from Gratiot's store, where they were awaiting the agent's arrival. Overnight, the old chiefs calmed the warriors, and in the morning the Lakota camps hurried north, casting a great cloud of dust into the sky.

Curly rode with his mother's people, the Brulé, towards the Snake River. As they stopped to make camp, Curly, who had seen Conquering Bear cut down by the soldier bullets, now caught a glimpse of the dying chief, his eyes hollow, his skin jaundiced. Shocked and confused, Curly leapt on his pony and rode away, alone.

Crying For a Vision
The Lakota believed that a sacred force pervaded every aspect of their life, so that their very existence was sacred. Anything mysterious was called *wakan*; the omnipotent deity was the Great Spirit, Wakan Tanka. One of the sacred seven rites of the Oglala was Hanblechyapi – Crying For a Vision – through which a young man sought guidance from the Sacred Powers. After purifying himself and under guidance from a holy man, the visionary fasted until he received some portent of his sacred power or 'medicine'.

Curly, though, went out alone and unprepared. He hobbled his horse in a holy place, in the Nebraska sandhills, where the Oglala Roan Eagle had a pit for catching eagles. For three days, Curly lay on the gravel, stripped to his breech-cloth, staring into the sky, sharp stones between his toes to keep him awake. Finally, feeling unworthy of a vision, he

Lakota pipe of about 1885. The bowl is of catlinite, the wooden stem wrapped with quillwork and adorned with the bighorn, deer, turtle and buffalo – all important figures in the religion of the Plains tribes.

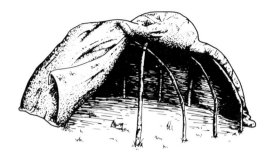

returned shakily to his horse. Suddenly, the earth reeled; with his stomach churning, Curly fell into the shade of a cottonwood tree.

He saw his horse start towards him, a light-haired man on its back. The horse was changing its hue, and floating above the ground. The man on its back wore a simple shirt and blue leggings. He had no face paint, and the central feather from a hawk's tail hung from his loose hair. A few beads adorned his scalp lock, and a small brown stone was tied behind one ear. He spoke no words, but Curly heard the warrior instruct him not to wear a war-bonnet or tie up his horse's tail before battle; Curly should also cast dust over his horse before fighting, and should never take anything for himself.

The man rode through a crowd of warriors, their arrows disappearing before they could hit him. Then he plunged into a fierce storm, now wearing only breechcloth and moccasins. Hailspots were dotted across his body, and a flash of lightning painted across his face. Over the man's head flew a red-backed hawk. The warrior's own people seemed to be holding him back, until they clasped his arms and engulfed him.

Then Curly awoke, being roughly shaken by his father, admonishing him for leaving camp alone.

It was three years before Curly told his father of his vision. Then the holy man, immersed in the scorching vapours of a sweat lodge, explained to his son that the vision he had seen was of himself, Curly. His father went on to say how he must dress as he had in the vision, a small stone behind his ear, a hawk over him. He must always be first in battle and through the power of thunder and the guidance of the hawk, he would be impervious to the bullets of his enemies. His path would be dark, but he should trust his vision, for it held great power.

Curly now had the Sacred Powers within him and continued to pray to them. Black Elk, the Oglala holy man, and Curly's cousin, described the powers graphically:

You have all heard of our great chief and priest Crazy Horse, but perhaps you did not know that he received most of his great power through the 'lamenting' which he did many times a year, and even in the winter, when it is very cold and very difficult. He received visions of the Rock, the Shadow, the Badger, a prancing horse, the Day, and also of Wanbli Galeshka, the Spotted Eagle, and from each of these he received much power and holiness.

In the sweat-lodge, a low dome of skins over a framework of willow saplings, the Indians purified themselves prior to religious rituals, in scorching vapours released by pouring water over red-hot rocks set in a central pit.

Crazy Horse – 'A Great Name'

The day after Curly's return to camp, Conquering Bear's body was wrapped in a buffalo robe and raised on a scaffold. In the Moon of Hairless Calves, 13th November, Conquering Bear's relatives Spotted Tail, Red Leaf and Long Chin avenged him by attacking a mail coach on the Holy Road, killing three white men.

Ignoring evidence to the contrary, Secretary of War Jefferson Davis declared the 'Grattan Massacre' to be the 'result of a deliberately formed plan' by the Lakota. A new agent from West Point, Thomas S. Twiss was appointed; and on 24th August 1855, General William S. Harney led a punitive expedition of six hundred men from Fort Kearney, Nebraska. The white-bearded general, later known as 'the Butcher', declared: 'By God, I'm for battle – no peace!'

Agent Twiss ordered all Lakota to move south of the Platte or be considered hostile. Most complied, but Little Thunder's Southern Brulé camp, which contained the lodges of Spotted Tail, Red Leaf and Curly's family, insisted on waiting for the meat from a buffalo hunt to dry.

On 3rd September, Harney marched his infantry into the camp on the Bluewater. Little Thunder parleyed while the women struck the lodges and prepared to flee; Harney talked while his cavalry secretly encircled the village. When the cavalry were discovered, the camp was thrown into confusion, and Harney's troops attacked the village without mercy.

Curly, away taming a mustang, returned to the camp only to witness the carnage left by the Butcher. Eighty-six of his people lay dead, including many children, and women with their dresses thrown back over their heads. The sight of so many relatives dead in their strong camp – unheard of among the Lakota who mourned even a single warrior's death – filled Curly with a bitterness that choked him.

Harney marched seventy women captives to Fort Laramie. There he withheld the Lakota annuities until 18th October, when Spotted Tail and the other mail-coach attackers, singing their death-songs, surrendered. They were imprisoned, and on the same day the humbled Lakota headmen touched the pen to another treaty at Fort Pierre.

Before the attack on the Blue Water, Curly had made his first kill at the age of thirteen. Joining a Brulé raid against the Omaha Indians, he saw an enemy sneaking through the undergrowth, and fired an arrow with great accuracy. Rushing to scalp his victim, Curly found it to be a woman. Although killing a woman was not considered disgraceful among the Lakota, Curly was sickened and left the scalp intact. On the journey home from this battle, in which the famous Omaha chief Logan Fontanelle was killed, the Lakota warriors teased Curly in song:

> A brave young man comes here,
> But a foolish one,
> Without a good knife

Magnificent Oglala eagle feather trailer bonnet. Only the tribe's ablest defenders claimed the right to wear such a bonnet. Imbued with the eagle's spiritual power, the bonnet was skilfully designed to sway and shimmer in the gentlest breeze, evoking the eagle's own movements.

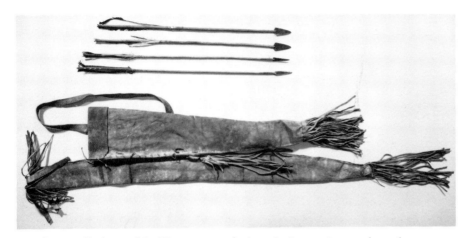

Curly was living with Cheyenne relatives in June 1857, when they were attacked on Solomon River by six troops of cavalry and three companies of infantry under Colonel Sumner. The Cheyenne medicine man Ice had given the warriors a sacred protection against the soldiers' bullets, but, ironically and inexplicably, Sumner ordered a sabre charge. The Cheyennes scattered in confusion, and Curly watched as yet another Indian village was put to the torch.

With a growing resentment towards the whites, Curly returned to his Oglala people. In the summer of 1857, they met with the Hunkpapa, Miniconjou, Sans Arcs, Blackfeet and Two Kettles tribes for a council at Bear Butte in the Black Hills. Only Spotted Tail's Brulé chose to stay away. As many as 7,500 Lakota gathered to declare their determination to unite against the white man's threat to their lands. When the earth grew bare, each band moved off for winter with a new gladness in its heart. Now Curly spoke to his father of his vision, and his adult life began.

Bowcase, quiver and arrows, probably Lakota. The bowcase and quiver are made from heavy, tanned skin, stained ochre brown and painted with green and red transverse lines. Such traditional weaponry of the warrior co-existed for some time with the repeater rifles.

A Warrior's Title

The Holy Road scared the buffalo away from the Black Hills. Consequently, the Oglala began to move north-west into the Powder River country. Though Old Smoke's Loafers remained at Fort Laramie, Red Cloud's Bad Faces, Red Dog's Oyukhpe, Sitting Bear's True Oglala and the Hunkpatila of Old Man Afraid of His Horses all migrated into the lands of their Miniconjou and Sans Arcs cousins. Horse Creek was forgotten as the Lakota warriors once more drove the Crow, Arapaho and Shoshoni from their lands.

In 1857, the Upper Platte Agency was moved from east of Laramie at Rawhide Butte Creek to Deer Creek on the North Platte, one hundred miles west of the fort. This agency suited the Powder River Lakota far more than those Indians still living near Laramie, though many whispered that Agent Twiss sold most of the Lakota annuity goods for his own gain.

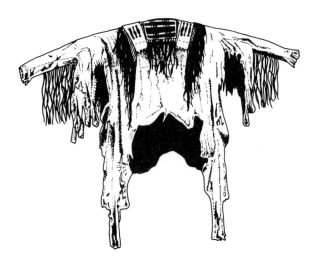

In the summer of 1858, Curly, with his friends High Back Bone and Lone Bear, and his brother Little Hawk, joined a war-party against the Arapaho. They rode further west than Curly had ever been, into central Wyoming, where the Oglala 'wolves' or scouts discovered an Arapaho camp. Then, the warriors stripped to their breechcloths and prepared for war, dressing in preparation for death, and donning the medicine talismans that linked them with the Sacred Powers.

Curly tied a small, brown stone into his hair behind his ear, and hung an eagle bone whistle around his neck. He fastened a single hawk feather into his scalp-lock, so that his vision-spirit would be flying above him. This war medicine had been prepared by Curly's friend Chips, a holy man whose power came from visions of sacred stones. Scattering a handful of gopher dust over himself and his horse, Curly was prepared for war.

The Lakota were discovered heading toward the camp, and a few Arapaho warriors dug in behind some hill-top rocks, from where they held the Lakota at bay for nearly two hours. Suddenly, Curly urged his horse forward, and charged in amongst the Arapaho, counting coup. He charged them twice more, their arrows always missing – for he was now the man of his vision fighting in the *real world*, the sacred world. Two Arapaho rode out to meet him but Curly killed them both with arrows, then leaped down to take their scalps. This broke Curly's taboo never to take anything for himself, and with his medicine violated he felt an arrow crash into his leg. Curly limped to safety, and the war-party rode home.

At the victory dance that night, while the other Lakota warriors boasted of their deeds, Curly shied away.

'It was just his nature,' his friend He Dog recalled. 'He was a very quiet man, except when there was fighting'.

Curly's bravery, though, brought him great honour, Chips explained: 'When we were young all we thought about was going to war with some other nation; all tried to get their names up the highest, and whoever did

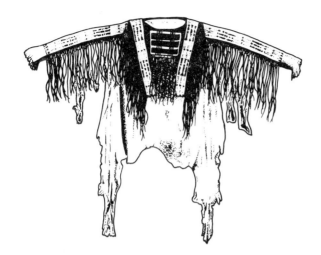

so was the principal man in the nation; and Crazy Horse wanted to get to the highest station and rank.'

Curly's father feasted the Hunkpatila headmen, announcing that he would now be known as Worm; then walked slowly among the lodges, singing:

> *My son has been against the people of unknown tongue,*
> *He has done a brave thing;*
> *For this I give him a new name, the name of his father,*
> *And of many fathers before him*
> *I give him a great name,*
> *I call him Crazy Horse.*

Respect, Vision and Anger

The following years were good ones for the Lakota living on the river they called the Powder, after the seams of lignite on its banks. The buffalo were plentiful, though another ocean of white emigrants swept across their lands in 1858, when gold was discovered in Colorado.

In 1860, John Loree, the new agent on the Upper Platte, relocated the Lakota agency back east of Laramie. The Loafers and the Corn band of the Brulé agreed to settle on a reservation; but the Powder River Lakota were furious when their annuity goods of 1863 became 'hoes and plows' instead of guns and bullets.

From 1861 to 1865, the white men fought amongst themselves, and their soldiers moved south. Following the 1862 Minnesota massacre of 450 whites by Santee warriors, volunteer troops were rushed to Fort Laramie. The time was ripe to drive the settlers from their lands, but the Lakota on the Powder seemed to have escaped the white man's evils, and were content to see the lodges fat with buffalo meat.

Crazy Horse grew to be a respected man during this time on the Powder. He carried much meat to his mother's lodge and was the bravest of the warriors in the raids against the Crow and Shoshoni. In the Moon of Making Fat, June 1861, he joined a party of Cheyenne and Lakota warriors in raiding the horse herd from Chief Washakie's Shoshoni on the Sweetwater River, Wyoming.

Crazy Horse and his younger brother were guarding the rear of their war party. After a lot of fighting, Crazy Horse's pony gave out. Crazy Horse turned it loose and the younger brother, who did not want to leave him, turned his own pony loose. Two of the enemy, mounted, appeared before them for single combat. Crazy Horse said to his brother, 'Take care of yourself – I'll do the fancy stunt.' Crazy Horse got the best of the first Shoshoni, the other one ran away. He got the horses of the two Shoshones and they caught up with the party. They had saved themselves and their party and got the two horses and the scalp of the Shoshone who was killed.

(Short Bull)

Lakota medicine pouch of raw hide decorated with beadwork, holding a pebble. Stone-dreamer medicine was an important protective power, which Crazy Horse employed in battle.

With such deeds, Crazy Horse became a popular leader of war-parties, all wishing to share his success and his strong medicine. He had acquired a new medicine, recalled by the brother of his first wife:

During war expeditions, he wore a little white stone with a hole through it on a buckskin string slung over his shoulder. He wore it under his left arm. He was wounded twice when he first began to fight but never since – after he got the stone. A man named Chips, a great friend of his, gave it to him.

(Red Feather)

Crazy Horse continued to lament and received a vision of the Thunder-beings, 'who come fearfully but bring goodness' as Black Elk described them. When flurrying snow filled the sky, Crazy Horse left camp alone to make the ancient snow-thunder medicine, finding that the snow-flakes, like the arrows of his enemies, could not touch him. Crazy Horse joined a medicine society called the Thunder Cult, and consequently rode into battle wearing only breechcloth and moccasins, his hair flying loose. He painted white hailspots across his chest and a forked zig-zag of lightning across his face to invoke his medicine. So prepared, he could not be harmed in battle, providing he always fought from the front, as He Dog recalled: 'Crazy Horse always led his men himself when they went into battle, and he kept well in front of them.'

In the summer of 1862, Crazy Horse stayed in the Bad Face Oglala camp, where he often stood with Black Buffalo Woman, niece of Red Cloud, their heads enfolded by a courting blanket. When Red Cloud sent word that he was to lead a war-party against the Crow, Crazy Horse joined up along with Little Hawk, High Back Bone, Lone Bear and the Bad Face brothers, No Water and Holy Bald Eagle (or Black Twin). As the warriors departed, No Water turned back, claiming that he had a toothache, bad medicine for a warrior whose power was derived from the teeth of the grizzly bear.

When the war-party returned two weeks later, singing victory songs, Crazy Horse learnt that No Water had married Black Buffalo Woman. His brother, Black Twin, was an influential man, and many people whispered that Red Cloud had arranged the marriage in order to bring power to his family. Crazy Horse rode away alone, returning with two

Crow scalps, which he threw to the dogs, for they were taboo to him. His anger and jealousy were to drive another wedge into the Oglala some years later.

Lighting the Flame

South of the Powder River, there were frequent clashes between the Cheyenne and volunteer soldiers who had replaced Civil War troops. Cheyenne headmen struggled to restrain their hot-blooded warriors, and Crazy Horse joined their attacks against emigrants still flooding along the Holy Road. Tension culminated on 29th November 1864 in a barbaric attack on friendly Cheyenne under Black Kettle, camped under a truce flag at Sand Creek. Colonel J.M. Chivington's 700 soldiers – including the Colorado Third's murderous 100-day volunteers – killed over 130 Cheyenne, mostly women and children. They mutilated the Indians' bodies, later displaying the Cheyenne women's pubic hair during the intermission of a Denver theatre show; the Plains were set aflame.

In December the Cheyenne sent the war-pipe to the Arapaho, Little Thunder's Southern Brulé and Bad Wound's Southern Oglala, who all smoked to indicate their participation in the war with the white man. Some nine hundred lodges from the various tribes gathered on Cherry Creek. Then they began moving slowly up the Platte, towards the Powder River Lakota. On 7th January 1865, a war-party of 1,000 warriors attacked Julesburg stage station, killing eighteen people. Crazy Horse joined a second attack on 2nd February, to plunder the station's remaining goods. In May, the Cheyenne joined the Oglala on Tongue River, while troops released from the Civil War reinforced the Platte.

The Oglala chiefs Two Face and Blackfoot now sought peace by taking a prisoner of the Cheyenne, Mrs Eubanks, to Fort Laramie. But their plan backfired; following her hysterical account of captivity, Laramie's temporary commander hanged the two chiefs. Their bodies, with artillery chains around their necks and iron balls dangling from their ankles, were left to swing from the fort's walls, driving the Lakota to fresh fury. Even the Loafers now fled to the Oglala camps, when the army attempted to march them unarmed to Fort Kearney in the heart of Pawnee territory.

That summer, the Lakota and Cheyenne performed their religious ceremonies together. Crazy Horse, who had eight horses shot from under him during his life, received from Chips a new protective stone to tie into his horse's tail. On 25th July 1865, he was one of twenty decoys who led an attack against the Platte Bridge stage station. Wearing his thunder medicine paint, Crazy Horse lured the station's troopers across the Platte towards 1000 concealed warriors. Impatiently, they sprung the trap prematurely, and the soldiers retreated safely. The following day, Crazy Horse led an attack against a relief column from the station, in which 29 troopers of the 11th Ohio Cavalry were killed.

Whilst not in Crazy Horse's nature to wear the flamboyant war bonnet, this unusual horn headdress has been attributed to him. It is a medicine bonnet of buffalo horns and hair, ermine, gold eagle wing pointers and 'fluffies', with owl and hawk feathers. It was used in ceremonies, dance, or perhaps in war to invoke its owner's guardian spirits.

The New Chief

That summer the southern half of the Northern Oglala renewed their chiefs. The people gathered around a great council lodge painted with sacred designs, in which sat the seven Wicasa Itacans, the greatest of the elders – the Big Bellies – with Old Man Afraid of His Horses seated in the middle. Then the chiefs of the warrior societies, finely dressed, rode through the village calling the names of those men selected to become the Wicasas or 'shirt-wearers'. The first three – American Horse, Young Man Afraid of His Horses and Sword – were all sons of Big Bellies. Then the warriors cried the name of a poor holy man's son, and the women trilled joyfully as Crazy Horse silently walked forward.

The people feasted and smoked before the four shirt-wearers each fastened a feather in their hair and donned their ceremonial shirts. These were made from two bighorn skins coloured with pigment in two halves, blue and yellow, or red and green. From Crazy Horse's quilled sleeves hung 240 hair-locks, symbolising his coups, and the people he was to protect. An old man instructed the shirt-wearers on their duties; to promote harmony, be generous, and always place the People before themselves. He Dog, who joined Red Cloud, Holy Bald Eagle and Big Road in the Bad Face's own investiture, recalled:

When we were made chiefs, we were bound by very strict rules as to what we should do and not do, which were very hard for us to follow. I have never spoken to any but a very few persons of what they made us promise then.

Red Cloud's War

Our nation is melting away like the snow on the sides of the hills where the Sun is warm, while your people are like the blades of grass in spring when the Summer is coming.
(Red Cloud, 1870)

In August 1865, three soldier columns under General Connor and Colonels Cole and Walker had invaded the Powder River country, under orders to kill 'every male Indian over twelve years of age'. While Connor established what would later become Fort Reno, Cole and Walker suffered repeated attacks from the Lakota including Crazy Horse. Their troops reached the fort in a state resembling that of a band of starving tramps rather than US soldiers. Governor Newton Edwards of Dakota Territory had meantime obtained treaty signatures from the already peaceful Lakota camps on the Missouri;

Like the old woman trying to catch the dog with a piece of meat in one hand and the butcher knife in the other.

(Sandoz)

'Winter of the Hundred Slain'

As part of President Grant's post-Civil War Peace Policy, the new treaty was sent to Colonel Maynardier at Fort Laramie. He was to obtain the hostile chiefs' signatures, guaranteeing the safety of miners following the Bozeman Trail to Montana. The council opened on June 13th 1866, with Red Cloud, Old Man Afraid and Spotted Tail all present. The Indians then learned of Colonel Henry B. Carrington's presence nearby. Carrington, with 700 men of the 18th Infantry, had marched from Fort Kearney, Nebraska with orders to establish forts on the Bozeman Trail regardless of the council's outcome.

Red Cloud stalked up to the commissioners, roaring: 'Great Father sends us presents and wants new road. But White Chief goes with soldiers to steal road before Indian says yes or no!'

The Oglala marched away, to defend their lands, while the friendly chiefs signed another meaningless treaty.

Carrington marched to Fort Reno, then on to the eastern foothills of the Bighorns. There, he began building Fort Phil Kearny, between Big Piney and Little Piney Creeks. In August he sent 150 men north to establish the third fort on the Bozeman Trail, Fort C.F. Smith on the Bighorn River. Red Cloud gathered 3000 warriors on the Tongue River, and between August and December of 1866, Lakota attacks claimed 154 lives and captured nearly 700 livestock. The Bozeman Trail was no safer than before, and wood or hay-cutting expeditions from Phil Kearny became treacherous undertakings.

In December, the Moon of Frost in the Tipi, the Miniconjou Chief White Swan died, after telling his people: 'Try to kill white men, for the white men have come here to kill you. I am about to die. I can kill no more. Therefore I look to you. Carry on.'

So the Miniconjou sent the war-pipe to the Oglala, who sent their finest warriors under Pawnee Killer and Crazy Horse to join a great attack on the fort. In attacks on the 6th and 19th December, the warriors had already discovered that the wood train was vulnerable to assaults from Lodge Trail Ridge north of the fort, beyond which nothing could be seen by the soldiers.

On the 20th December, some 2000 Oglala, Miniconjou, Brulé, Cheyenne and Arapaho warriors rode south along the Tongue. They wore blanket leggings and buffalo robes, with red Hudson's Bay blankets wrapped about their waists against the cold. On a snow-covered plain, the Lakota warriors formed a long line. From among them rode a *winkte*, a man who dressed and spoke like a woman, and was believed to hold *wakan* powers. With a black blanket drawn about his head, and blowing an eagle-bone whistle, the *winkte* rode his sorrel horse in zig-zags over a hill, searching for an enemy. He reappeared shortly, asking the Lakota chiefs, 'I have ten men, five in each hand; do you want them?' The chiefs said this was not enough. The *winkte* rode away and returned twice more, but the chiefs declined his offers of twenty and fifty men. When the *winkte* returned a fourth time, he fell from his horse, his

Lakota-type bow, quiver and bow case. The quiver and case are of deerskin, decorated with wool and beadwork. The bow is of recurved wood, further strengthened with sinew backing, with a string of sinew. Such short bows could loose arrows with great power and frequency from horseback, and were often preferred to firearms before the introduction of repeating rifles.

hands falling heavily to the ground. He shrieked, 'Answer me quickly, I have a hundred or more,' and the warriors, with a roar, began to count coup over the *winkte* in anticipation of the hundred victims he had delivered.

On the morning of 21st December 1866, the warriors prepared for war, Crazy Horse painting the lightning across his face but keeping his blanket tied around him against the cold. At the fork of Prairie Dog Creek, the Lakota chiefs Black Shield and Black Leg selected two warriors from each tribe to act as decoys – and Crazy Horse received the great honour of leading them.

The main war-party rode south-west, crossed the Bozeman Trail, and concealed themselves behind Lodge Trail Ridge. A smaller group circled westwards along the valley between the ridge and the Bighorns, to await the wood train travelling west below the Sullivant Hills. The wood train left late in the morning and, when attacked, corralled some 1½ miles from Fort Phil Kearny. Carrington prepared a relief force under the command of William J. Fetterman, who had once boasted, 'Give me eighty men and I would ride through the whole Sioux nation.' Carrington ordered him to: 'Support the wood train, relieve it, and report to me. Do not engage or pursue Indians at its expense. Under no circumstances pursue over the ridge . . .'

Fetterman led exactly 80 men from the fort. As they emerged, the Indians attacking the wood train withdrew, and Crazy Horse led the decoys over Lodge Trail Ridge. They were scattered by a shot from the fort's howitzer, but Crazy Horse feinted towards Fetterman, waving his red blanket. He slapped his horse with one hand, restraining it with the other, and Fetterman pursued him eagerly.

Retreating slowly, the decoys led the soldiers over the ridge, beyond sight of the fort, and up to Reno Creek. As the cavalry broke away to give chase, the decoys rode in zig-zags to signal the attack. The uncharacteristically well-disciplined Indians now broke from cover, 2000 warriors sweeping up behind the soldiers.

Two Lakota were killed as they charged in to count coup on the infantry. Then the sky was darkened with arrows, and the walking soldiers all fell. Fetterman raised his revolver to his temple and squeezed the trigger.

Some 400 yards to the north, the cavalry fought to the top of the ridge, and released their horses. The Indians clambered slowly up the slippery slope before mounting a charge. Then the last of the soldiers were clubbed to the ground, their blood freezing as it met the icy air.

The warriors stripped the soldiers and mutilated their bodies terribly. A dog seen running from the scene was impaled with an arrow, in order that nothing at all of the enemy force should survive. Crazy Horse, who had been prominent in the fighting, now held Lone Bear in his arms, as his friend died from his wounds. He mourned for the dead Lakota, but it

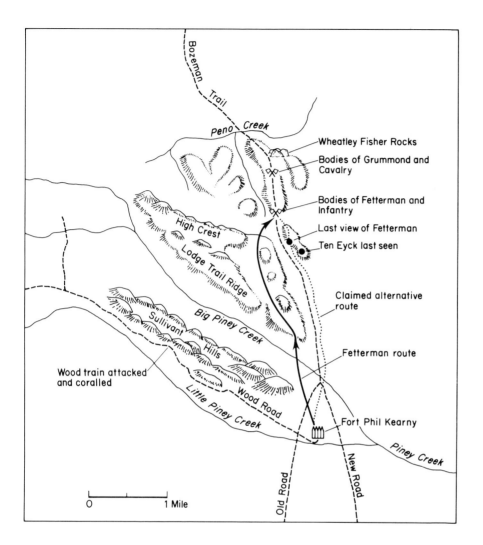

The Battle of the Hundred Slain – the Fetterman Massacre – Fort Phil Kearny, 21 December, 1866.

had been a good day to die. The whites would call the battle 'the Fetterman Massacre'; but Crazy Horse, because of the *winkte* prophecy, called it 'the Battle of the Hundred Slain'.

The Wagon Box Fight

Instead of attacking Fort Phil Kearny, the Indians now divided, seeking shelter from the winter snows. The U.S. government reacted with horror to the worst defeat to date of the Army in the Indian Wars; and Carrington was relieved of his command on 23rd January 1867. While the friendly Lakota signed another treaty in April, Crazy Horse led raids near Fort Reno. In the summer, the hostiles gathered for their Sun Dance, and took the war 'out of the bag' once more. In July, the Cheyenne went north to attack Fort C.F. Smith, while Crazy Horse and Young Man Afraid led 500 Lakota against Fort Phil Kearny.

The Indians often modified their guns, as with this 1869 single-shot Springfield infantry rifle, used at the Little Bighorn. Its barrel has been shortened for use on horseback and repaired with rawhide binding. Also, its sights have been altered and brass tacks added for decoration in typical design.

Hunkpapa Society lance (detail opposite), captured by an Indian army scout in 1881. The steel blade is adorned with hawk feathers, horsehair and red ribbon. The willow shaft is wrapped with quillwork, weasel-skins and weasel-skin pendants. Otter-skin binding on lances was more common, and weasel-skins here may represent the warrior's membership of a dreamer cult, or simply be a part of his personal medicine.

Crazy Horse again led the decoys in attacking a wood-cutting party. His purpose was to draw the soldiers from a corral of wagon boxes that had been constructed west of the fort. However, the main body of warriors raced from hiding prematurely, intent upon capture of the fort's horse herd. The woodcutters escaped to the fort under covering fire from the wagon boxes. The Lakota circled the corral, but were held at bay by Captain James Powell and 30 men armed with the new Springfield breech-loading rifles and delivering a withering cross fire.

The warriors withdrew, and Crazy Horse formed them into a slowly advancing wedge on foot. One soldier later said, 'It chilled my blood . . . hundreds and hundreds of Indians swarming up a ravine about ninety yards to the west of the corral . . . it looked for a minute as though our last moment on earth had come.' Yet the Lakota could not reach the corral, and when reinforcements appeared from the fort, Crazy Horse had to withdraw. This, the Wagon Box Fight of 2nd August 1867, was almost a repetition of the Hayfield Fight of the previous day, with the Cheyenne turned back by the superior fire-power at Fort C.F. Smith.

The government, though, had grown tired of the expenditure of lives and money on Red Cloud's War. A new peace commission met with Old Man Afraid in November, then returned with a wagon-load of goods for Red Cloud in April 1868. While the government representatives kicked their heels, Red Cloud sent a message, saying: 'We are on the mountains looking down on the soldiers and the forts. When we see the soldiers moving away and the forts abandoned, then I will come down and talk.' On 27th July, Fort C.F. Smith was abandoned, and was set ablaze by Crazy Horse's warriors the following dawn. Some days later, Little Wolf's Cheyenne burned Fort Phil Kearny to the ground. Red Cloud finally arrived at Laramie on 4th November. He 'washed his hands with the dust of the floor' and touched the pen to the 1868 Laramie Treaty. This established a Lakota reservation spanning South Dakota and declared the Powder River country 'unceded Indian territory'. It also instructed the Indians to settle on farms; this Red Cloud ignored, departing to hunt on the Powder once more.

Crazy Horse never came to Fort Laramie, instead leading his camp north-east to join Sitting Bull's Hunkpapa. Here He Dog recounted, 'the older more responsible men of the tribe conferred another kind of chieftainship on Crazy Horse. He was made war chief of the whole Oglala tribe. A similar office was conferred on Sitting Bull by the Hunkpapa tribe.'

Defending the Black Hills

Crazy Horse led raids against the Crow in the summer of 1869. He quickly comprehended the Laramie treaty's implications when he attempted to trade for powder and lead on the Platte and was fired on by soldiers. The Indians had either to move on to a reservation, or stay on Powder River without trading; and Crazy Horse naturally took the second option.

The following summer, Crazy Horse and He Dog led a raid against the Crow, east of the Big Horns:

When we came back, the people came out of the camp to meet us and escorted us back, and at a big ceremony presented us with two spears, the gift of the whole tribe, which was met together. These spears were each three or four hundred years old and were given by the older generation to those in the younger generation who had best lived the life of a warrior.

(He Dog)

In the next raid against the Crow, Crazy Horse and He Dog were elected lance-bearers of the Kangi Yuha or Crow-Owners, one of the Oglala warrior societies. Such officership was accorded great honour and carried special obligations in battle. When the raiders reached the Crow reservation, Crazy Horse took the crow-skin society lance from its case and passed it over the smoke of a sweetgrass fire. The lance's red-painted shaft was wrapped in otter fur, with eagle and owl feathers at one end; below its spear-head was bound the stuffed skin of a crow.

The Bad Heart Bull manuscript records Crazy Horse's first conflict as a lance-bearer as the battle 'When They Chased the Crows Back to Camp'. He Dog led the Lakota in stealing the Crow camp's horses, the Crow warriors making a determined pursuit. Crazy Horse, as a crow-lance bearer, was obliged never to retreat, and rallied his men. They countercharged, driving the enemy back amongst their own lodges, and lifting thirteen scalps. A Crow captive later said that his people 'knew Crazy Horse had a medicine-gun that never missed, and that he was bullet-proof.'

Black Buffalo Woman

Ten days after this battle, while No Water was away hunting, Crazy Horse rode from his Oglala camp with Black Buffalo Woman at his side. When No Water returned, he pursued and caught up with the eloping couple on the Powder. Borrowing a revolver from Bad Heart Bull, No Water burst into the lodge, where the two were seated with friends including Little Big Man and He Dog's brother, Little Shield.

'My friend, I have come!' cried No Water and shot Crazy Horse in the face from only four feet away. His upper jaw shattered, Crazy Horse slumped forward into the fire.

No Water fled, telling his friends that he had killed the Hunkpatila

Rear view of a magnificent southern Lakota war-shirt of about 1870. Originally accredited to Crazy Horse, the Nebraska State Historical Society now associate the shirt with Greasing Hand, because it was acquired at Pine Ridge Agency, which was established in 1878 after Crazy Horse's murder. Greasing Hand married Crazy Horse's widow Nellie Larrabee, and, settling at Pine Ridge, assumed his predecessor's name; though it is not inconceivable that he also inherited Crazy Horse's shirt. Whatever its history, the shirt is a good example of the type presented to Crazy Horse upon his election as a Shirt Wearer. It has a blue-dyed upper, and yellow-dyed lower half, and is adorned with 291 hair-locks. The predominantly white beadwork, with red crosses, and dark green panels with red lines and borders of blue triangles is typical of the Southern Lakota.

shirt-wearer. They built him a sweat lodge in order to purify him of the murder. Meanwhile, Crazy Horse's followers, unable to find No Water, shot the mule he had left behind, and Crazy Horse himself was carried to the lodge of his uncle Spotted Crow.

The Oglala circle again lay shattered, and the Hunkpatila demanded that No Water be turned over to them. No Water sheltered in the Bad Face camp of Holy Bald Eagle, who told him, 'Come and stay with me and if they want to fight us, we will fight.'

An internecine struggle was prevented only by the mediation of Crazy Horse's uncles, who sent Black Buffalo Woman to Bad Heart Bull's lodge to be returned to No Water. She later gave birth to a light-haired girl, whispered to be Crazy Horse's daughter. But when No Water sent three ponies to Worm, the matter was supposedly closed.

Crazy Horse slowly recovered, a scar remaining below his left nostril. He later met No Water on a hunting trip, and pursued him all the way to the Yellowstone; after which No Water took to living at Red Cloud Agency. The repercussions of the incident were serious, for the Big Bellies decreed that Crazy Horse had put his interests before those of the tribe, and must return his ceremonial shirt.

Because of all this, Crazy Horse could not be a shirt-wearer any longer. When we were made chiefs we were bound by very strict rules . . . I have always kept the oaths I made then, but Crazy Horse did not . . . The shirt was never given to anybody else. Everything seemed to stop right there. Everything began to fall to pieces. After that it

In the 'Battle Where They Chased The Crows Back To Camp', of 1870, the Lakota are led by Crazy Horse, his status indicated by carrying the ancient Crow-lance of the Kangi Tuha or Crow-Owners warrior society.

seemed as if anybody who wanted to could wear the shirt – it meant nothing. But in the days when Crazy Horse and I received the shirts, we had to accomplish many things to win them.

(He Dog)

As he recovered, Crazy Horse took a new wife, Black Shawl, but soon suffered a new blackness in his heart. A war-party returned from south of the Platte to report the death of his brother Little Hawk, shot by white miners. Wearily, Crazy Horse rode south, found his brother's body, and raised it on a scaffold.

When the summer was passed, Crazy Horse and High Back Bone led a large party against the Shoshoni. Finding the ground at Wind River treacherous, Crazy Horse asked, 'I wonder if we can make it back to Cone Creek? I doubt if our horses can stand in this slush. They sink in over their ankles.'

Angrily, High Back Bone replied: 'This is the second fight he has called off in this same place! This time there is going to be a fight. The last time you called off a fight here, when we got back to camp they all laughed at us. You and I have our good name to think about. If you don't care about it you can go back. But I'm going to stay here and fight.'

Reluctantly, Crazy Horse acquiesced, but the two *kolas* were soon guarding a Lakota retreat. High Back Bone's horse was wounded and a Shoshoni charge engulfed the great warrior.

Seeking High Back Bone's body, Crazy Horse returned four days later, but found only bones left by the coyotes. After losing his chieftainship, his brother and his greatest friend, he would now fight with no fear of death.

Skirmish with Longhair

In the spring of 1871, Crazy Horse's Oglala band drifted northward, strengthening their relations on the Yellowstone with the northern Lakota, the Hunkpapa, Miniconjou and Sans Arcs. There, Black Shawl gave birth to Crazy Horse's daughter, who was called They Are Afraid of Her.

In the summer that followed, Crazy Horse fought in the Second Arrow Creek Fight, called the 'Time When Yellow Shirt Was Killed by the Crow'. Crazy Horse is depicted at this battle in the Bad Heart Bull manuscript, wearing breech-cloth, moccasins and a cape, and shown leaving his wounded horse. This is confirmed:

Crazy Horse charged the Crows, his horse was shot under him, and he was surrounded by the enemy. The Oglala tried to help him but could not get near him. A man named Spotted Deer made a last effort to reach him. He broke through the enemy and Crazy Horse got on to his pony behind him and they made a charge for the open. They made it back to the Sioux lines, riding double and closely pursued.

(Short Bull)

That August, a surveying party protected by Major E.M. Baker's 2nd

Seized by Little Big Man, as foretold in his vision, Crazy Horse receives a fatal thrust from the bayonet of Private William Gentles, outside Fort Robinson guard house, 5th September 1877.

Cavalry, plotted the Northern Pacific Railroad's continuation along the Yellowstone. They fought a long-range engagement with Sitting Bull and Crazy Horse on the fourteenth, and were eventually turned back.

In the winter, Crazy Horse's following fell to about fifty lodges, but increased to some 200 when the agency Indians came north for the buffalo and the Sun Dance the following summer.

A new surveying party hammered stakes along the Yellowstone in June 1873, protected by General D.S. Stanley's troops, and the 7th Cavalry of General Custer, who the Indians called Pahuska, or Long Hair. On 4th August, Crazy Horse and five other decoys attacked Custer's advance party of some ninety men. When Long Hair refused to be drawn, 300 Indian warriors burst from cover and drove the soldiers back into a grove near the mouth of Tongue River. When Custer eventually counter-attacked, his heavy cavalry horses were outrun by the Indians' fleet-footed ponies.

There were skirmishes for the next seven days, before the Indians forded the Yellowstone, a manoeuvre beyond the troopers' capabilities. At dawn on 11th August, the Lakota warriors re-crossed the river, killing four soldiers and shooting Long Hair's horse from beneath him, before being driven off. The surveyors returned east, where their work came to nothing with the bankruptcy of the Northern Pacific Railroad. Meanwhile, Crazy Horse wintered on the Powder.

The Thieves' Trail

In 1874, rumours began to circulate among the white settlements that there was gold in the Black Hills. Though the 1868 Laramie Treaty guaranteed this land to the Indians 'so long as the grass shall grow', General Sheridan sent an expedition to investigate. On 2nd July, Long Hair led 1200 men, including miners and geologists, from Fort Abraham Lincoln on the Missouri, into Pa Sapa. He sent back reports telling of gold 'from the grass roots down,' precipitating a gold rush into the Lakota lands. Custer also commented that he 'could whip all the Indians in the north-west with the Seventh Cavalry.' The Lakota now called Long Hair 'thief' and the route he had taken 'the Thieves' Road'.

Crazy Horse had a more personal cause for grief. When he returned from raiding the Crow, he found Black Shawl with her hair cut and her dress ripped in mourning – and his daughter dead from cholera. He rode to Crow country to find the scaffold that held her tiny body, and mourned for three days.

Unrest about the Black Hills invasion grew at Red Cloud Agency, and many Lakota rode out to join Crazy Horse at the summer's end, taking their allegiance away from Red Cloud forever. Buffalo were scarce that harsh winter, but in the spring Crazy Horse led the Lakota and Cheyenne in frequent attacks against the miners that were flocking into Pa Sapa's heart. In the summer of 1875, Crazy Horse's Oglala, Sitting Bull's

Hunkpapa, Spotted Eagle's Sans Arcs, and Miniconjou under Touch the Clouds, all joined the Cheyenne in a great Sun Dance.

At the end of summer, Young Man Afraid and the interpreter Louis Richards brought tobacco to Crazy Horse's camp, asking him to meet a commission from Washington at Red Cloud Agency. Crazy Horse said simply, 'One does not sell the earth upon which the people walk.'

The council opened on 20th September, eight miles east of the Lakota agency, with twenty thousand Lakota, Cheyenne and Arapaho present. Senator William Allison proposed the purchase of mining rights for the Black Hills, and gave the Indians three days in which to discuss the matter. They reconvened on 23rd September, each band's warriors galloping down from the hills firing their guns, until thousands of Indians surrounded the commissioners' council tent.

About noon, Red Cloud prepared to open the council. There was a sudden movement in the Indian ranks; Little Big Man, Crazy Horse's emissary, burst from among the warriors. Mounted on a fine, grey pony, wearing only breech-cloth and war-bonnet, blood ran down his chest from the freshly opened scars of the Sun Dance. Brandishing a Winchester and shells, and with two revolvers in his belt, Little Big Man declared that he was going to kill the white men who had come to steal the Lakota lands.

The Indian police immediately overpowered him, but only Young Man Afraid's dignified entreaties quieted the excited warriors.

The commissioners quickly scuttled back to Fort Robinson, and Crazy Horse's voice had been heard. On 20th September the commissioners proposed to purchase the hills for $6,000,000, but were told by Spotted Tail that the price was too small. The Lakota left the agencies in large numbers to join the Powder River camps as it became clear that the whites, unable to purchase the Black Hills, would try to steal them.

The commissioners recommended that 'if the Government will interpose its power and authority, they (the Indians) are not in a position to resist.' On 3rd November, President Grant told General Sheridan that the Indians must be forced on to the reservations so as to solve the Black Hills problem. On 9th November, Indian Inspector E.C. Watkins toured the Lakota lands and recommended that the government 'send troops against them in the winter . . . and whip them into subjection.'

Thus, on 6th December, Red Cloud Agent James Hastings was instructed to send messengers to the Lakota, notifying them that 'unless they shall remove within the lands of their reservation (and remain there) before the 31st January, they shall be deemed hostile, and treated accordingly by the military force.'

Indian runners battled through blizzards to Crazy Horse's camp on the Tongue, where Black Twin told them the snow was too deep and the ponies too thin for the camp to move into the reservation. Then Crazy Horse led his people north to join Sitting Bull.

Eagle talon medicine bundle adorned with cloth and beadwork wrapping with brass bells. This magnificent talisman conveyed the eagle's power to strike its prey to a warrior who had received such a blessing in a vision-quest. Such symbols of medicine remained important to a visionary like Crazy Horse for the whole of his life.

On 8th February 1876, Sheridan ordered Generals Crook and Terry to prepare for military operations on the Powder, Tongue, Rosebud and Bighorn headwaters 'where Crazy Horse and his allies frequented.'

As spring brought fresh herds of buffalo, He Dog took a dozen lodges to join Old Bear's Cheyenne camp – and on 17th March 1876, Crook's advance force of six cavalry companies under Colonel J.J. Reynolds fell upon the camp. The Indians fled, while the soldiers burned their lodges and possessions. Mistakenly, the troops believed they had destroyed the camp of Crazy Horse, whom Captain J.G. Bourke described as, 'justly regarded as the boldest, bravest and most skilful warrior in the whole Sioux nation.'

It was, though, Crazy Horse's village that took in the refugees after a flight of three days. The Oglala headmen cried out 'Cheyenne, come and eat here', while Crazy Horse told them, 'I'm glad you are come. We are going to fight the white man again.'

Short Bull later said, 'If it had not been for that attack by Crook on Powder River, we would have come in to the agency that spring, and there would have been no Sioux war.'

Greatest Victory

Crazy Horse led his people north to join the ever growing camp of Sitting Bull. This great camp lumbered on to new grass every few days; as they moved, another cluster of horses would haul their travois into the long column, bringing families fresh from the agencies. By May, the Rosebud valley was filled with lodges. In June, Sitting Bull offered one hundred pieces of flesh at the Hunkpapa Sun Dance and received a vision of many soldiers falling into camp. Wakan Tanka told him: 'I give you these because they have no ears.'

Rosebud

After the Sun Dance, the camp moved to Ash Creek on the Little Bighorn, where Cheyenne scouts rode in howling like wolves, proclaiming the discovery of many Blue Coats on the Rosebud. These were the 1,047 soldiers under Crook that had marched north from Fort Fetterman on 20th May, with 262 Crow and Shoshoni scouts. Meanwhile, 460 men under Colonel John Gibbon, were marching east along the Yellowstone from Fort Ellis, Montana; and 925 men including Custer's 7th Cavalry were marching west from Fort Abraham Lincoln under Brigadier-General Alfred Terry.

On 16th June, Crazy Horse led a force of at least 1,500 warriors against Crook. Nearing the headwaters of the Rosebud at dawn on 17th June 1876, he stopped to prepare for battle, applying his snow-thunder paint and fastening the stuffed skin of a red-backed hawk in his hair.

Crook's forces were camped on both sides of the Rosebud and the first intimation they received of danger was the appearance of an Indian scout, screaming, 'Lakota! Lakota!' Crazy Horse, the majority of his warriors concealed behind bluffs, led the first attack from the north-west, but was held by the Crow and Shoshoni scouts. Then the infantry's arrival pushed the Lakota back to a ridge a mile north of Rosebud Creek. The Indians then attacked further east, but were driven west by a cavalry charge under Captain Mills. They rallied on a second line of hills, making bravery runs, slapping their buttocks and taunting the soldiers. The correspondent John Finerty reported, 'One chief, probably the late, lamented Crazy Horse, directed their movements by signals made with a pocket mirror . . .'

The soldiers drove the Indians back from a second ridge, then a third, only to see their ranks arrayed on the next crest. Colonel Royall's men became surrounded on a south-easterly hill, while the Indian scouts, supported by cavalry, drove the Lakota westwards. Crook's remaining troops skirmished on the edge of the valley:

The soldiers first got the Sioux and the Cheyenne on the run. Crazy Horse, Bad Heart Bull, Black Deer, Kicking Bear and Good Weasel rallied the Sioux, turned the charge, and got the soldiers on the run. When these five commenced to rally their men that was as far as the soldiers got.

(Short Bull)

He Dog, a life-long friend of Crazy Horse, pictured in 1930 when, aged ninety-two, he provided Eleanor Hinman with a remarkable history of his comrade the Oglala chief. His memory of events gave him the status and rôle of tribal chronicler. Other old-timers, when interviewed, often simply replied: 'He Dog will remember that'.

In one clash, Jack Red Cloud, son of Oglala chief Red Cloud, was surrounded by Crow scouts, who snatched off his war-bonnet, which he had no right to wear, and whipped him. They laughed at his pleas for mercy, until Crazy Horse swept down and snatched the boy to safety.

Crook drew his men into a tighter circle, while his snipers pinned down the Indians from a ridge in the north-west, and the 9th Infantry supported Royall. Then he ordered Mills to go north, along a thin defile towards where he believed the Indian camp to be. Crazy Horse – crying 'today is a good day to fight, today is a good day to die,' – led a fresh onslaught against Crook's weakened force. Only by recalling Mills, who swept around into the Indians' flank, did Crook save his command.

The warriors withdrew, having demonstrated a new determination and co-ordination in their fighting. Crook claimed a victory, but had lost 28 dead with 56 wounded – and expended 25,000 rounds of ammunition and all his supplies. He was out of the summer campaign, returning to his Goose Creek base camp, where he stayed until July, licking his wounds.

Battle On The Greasy Grass

Six nights after the Rosebud battle, the Indians found a new campsite, their smoke-tinted tipis stretching for three miles along the west bank of the Little Bighorn, in the valley they called the Greasy Grass. Ten thousand people gathered there. The Cheyenne camped in the north,

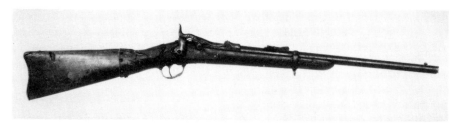

then the Brulé, Sans Arcs, Oglala, Blackfoot and Miniconjou circles, with the Hunkpapa in the south.

Terry and Gibbon had met up above Rosebud Creek, aware of the Indian camp on the Little Bighorn, but oblivious to Crook's defeat. Councilling on the steamer *Far West*, they proposed to surround the camp by sending Custer south while Gibbon swept west and attacked from the north. On 22nd June, Custer led 31 officers and 586 soldiers of the 7th Cavalry, with 33 Indian scouts and 20 civilians, south along the Rosebud. He had turned down the offer of three cumbersome Gatling guns and four troops of the 2nd Cavalry, and carried rations for only fifteen days. As they departed, Gibbon remarked, 'Now Custer, don't be greedy but wait for us.' Custer replied, ambiguously, 'No, I will not.'

When his scouts found the Indian village's trail, Custer swung west immediately, making a forced march on the night of 24th June. His scouts became animated over their discovery of sandpictures, depicting Sitting Bull's vision; and the Arikara warrior Bloody Knife warned that the camp held more Indians than the soldiers had bullets. Nevertheless, at noon on Sunday 25th June 1876, Custer prepared to attack the village, hidden to the west behind bluffs and trees. Leaving the pack-train behind, he divided his men into three groups: Captain F.W. Benteen scouted south-west with 113 men; Major M.A. Reno took 131 men south; Custer hurried north with 215 men, along the bluffs above the valley in which the camp lay.

Lakota women, digging turnips, alerted the camp to Long Hair's presence, and the warriors dressed hurriedly for death. Suddenly at about 3.00 p.m., Reno's men hit the southern end of the village, cutting down those women and children standing out in the open. The Hunkpapa rallied and turned Reno's hesitant charge. Crazy Horse 'rode with the greatest daring' up and down in front of Reno's skirmish line and as soon as these troops were driven across the river, he went at once to Custer's front and 'there became the leading spirit.' Reno's men were driven across the Little Bighorn, digging in to the bluffs where they were supported by Benteen's arrival at 4.15 p.m.

Short Bull first saw Crazy Horse after Reno's retreat:

'Too late! You've missed the fight!' we called out to him. 'Sorry to miss the fight!' he laughed, 'but there's a good fight coming over the hill.'

I looked where he pointed and saw Custer and his blue coats pouring over the hill. I thought there were a million of them.

'That's where the big fight is going to be,' said Crazy Horse, 'We'll not miss that one.' He was not a bit excited; he made a joke of it. He wheeled and rode down the river, and a little while later I saw him on his pinto pony leading his men across the ford. He was the first man to cross the river. I saw he had the business well in hand. They rode up the draw and then there was too much dust – I could not see any more.

As Custer continued along the eastern bluffs, he was turned away by warriors led by the Hunkpapa Gall, and forced to continue north. Crazy Horse swept through the heart of the Indian camp, hearing a growing thunder of hooves behind him. He emerged from the Cheyenne camp with a thousand warriors at his heels, and galloped across the ford, encircling Long Hair.

Custer's troops were retiring 'step by step' from Gall's attack. Lieutenant Calhoun's L Company was engulfed, and the Companies of Lieutenant A.E. Smith and Captain Thomas Custer were swept into Deep Coulee Ravine. Meanwhile, Long Hair Custer, with Captain G.W. Yates' Company, was ascending the highest point on the ridge –

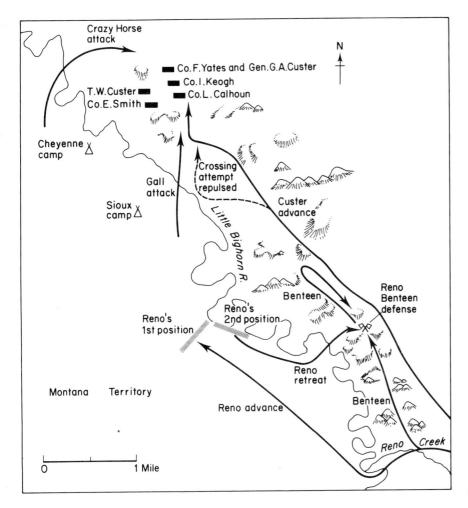

The Battle on the Greasy Grass – the Little Bighorn – fought on 25th June, 1876.

87

Lakota shield cover of tanned skin is painted with protective medicine designs, in black, white, yellow, red, green and bright blue; the central feature probably depicting the Eagle or Thunderbird. While a shield of rawhide padded with hair could deflect a low-velocity musket-ball, the importance of its medicine designs was such that sometimes only the flimsy, protective cover was carried into battle.

now called Last Stand Hill – when Crazy Horse emerged over its crest. Brandishing a Winchester rifle, and swinging his war-club, he led his screaming, painted warriors crashing through Custer's command. By 5.00 p.m., within an hour-and-a-half of the attack, not a soldier remained alive.

Crazy Horse the Sioux chief, was the bravest man I ever saw. He rode closest to the soldiers, yelling to his warriors. All the soldiers were shooting at him, but he was never hit.

(Arapaho Warrior)

Reno and Benteen remained entrenched through the night, and when the wolves reported Gibbon's approach the next day, the Indian camp moved off towards the Bighorns. Crazy Horse rode off alone to a butte near Reno Creek, and engraved in the sand a horse and a snake with lightning marks, the signs of his vision.

Surrender and Death

Inevitably, the huge Indian camp divided, and many Indians returned to the agencies. Here they were forced to sign away the Black Hills on threat of having their rations stopped. Crazy Horse renewed his attacks against the miners. Then, in August, Crook and Terry set out to hunt him once more. On 9th September 1876, Crook's advance detachment under Captain Mills struck a camp of Oglala and Miniconjou under Iron Plume. Most of the Lakota escaped, and Crazy Horse led a counter-attack against Crook, but was fought off by superior numbers.

Crook returned from the field in October in order to enlist scouts from the Lakota agencies who would hunt for their own people in his winter campaign. Colonel Ranald Mackenzie was dispatched to find Crazy Horse; instead he struck Dull Knife's Cheyenne camp at dawn on 25th November. The Cheyenne suffered forty dead; losing all their belongings, they fled desperately through the snow. Twelve Cheyenne children froze in their mothers' arms on the first night of the flight, and eleven more nights passed before they reached the camp of Crazy Horse.

'We helped the Cheyennes the best we could. We hadn't much ourselves,' Short Bull recalled. Wooden Leg, the Cheyenne, remembered 'Oh, how generous were the Oglala!' Yet Bourke wrote that: 'Crazy Horse was indifferent to the sufferings of his allies, and turned the cold shoulder upon them completely.'

Certainly, from this time, the Cheyenne seemed to be the first of Crazy Horse's friends suddenly to turn against him.

The Oglala and Cheyenne village moved up the Tongue. With his people hungry, Crazy Horse sent a delegation under Packs The Drum (Sitting Bull) to seek terms with Colonel Miles at Fort Keogh. As they

Shield cover, bearing blue, red and yellow medicine symbols including the Thunderbird. It has been attributed to Crazy Horse and according to its documentation, it was captured by General Lawton, who 'might have been attached to Miles' Command.'

approached the fort under a white flag, Miles' Crow scouts shot down five of the Lakota, leaving them bleeding in the snow; so ending the peace talks.

Now, even Crazy Horse's own people tried to sneak away to the agencies, so that his faithful warriors had to shoot the horses of the renegades in order to make them stay.

Following skirmishes on 1st and 3rd January 1877, some 500 infantry under Miles struck Crazy Horse's camp on 8th January. Miles' faltering charge through deep snow was held by Crazy Horse and just three others, while the rest of the camp fled. A blizzard forced Miles back to Fort Keogh, Crazy Horse following him all the way in a forlorn attempt to rescue some captured women.

In January, Red Cloud's nephew Sword led an Oglala delegation from the agency to beg Crazy Horse's surrender; but he refused their tobacco. Then, the half-breed Big Leggins Johnny Brughier brought in the captured women with an offer that Crazy Horse should surrender to Miles.

In March, Spotted Tail led 250 Brulé to Crazy Horse's camp, with promises from Crook of the Oglala chief's own agency if Crazy Horse surrendered at Fort Robinson. Crazy Horse, seeing his people truly divided, stayed away from camp during Spotted Tail's visit. He left a message with Worm, saying he shook hands with his uncle, and would bring in his people when the weather permitted.

Spotted Tail, the outstanding Brulé headman, with his wife and daughter, in Nebraska about 1879. Though remembered as one of the most fearless of all Lakota warriors, Spotted Tail became a leading advocate for peace with the whites after 1864.

89

Crazy Horse councilled on the Powder River with Little Wolf, He Dog and Ice of the Cheyenne, and listened as old Iron Hawk told him: 'You see all the people here are in rags, they all need clothing, we may as well go in.' With the buffalo dying and his people's spirit broken, Crazy Horse headed towards the agency. Red Cloud met him on 27th April, saying, 'All is well; have no fear; come on in.' Thus he stole the 'honour' of Crazy Horse's capture from Spotted Tail.

On the morning of 6th May 1877, Crazy Horse met Lieutenant 'White Hat' Clark, commanding officer at Red Cloud Agency, some seven miles out from the agency. Crazy Horse smoked with Clark, then held out his left hand, saying: '*Kola*, I shake with this hand because my heart is on this side; I want this peace to last forever.' He then gave his war-shirt to Red Cloud.

Shortly after noon, Crazy Horse's people approached the agency, led by Clark and Red Cloud's Indian police. At Crazy Horse's side rode He Dog, Little Hawk, Little Big Man, Old Hawk and Bad Road; and behind them rode a finely disciplined column of warriors, painted and dressed in their finest costume. For two miles behind them, the women and children rode in silence, the hooves of 2,000 Oglala ponies rumbling across the ground. Nearing the fort, Crazy Horse began to sing, softly and deeply, the peace song of the Lakota. All the warriors took up the chant, then the women and children, until the voice of nearly 900 people echoed through the valley. 'By God! This is a triumphal march, not a surrender!' one officer remarked.

While the Oglala women raised the lodges on the banks of the White River, the warriors surrendered their ponies to Red Cloud's eager followers. Then Clark searched the Oglala lodges, confiscating 117 guns, including Crazy Horse's three Winchesters. Clark was all the while guarded by his Cheyenne scouts. Crazy Horse's old friends, including Little Wolf and Morning Star, were hidden, painted for war, behind a ridge; waiting to attack the Oglala.

Of his surrender, Luther Standing Bear said that Crazy Horse, 'foresaw the consequence . . . it meant submission to a people whom he did not consider his equal . . . Crazy Horse feared no man and when he did surrender, it was not from volition on his part, but because his people were tired of warfare.'

The Prophecy Fulfilled
After his surrender, Short Bull recalled Crazy Horse's words to Clark:

He said 'There is a creek over there they call Beaver Creek; there is a great big flat west of the headwaters of Beaver Creek; I want my agency put right in the middle of that flat'. He said the grass was good there for horses and game. After the agency was placed there, he would go to Washington and talk to the Great Fathers. It was the only cause of misunderstanding at that time. Crazy Horse wanted to have the agency established first, and then he would go to Washington. The officers wanted him to go to Washington first.

The difference of whether Crazy Horse should go to Washington before or after the site of the agency was settled upon brought on all the trouble, little by little.

(Short Bull)

The officers at Fort Robinson were understandably fascinated by Crazy Horse, and Red Feather recalled: 'All the white people came to see Crazy Horse and gave him presents and money. The other Indians at the agency got very jealous.' The old rivalries between the Bad Faces and the Hunkpatila resurfaced and Crazy Horse attracted an increasing number of enemies. When Crook granted him permission for a feast and a buffalo hunt, Red Cloud and Spotted Tail immediately spoke against Crazy Horse to their agents.

Then, when Crazy Horse finally decided to go to Washington, the Red Cloud Lakota whispered to him of the great danger he was in. 'Other Indians were jealous of him,' Little Killer said, 'and afraid that if he went to Washington they would make him chief of all the Indians on the reservation. These Indians came to him and told him a lot of stories. After that he would not go there.' According to Carrie Slow Bear, 'Another Indian told him they would kill him either at Fort Robinson or Washington . . . Little Big Man told him that.'

In August of 1877, Crook asked the Oglala to help him fight the Nez Perce. While his people signed up, proudly parading their new guns and

Little Big Man, who in 1875, as Crazy Horse's lieutenant, threatened to kill the Black Hills commissioners. After surrendering with Crazy Horse, he switched allegiance, and schemed to supplant the Oglala chief, pinioning Crazy Horse's arms when he was killed. Lt. Bourke said of Little Big Man: 'In appearance he was crafty, but withal a man of considerable ability and force;' however the reservation Lakota spoke of him as a trouble-maker.

91

Touch the Clouds, the dignified seven-foot tall Miniconjou warrior and chief who shared Crazy Horse's fight for the Lakota's traditional freedom. Greatly feared by his enemies, he surrendered at the Spotted Tail Agency, Camp Sheridan, at the head of a singing column of warriors, on 14 April, 1877. There, Crazy Horse sought Touch the Clouds' protection when escaping arrest on the 4th September.

horses, Crazy Horse refused. Red Feather explained: 'When he came to the agency, the soldiers had made him promise not to go on the warpath any more. They told him not to fight and then to fight.' When Clark persisted in asking him to enlist, Crazy Horse snapped, 'If the Great Father wants us to fight we will go north and fight until not a Nez Percé is left.' The translator, Frank Grouard, maliciously translated this as, 'until not a white man is left.' Then Crazy Horse, exasperated by affairs at Red Cloud Agency, threatened to take his people north again, and the white officers were thrown into panic.

Crook was summoned, arriving at the Red Cloud Agency on 2nd September 1877. Two officers, Randall and Bradley, visited Crazy Horse, giving him a knife and two cigars, and the Indians were told to move across the creek for a council with Crook. Crazy Horse refused, suspicious of his white visitors.

He thought the gift of the knife meant trouble coming. He thought they shook hands with him as if they did not mean him any good. He was afraid there would be trouble at that council.

(He Dog)

When He Dog asked if this meant that Crazy Horse would be his enemy if he moved across the creek, Crazy Horse, laughing, replied:

'I am no white man! They are the only people that make rules for other people that say, 'If you stay on one side of this line it is peace, but if you go on the other side I will kill you all. There is plenty of room; camp where you please.'

When Clark asked He Dog to persuade his friend to attend, Crazy Horse replied, 'Some people over there have said too much. I don't want to talk to them any more. No good would come of it.'

As an ambulance carried Crook and Clark to the council, Red Cloud's cousin Woman's Dress rode up. He often loafed with Long Chin and Lone Bear near Crazy Horse's lodge, blankets about their heads; and he announced that Crazy Horse meant to kill Crook.

Crook returned immediately to Fort Robinson, and the next day told the Lakota chiefs, 'that they must preserve order in their own ranks and arrest Crazy Horse'. Red Feather heard White Hat offer '$100 and a sorrel horse to any Indian who would kill Crazy Horse,' and hurried to warn the betrayed Oglala of his fate.

At 9 a.m. on 4th September, eight companies of infantry left Fort Robinson for Crazy Horse's village, Clark leading 400 warriors including Red Cloud, Little Wound, American Horse and Young Man Afraid. They reached Crazy Horse's village only to find the lodges scattered, Crazy Horse having taken his wife to Spotted Tail Agency. Clark offered $200 to the first man to catch him, and it was No Water who led the pursuit. By riding hard downhill, and walking uphill, Crazy Horse reached Spotted Tail Agency that evening, while No Water killed two horses in a vain attempt to catch him.

Crazy Horse spent the night under the protection of the seven-feet Miniconjou chief Touch The Clouds. Assured that he could eventually settle at Spotted Tail Agency, Crazy Horse left to return to Red Cloud Agency in the morning, escorted by Touch The Clouds, Agent Lee and Spotted Tail's soldiers. Lee described Crazy Horse as being like, 'a frightened, trembling wild animal brought to bay, hoping for confidence one moment and fearing treachery the next. He had been under a severe strain, and it plainly showed.'

When Crazy Horse reached White River, some 10,000 Lakota had gathered at the agency. He Dog met him, warning, 'Watch your step – you are going into a bad place.' Crook had ordered Bradley to 'capture this chief, confine him, and send him under guard to Omaha.' So, while Crazy Horse was led into the adjutant's office at Fort Robinson, Lee was told that Bradley would not see the chief, and that he must be placed in the guardhouse.

Under the charge of Captain James Kennington, Crazy Horse was led towards the prison, still believing Lee's assurances that he could speak to the commanding officer. The Indian policemen Turning Bear, Wooden Sword, Leaper and Little Big Man escorted him. Passing a soldier with a bayonetted rifle, Crazy Horse saw the tiny cell's barred windows. He

Crazy Horse boasted that he would never allow the white man's camera to 'steal his shadow'. No fully authenticated image of him exists, although several photographs have been published purporting to be him. Of these, this old tin-type is the most likely to be authentic. It originated with Ellen Howard, daughter of the scout Baptiste Garnier (Little Bat) whose wife was Crazy Horse's cousin. She claimed that Little Bat and the infamous scout Frank Grouard persuaded Crazy Horse to have the photograph taken near Fort Laramie, about 1872. It bears a fascinating resemblance to written descriptions of Crazy Horse, and was authenticated as being him by Jake Herman, Fifth Member of the Oglala Sioux Tribal Council, after consultation with the Lakota elders.

smelled its foul stench and realised for the first time that he was to be imprisoned. Drawing a knife, he reeled around, slashing Little Big Man across the forearm. Then Little Big Man grasped his old friend's arms, echoing Crazy Horse's vision. American Horse and Red Cloud screamed, 'Shoot to kill!' Kennington bellowed, 'Stab the son of a bitch!'

His arms pinioned, Crazy Horse felt the bayonet of Private William Gentles pierce his back. Then it was thrust again, through his kidneys. Falling into Little Big Man's arms, Crazy Horse whispered, 'Let me go, my friends. You have got me hurt enough.' He Dog stepped up and Crazy Horse asked, 'See where I am hurt. I can feel the blood flowing.' Then Touch The Clouds picked up the Oglala gently in his arms, and carried him in to the adjutant's office.

Worm and Touch The Clouds spent the night beside Crazy Horse, who told them, 'I am bad hurt. Tell the people it is no use to depend on me any more now.' He died early in the morning of 6th September 1877. Touch The Clouds spoke quietly: 'It is good; he has looked for death and it has come.' Only now did the Lakota realise that they had killed their great warrior and chief through their fears and jealousies. One elder said later, 'I'm not telling anyone – white or Indian – what I know about the killing of Crazy Horse. That affair was a disgrace and a dirty shame. We killed our own man.'

Crazy Horse's body was placed in a coffin and carried on a travois to be placed on a scaffold at Spotted Tail Agency. When the Lakota were moved to a new agency on the Missouri, Worm broke away from his people. Wrapping his son's bones in a buffalo robe, he placed them on a scaffold, in an unknown place near Chankpe Opi Wakpala, Wounded Knee Creek:

His father hid his body so not even my sister (Black Shawl) knew where it was buried. Before he was buried a war-eagle came to walk on the coffin every night. It did nothing, only just walked about.

(Red Feather)

Chronology of Events

1830	Indian Removal Act.
1831	Fort Pierre built in the Dakotas.
1834	Fort Laramie established. Oglala head south.
1841	First large wagon-trains cross the Plains.
	Bull Bear murdered in Old Smoke's camp.
	AUTUMN: Curly born on Rapid Creek.
1845	15 JUNE: Colonel Kearney meets Oglala and Brulé at Laramie.
1849	Troops stationed at Fort Laramie.
	Cholera sweeps the Plains.
1850	Smallpox sweeps the Plains.

1851	Horse Creek council and treaty signing.
1854	19 AUGUST: Lieutenant Grattan's party killed.
1855	3 SEPTEMBER: Blue Water Massacre. General Harney destroys Little Thunder's camp.
1857	29 JULY: Colonel Sumner fights Cheyenne on Solomon River.
1857	SUMMER: Bear Butte Indian council.
	Upper Platte Agency moved west of Laramie.
1858	Curly kills two Arapaho and is named Crazy Horse.
	Colorado gold-rush.

1860	Upper Platte Agency moved back east of Laramie.
1861–5	American Civil War.
1862	No Water marries Black Buffalo Woman.
1864	Sand Creek Massacre. Colonel Chivington attacks Black Kettle's Cheyenne
1865	7 JANUARY: First Julesburg Station attack.
	2 FEBRUARY: Second Julesburg Station attack.
	14 JUNE: Loafers flee en route to Fort Kearney.
	25–26 JULY: Platte Bridge Station attack.
	SUMMER: Crazy Horse is made a Shirt Wearer.
	AUGUST: Powder River expeditions under General Connor and Colonels Cole and Walker.
1866	JUNE: Carrington meets Red Cloud at Laramie.
	AUGUST: Forts Reno, Phil Kearny and C.F. Smith established on Bozeman Trail.
	21 DECEMBER: The Battle of the Hundred Slain (Fetterman Massacre).
1867	23 JANUARY: Carrington relieved of command at Fort Phil Kearny.
	1 August: Hayfield Fight.
	2 AUGUST: Wagon Box Fight.
1868	JULY: Forts C.F. Smith and Phil Kearny abandoned.
	NOVEMBER: Red Cloud signs Laramie Treaty.
	Crazy Horse recognised as Oglala war chief.
1870	SUMMER: Crazy Horse and He Dog carry crowlances in battle 'When they chased the Crows back to Camp.'
	No Water shoots Crazy Horse after elopement with Black Buffalo Woman.
	Little Hawk killed.
	AUTUMN: High Back Bone killed.
1871	Crazy Horse's daughter They are Afraid of Her born.
1872	SUMMER: Second Arrow Creek Fight.
1872	AUGUST: Major Baker's Northern Pacific Railroad Yellowstone survey.
1873	JUNE: Generals Stanley and Custer's Yellowstone survey.
1874	JULY: Custer's Black Hills expedition.
	Crazy Horse's daughter dies.
1875	SUMMER: The Lakota and Cheyenne hold great Sun Dance.
	SEPTEMBER: Black Hills commission fails to purchase Pa Sapa.
	6 DECEMBER: Indians ordered on to reservations.
1876	17 MARCH: Colonel Reynold's attack on He Dog's Powder River camp.
	Sitting Bull's Sun Dance.
	17 JUNE: Battle of the Rosebud.
	25 JUNE: Battle of the Greasy Grass (Little Bighorn).
	9 SEPTEMBER: Captain Mills attacks Iron Plume camp at Slim Buttes.
	25 NOVEMBER: Colonel Mackenzie attacks Dull Knife's Cheyenne.
	DECEMBER: Crazy Horse's emissaries killed at Fort Keogh by Colonel Miles' Crow scouts.
1877	8 JANUARY: Miles attacks Crazy Horse camp.
	Sword's Oglala delegation asks Crazy Horse to surrender.
	MARCH: Spotted Tail's Brulé delegation asks Crazy Horse to surrender.
	27 APRIL: Red Cloud claims honour of Crazy Horse surrender.
	6 MAY: Crazy Horse surrenders at Red Cloud Agency.
	6 SEPTEMBER: Crazy Horse killed.

Bibliography

Adams, A.B. *Sitting Bull* New English Library, 1975.

Ambrose, S.E. *Crazy Horse and Custer*, Purnell, 1975.

Bad Heart Bull, A. *A Pictographic History of the Oglala Sioux* University of Nebraska, 1967.

Bourke, J.G. *On the Border with Crook* Time Life, 1980.

Brandon, W. *American Heritage Book of Indians* American Heritage, 1982.

Brown, D. *Bury My Heart At Wounded Knee* Barrie & Jenkins/Pan, 1970.

Brown, J.E. *The Sacred Pipe* Penguin, 1971.

Finerty, J.F. *War Path and Bivouac* University of Oklahoma, 1961.

Grinnel, G.B. *The Fighting Cheyennes* University of Oklahoma, 1915.

Hinman, E.H. *Oglala Sources on the Life of Crazy Horse* Nebraska State Historical Society, 1976.

Hook, J. 'Crazy Horse' in *Military Illustrated* June/July, 1986.

Hook, J. *The American Plains Indians* Osprey, 1985.

Hyde, G.E. *Spotted Tail's Folk*, University of Oklahoma, 1961.

McCluhan, T.C. *Touch the Earth,* Sphere 1971.

Marquis, T.B. *Wooden Leg*, University of Nebraska 1931.

Powell, P.J. *People of the Sacred Mountain*, Harper & Row 1981.

Sandoz, M. *Crazy Horse*, Bison, 1961.

Swanton, J.R. *The Indian Tribes of North America,* Smithsonian Institution, 1952.

Taylor, C. *Warriors of the Plains*, Hamlyn, 1975.

Vaughn, J.W. *Indian Fights,* University of Oklahoma, 1966.

Vestal, S. *Sitting Bull*, University of Oklahoma, 1956.

Chief Joseph

GUARDIAN OF THE NEZ PERCE

Studio portrait of Chief Joseph in 1877 when he was 37 years old. He wears blanket coat and leggings, cotton shirt, loop necklaces and moccasins, with his hair in ornamented plaits and the usual swept-up fringe. A fur quiver is visible to Joseph's right, held by a thin strap across his chest.

Route of the Nez Perce on their epic 1,700-mile march from the Wallowa Valley to the Bear Paws, showing the major battles fought during their flight.

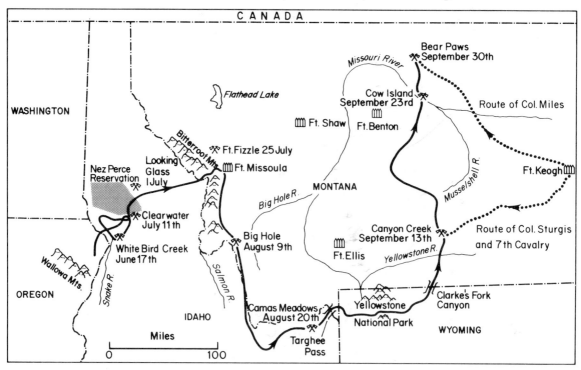

98

The Earth was created by the assistance of the sun, and it should be left as it was. . . .
The country was made without lines of demarcation and it is no man's business to divide
it. . . .

(Chief Joseph)

The whites told only one side. Told it to please themselves. Told much that is not true.
Only his own best deeds, only the worst deeds of the Indians, has the white man told.

(Yellow Knife of the Nez Perce)

Protector of the People

The story of the Nez Perce struggle to defend their ancient homeland is
one of the most outstanding in American history. Proudly, they maintained peace with the white men for seventy years, until finally they
became forced to take up arms, the reluctant tormentors of the US
Army. Yet the spirit, dignity and skill which characterised their struggle
won the Nez Perce many supporters, even among the white communi-
ties.

The Plateau culture region.

Their leader was Chief Joseph, a truly remarkable man. In an era of
violent conflict, his long struggle for peace with the white man remains
one of the most inspiring stories of the time. Thereafter, his leadership of
the Nez Perce, reluctantly into war, was magnificent. Though outnum-
bered the Nez Perce fought valiantly in a gallant but vain attempt to
reach Canada and to find sanctuary. Their journey was a battling retreat,
one of the greatest in all of military history.

The final defeat of the Nez Perce – almost in sight of their goal – and
their surrender, inspired Joseph's greatest adversary to befriend him. In
doing so, General Nelson Miles' own words tell everything about the
nature of Chief Joseph and his brave people:

The boldest and best marksmen of any Indians I have ever encountered. And Chief
Joseph was a man of more sagacity and intelligence than any Indian I have ever met.

Though Joseph spent much of his later life in exile from his beloved
Wallowa Valley, he was never subjugated, possessing a kind dignity that
was as powerful as his leadership when young. The absence of any
atrocities or aggressive acts on the part of Joseph's people sets the Nez
Perce conflict apart from all of the other Indian wars. Its character was
summarised by Joseph's warning to the defenders of Fort Fizzle in Montana:

We are going by you without fighting, if you will let us; but we are going by you
anyhow.

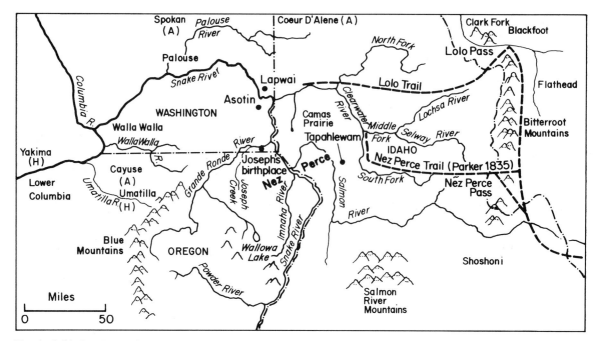

Homeland of the Nez Perce and the neighbouring tribes of the Shahaptian (H) and Salish (A) families that shared their Plateau culture.

The Nez Perce

The Nez Perce, in common with most North American Indian tribes, referred to themselves simply as 'The People' – Nimipu. Their first white visitors, William Clark and Meriwether Lewis, who 'discovered' the tribe in 1805, called them the Chopunnish. This name was probably a corruption of an old Nez Perce word *Tssop-nit-palu*, meaning 'The Walking People'. The explorers also called them 'Pierced Noses', since some of the tribe demonstrated a coastal trait of inserting dentalium through their noses. French trappers adopted this name, translating it to *Nez Percés*, which has been corrupted in English to their modern name of Nez Perces, or simply Nez Perce.

Homelands and Origins

Numbering less than 6000 souls, the Nez Perce roamed a traditional Plateau homeland of some 27,000 square miles, spanning western Idaho, south-eastern Washington, and north-eastern Oregon. A region of lush prairies, sheltered river valleys, towering highlands and precipitous canyons, it spanned the Clearwater Mountains in the north and Salmon River Mountains in the south. The Bitterroots formed their eastern borders, the Blue Mountains and Columbia River their western.

Settlement was concentrated in fishing villages on the tributaries of the Snake, Clearwater and Salmon Rivers. Each village had a headman, but tribal cohesion was apparent only in such co-operative ventures as organising large war, hunting or gathering parties.

100

They were a very bright and energetic body of Indians; indeed the most intelligent that I had ever seen. Exceedingly self-reliant, each man seemed to be able to do his own thinking and to be purely democratic and independent in his ideas and purposes.

(Col. Nelson Miles)

Archaeological remains indicate that the Nez Perce's ancestors occupied caves in the region over 8000 years ago. However, the Nez Perce themselves placed their origins in the blood of a mythical monster slain by the culture hero Coyote. They were the most powerful in the Shahaptian family, which also included the Palouse, Walla Walla, Umatilla, Wanapum, Klickitat, Yakima and Cayuse tribes. Their Plateau culture was shared also by the Salish family of tribes to the north, which included the Salish (Flathead), Spokan, Skitswish (Coeur d'Alênes), Kalispel (Pend D'Oreilles), Okanogan, Sans Poil, Colville, Senijextee (Lake), Ntlakyapamuk, Lilooet, Shuswap, Columbia, Methow and Wenatchee. The Nez Perce feuded with the Spokan and Skitswish, but their most bitter enemies were the Shoshoni, Bannock and Paiute tribes of the Great Basin region to the south.

The People

The Nez Perce were renowned as great travellers, especially following their acquisition of horses in the early eighteenth century. According to legend, their magnificent horse-herds were descended from a white mare and her colt, purchased with dentalium by a peace delegation to

Nez Perce toy cradleboard, front and back, of buckskin-covered board with beadwork decoration and buckskin fringe and carrying strap.

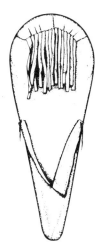

Flathead woman and child, painted by Paul Kane around 1850. The cradleboard is designed to compress the child's skull, creating the flattened head seen on the mother. The Nez Perce borrowed this trait, along with their nose piercing from their original neighbours among the North West Coast tribes.

The distinctively marked Appaloosa ponies – the 'spotted horses' – took their name from the Palouse Indians, but were especially bred by the Nez Perce. They were used in the desperate flight of Joseph and his people.

Nez Perce war-bonnet of 1860–90. It is constructed from eagle feathers, horse-hair, red cloth, ermine pendants, buffalo-horn strips, beadwork and brass bells. Such headdresses denoted accomplished warriors and were adopted from the Plains tribes.

the Shoshoni. The animals thrived in the rich grasslands, and by 1750 had become central to Nez Perce life. The tribe developed a unique aptitude for horse-breeding, and Meriwether Lewis described them as having a method of gelding 'preferable to that practiced by ourselves'. Through selective breeding, the Nez Perce produced thousands of outstanding horses, including the magnificent Appaloosa ponies – the famous 'spotted horse'.

The mounted Nez Perce developed far greater contact with distant tribes. Westward trips to the Dalles increased in frequency, improving trade with North-west Coast tribes like the Yakima, and introducing to the tribe such coastal traits as nose-piercing and the artificial flattening of babies' heads. More importantly, mounted hunters followed the Lolo and Old Nez Perce trails east over the Bitterroots, and joined bands of Flathead and even Crow in hunting buffalo on the Plains. The Nez Perce hunters carried with them trade goods of dried fish and roots, craftwork of basketry and horn, and shells obtained at the Dalles. They returned laden with buffalo robes and meat, as well as Plains-style costume and artefacts such as magnificent eagle-feather war-bonnets. In this way, the Nez Perce developed a distinctive culture fused from their own traditions and those of the Plains and North-west Coast. This fusion was reflected in their unique ability to communicate in both the sign language of the Plains tribes, and the Chinook trade jargon of the coastal peoples.

New Wars and Weapons

Returning from the buffalo country, Nez Perce warriors boasted of battles with strange peoples: the Blackfoot and Gros Ventre of Canada, the Assiniboin and Crow of the central Plains. Soon the Nez Perce were participating in Plains-style warfare, raiding for horses, and for scalps when their own herds were stolen. Scouts led war-parties over great distances to the camps of their enemies. Before entering battle, the warriors stripped to breech-cloth and moccasins, some donning war-bonnets, then prepared their medicine bundles and applied sacred body paint to invoke the *Wyakin* medicine powers that gave them supernatural protection. Before they acquired firearms in the first years of the nineteenth century, the Nez Perce fought with clubs, lances and their most famous weapon, a bow of mountain sheep horn. The curled horn was boiled until pliable, stretched and straightened, then backed with deer sinew attached with a glue of salmon skin or sturgeon blood. The horn bow's power and beauty was worth the trade of a good horse on the Plains.

About 1755, the Blackfoot obtained firearms from the Hudson's Bay Company, and drove back the Shoshoni and Flathead, so exposing the Bitterroot valley. Allying themselves with neighbouring tribes, the Nez Perce thwarted Blackfoot aggression in a period of desperate warfare. By 1800, Nez Perce buffalo-hunting expeditions to the Yellowstone had become too dangerous, and five years later a council in the Kamiah valley resolved to obtain firearms for the tribe. Three warriors from the band of Chief Broken Arm (Tunnachemootoolt) made a perilous journey of some 1000 miles, beyond the lands of the Teton Sioux, to trade with the Hidatsa Indians. Incredibly, they returned safely, bearing the first six firearms among the Nez Perce. The Lewis and Clark expedition was able to provide powder and lead for the Nez Perce, a persuasive enough argument for their friendly relations with the white man.

Among the Nez Perce and Crow people, pieces of horn were glued together and bound with sinew to create a bow 'stronger, tougher, more elastic, and more durable than a bow of any other materials'. The horn bow was a popular weapon among the Nez Perce both for its power and beauty.

Corps of Discovery

According to tribal legend, the first Nez Perce to encounter a white man was a woman called Watkuweis, meaning 'Returned from a Faraway Country'. Captured by Blackfoot or Atsina Indians when accompanying buffalo-hunters to Montana in the late eighteenth century, she was sold to eastern Indians and then on to a French-Canadian at Red River. After giving birth to a child, Watkuweis ran away and journeyed back to her own people. She spoke kindly of the white men, whom she called Soyappo ('Long Knives') and when William Clark first entered the Nez Perce lands, Watkuweis, now aged and dying, apparently told her tribe: 'These are the people who helped me. Do them no hurt'.

The Lewis and Clark expedition, the Corps of Discovery, first entered the Bitterroot Mountains on 11th September 1805, seeking the Columbia River. A week later, they recorded reaching the 'Kooskooske' River, from the Nez Perce *Koos keich keich*, meaning Clearwater. Here Clark led six men ahead to secure much needed supplies. At the Nez Perce camp on Weippe prairie, and later in the Clearwater valley, the expedition met only kindness and help from the Nez Perce. Thus, Lewis and Clark left the area with a strong regard for the Nez Perce:

Among the most amiable men we have seen. Their character is placid and gentle, rarely moved into passion.

(Meriwether Lewis)

Bow-case and quiver, probably Nez Perce, of otterskin decorated with beadwork and pendants of ermine. Like many other aspects of Nez Perce design, it demonstrates a strong Crow influence.

Long Knives and Black Robes

In May 1806, Lewis and Clark re-entered the Nez Perce homeland, on their journey back from the Pacific. The previous summer they had left an American flag for Broken Arm, who had been absent leading a triumphant attack on the Shoshoni. Now, they presented all the Nez Perce headmen with medals. Then, through a series of interpreters, they called for the Nez Perce to cease making war upon other tribes, so that a trading post could be established. After witnessing a demonstration of 'magnetism, the spye glass, compass, watch, airgun and sundry other items', Broken Arm consented to this request. The other headmen indicated their agreement by attending a feast given by the chief, though the women of the village 'cried, wrung their hands, tore their hair, and appeared to be in the utmost distress', at the notion of this fundamental change to tribal life.

However, an elderly man assured the expedition of the tribe's 'warmest attachment and that they would always give them every assistance in their power; that they were poor but their hearts were good'. This tribal promise was the cornerstone of the Nez Perce's determined and continued friendship with the white man.

In July, the Nez Perce guided Lewis and Clark along the Lolo Trail and out of their lands, after receiving assurances that American traders would be sent to their country. Travelling east, Lewis encountered two men, Joseph Dixon and Forrest Hancock, trapping the Missouri west from Illinois. They were the vanguard of a legion of trappers, traders and mountain men who would pioneer American settlement of the far West. In December that year, Nez Perce traded at Kootenae House for the first time, and by 1810 they had obtained sufficient firearms to join the Flathead in a party of 150 that drove back the Blackfoot, whose hostility had plagued initial efforts of traders to penetrate westward.

In 1811, the ragged remnants of an expedition from John Jacob Astor's Pacific Fur Company sought refuge among the Nez Perce, and were guided safely to Fort Astoria on the lower Columbia. Among them was Donald Mackenzie, a 312-pound colossus, who returned the following year to build Fort Nez Perce on the confluence of the Snake and Clearwater Rivers. Mackenzie expected to exchange trade goods for beaver skins, but the Nez Perce refused to trap beaver, since it was not consistent with their seasonal existence. Mackenzie's men had to set the traps themselves. Then, when their supplies ran short, they had to exchange trade goods with the Nez Perce for horse-meat.

On 16th October 1813, the Pacific Fur Company sold out to the North West traders, having pushed relations with the Indians to their limit.

Mackenzie returned to Astoria, now Fort George, in 1816 and secured employment with the North West Company. Having councilled with the Nez Perce for two years, in July 1818, he re-established a fort in their name in the region of the Cayuse and Walla Walla Indians. For four years

he led beaver-trapping expeditions along the Snake with increasing success, while the Nez Perce warriors confined themselves to fleecing the less provident of Mackenzie's Iroquois henchmen. Mackenzie made futile attempts to negotiate a peace between the Nez Perce and the Shoshoni before his departure in 1821, when the North West and Hudson's Bay Companies were merged. Two years later, the traders' annihilation of a Piegan Blackfoot war-party cemented relations with the Nez Perce.

Between 1824 and 1830, the Nez Perce switched their allegiance from the British to the growing bands of free-spirited American mountain men, who traded generously and treated the Indians as equals. In 1832 at the Pierre's Hole rendezvous, the Nez Perce fought a long and decisive battle alongside the Americans against some transient Blackfoot. Twenty-five Blackfoot warriors were killed, while two Nez Perce chiefs were injured. They were Rotten Belly (Tackensautis) and Hallalhotsoot, called Lawyer by the Americans because of his shrewd diplomacy.

In February 1834, an American called Benjamin Bonneville penetrated

Headman Bull's Head with wife and dog travois. The Nez Perce absorbed much of the culture of the Plains, where the travois was used before the introduction of the horse.

105

the lower Nez Perce heartland west of the Snake in the continuing battle to win over trade from the British. Bonneville, called the 'Bald Headed Chief' by the Indians, visited the Asotin band of Nez Perce, where he administered medicine to the daughter of Flint Necklace, or Old Looking Glass, father of Chief Joseph's greatest ally. He also visited a settlement on Joseph Creek, on the Grande Ronde, whose headman was Chief Joseph's father, Tuekakas.

The 1834 Green River rendezvous was attended both by Nez Perce headmen and the burly, broad-jawed Methodist minister Jason Lee. His presence was transient, but other 'Black Robes' were shortly to follow in his footsteps. An interest in Christianity had first arisen among the Nez Perce when a Spokan and a Kutenai boy returned after four years at the Red River Church of England Mission School. Dressed as white men, speaking English and clutching bible and prayer-book in their hands, Spokan Garry and Kutenai Pelly caused a sensation. After meeting them, Nez Perce headmen including Lawyer and Timothy dispatched a delegation to St Louis in late summer 1831 to answer claims that 'the white man's religion was better than theirs, and that they would all be lost if they did not embrace it' (Catlin).

In May 1835, the pompous, purse-lipped Presbyterian minister Samuel Parker and his zealous assistant Dr Marcus Whitman left Liberty for Oregon, predicting that the 'Church-going bell will sound far and wide'.

Dispatching Whitman back east for reinforcements, Parker travelled extensively beyond the Salmon River Mountains, before reaching Fort Vancouver. He conducted sermons, and met many Nez Perce headmen, including Tuekakas, of whom he wrote: 'If there is one among this multitude who it may be hoped has been everlastingly benefitted by the gospel, I should believe it is this man'. Of the Nez Perce, Parker observed: 'I have nowhere witnessed so much subordination, peace and friendship as among the Indians in the Oregon Territory. The day may be rued when their order and harmony shall be interrupted by any instrumentality whatever.'

In July 1836, Whitman and his new wife Narcissa, accompanied by the stern, short-tempered Reverend Henry Spalding and his ailing spouse Eliza, hauled a wagon over what would become the Oregon Trail, to Fort Vancouver. While Whitman established his mission among the Cayuse, the Spaldings ventured 120 miles east to Lapwai, 'Place of Butterflies', on the Clearwater, where their mission grew slowly.

In July 1839, Spalding travelled to the village of Tuekakas – who became known as Old Joseph – in the beautiful Wallowa valley. Here he baptised and conducted Christian marriages for Old Joseph and his wife Khapkhaponimi (Asenoth), and for Tamootsin (Timothy) and his wife Tamar. Then on 12th April 1840, he baptised Old Joseph's newborn baby 'Ephraim', who as an adult would inherit his father's name, Joseph.

Thunder Travelling to Distant Mountains

Composite tipi, from Joseph's winter camp of 1901. This unusual variation on the Plains tipi design was favoured by some Plateau tribes, and particularly by the Nez Perce.

Joseph was born in the spring of 1840 in a cave near where Joseph Creek forks from the Grande Ronde River. Here, the Wellamotkin band of Nez Perce sheltered from winter snows in a village of tipis and circular pit-houses, centred on a large, rectangular council lodge, its floor dug below ground, its roof an A-shaped frame covered with tule mats. After the wildflowers blossomed in March, they journeyed south along the lush Wallowa valley to gather wild roots like kouse and camas.

Christian Childhood

After being baptised in the hands of Henry Spalding, Joseph spent much of his first seven years at the Lapwai Mission, where Eliza Spalding's growing band of helpers gave academic and religious instruction. During this time, Henry Spalding drove a wedge into the Nez Perce tribe, dividing them into Christians, who followed his preaching, and the 'heathen' faction, who maintained their traditional beliefs. This rent in the tribal fabric was torn wider by Dr Elijah White, Superintendent of Indian Affairs, who presented the Nez Perce with a set of rules to govern them, and demanded that they appoint a head chief. He selected Ellis, grandson of Red Grizzly Bear, a choice which angered Lawyer and Joseph and created more problems than it solved.

The increase in white settlement on the Columbia, which saw 3000 newcomers in 1845, led to growing fears among both Christian and 'heathen factions' of the Nez Perce. These matured in 1847, when wagons carried 4000 people along the Oregon Trail, along with an epidemic of measles. Over half the Cayuse tribe died, and while Whitman treated those he could, the rumour spread that the missionary was, in fact, poisoning the Indians. On the afternoon of 29th November 1847,

107

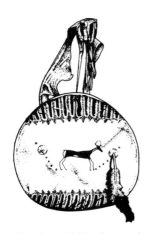

Nez Perce shield and cover of 1870. Made from buffalo hide and deerskin, it is decorated with eagle feathers. The original red, yellow and blue paint designs reflected the owner's medicine and his vision-spirit, the deer.

Cayuse chief Tilokaikt appeared at Whitman's home. He asked the doctor for some medicine, then as Whitman turned to fetch it, felled him with a tomahawk. In the ensuing massacre, eleven men, Narcissa Whitman and two children were savagely killed and forty-seven people captured, later to be ransomed.

Spalding, after being warned of his peril by Catholic priest Father Brouillet, fled from the massacre to Lapwai. On New Year's Day of 1848, friendly Nez Perce escorted him out of their lands to Fort Walla Walla. The Cayuse War raged from 1847 to 1850, in which year the Whitman Massacre ringleaders were hung, and the Indians' lands opened to homesteading by the Oregon Donation Land Law. Although Protestant missionaries were banned from the region, converts such as Lawyer and Timothy maintained the faith; by 1860 the Christian faction comprised two-thirds of the tribe.

Learning the Old Ways

Old Joseph retired to the seclusion of the Wallowa valley to escape the soldiers that marched through his country, but with whom he had no direct quarrel. Here, his son Joseph learnt the traditions and religion of his own people. The Nez Perce believed in an infinite number of spirits, all of them a part of one omnipotent deity and embodying a sacred Wyakin power, which was present in the land, elements and animals of their country. At the age of nine, Joseph was instructed by a holy man on how to attain his own guardian spirit or *Wyakin*. In the following years, he would have undertaken a vision quest similar to that described by the Nez Perce warrior Yellow Wolf:

I was a boy of about thirteen snows when my parents sent me away into the hills . . . to find my Wyakin. After going so many suns without food, I was sleeping. It was just like dreaming what I saw. A form stood in the air fronting me . . . . It was a Spirit of a wolf that appeared to me. Yellow-like in colour it sort of floated in the air. Like a human-being it talked to me – and gave me its power . . . . That was how I got named Yellow Wolf.

The recipient of a *Wyakin* participated in the winter ceremonial Guardian Spirit Dance, where he sang the medicine song taught by his *Wyakin*.

From his uncle, Joseph received the name Hin-mah-too-yah-lat-kekht, 'Thunder Travelling to Distant Mountains'. His younger brother, born two years after him, was named Ollokot – Frog – after a half-brother of Old Joseph. While Ollokot was boisterous and full of daring, the young Joseph demonstrated the gentle, dignified nature that would distinguish his later life.

Council at Walla Walla

When he was fifteen, Joseph travelled with his father to the Walla Walla valley, where Isaac I. Stevens, governor of newly formed Washington Territory and Superintendent of Indian Affairs, had called one of a series of treaty councils removing Indian land rights. On 24th May 1855, Lawyer, Old Joseph, The Wolf (Utsinmalikin), Three Feathers (Metat Waptass) and Red Wolf (Hemene Ilppilp) led 2500 Nez Perce to the council grounds, where Stevens' 100-strong entourage was camped with other tribes of the Columbia basin. The warriors approached:

Mounted on fine horses and riding at a gallop, two abreast, naked to the breech-clout, their faces covered with white, red and yellow paint in fanciful designs, and decked with plumes and feathers and trinkets fluttering in the sunshine.

They encircled the commissioners, singing and beating shields and drums, before dismounting and conducting a dance.

Prior to the council, Lawyer was given a paper proclaiming him head chief of the Nez Perce. Joseph himself recollected how, on 29th May, Stevens 'made known his heart':

He said that there were a great many white people in the country and many more would come; that he wanted the land marked out so that the Indians and white men could be separated. If they were to live in peace it was necessary, he said, that the Indians should have a country set apart for them and in that country they must stay.

For two weeks, Stevens cajoled the Nez Perce headmen, including Old Joseph, who had clear words for the commissioners:

These are my children. I see them all sitting here. Talking slowly is good. It is good for old men to talk straight; talk straight on both sides and take care of one another. It is not us we talk for, it is for our children who come after us.

Lawyer moved his lodge into the centre of the commissioners' camp and, under his influence, the chiefs seemed ready to sign. Their decision was delayed by the arrival of the formidable war chief of the Asotin band, Old Looking Glass, seventy winters old, at the head of a line of warriors. Brandishing a scalp freshly taken in Blackfoot country, he admonished the Nez Perce headmen:

My people, what have you done? While I was gone, you have sold my country. I have come home and there is not left me a place on which to pitch my lodge. Go home to your lodges. I will talk to you.

However, after a heated discussion, Lawyer's will prevailed; and on 11th June Stevens, calling for no speeches, conducted the treaty signing. Lawyer took up the pen first, followed by Old Looking Glass, Old Joseph, Old James and Timothy, until fifty-eight Nez Perce chiefs were recorded. They accepted $200,000 and a reservation embracing much of their traditional homeland, while retaining the rights to their traditional hunting and fishing grounds. While Joseph returned with his father to the Wallowa, now officially Nez Perce land, a delegation under Old Looking Glass accompanied Stevens to Blackfoot lands. There, in October, they negotiated a remarkable treaty, ending the ancient hostilities between the Blackfoot and the Nez Perce.

Prompted by Stevens' treaty at Walla Walla, there was an immediate

Ceremonial Nez Perce drum which is attributed to Joseph.

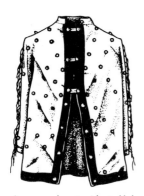

An unusual coat with studded decoration and ermine fringes, accredited to Chief Joseph.

rush east of the Cascades for land and for gold. The Indians were angered by this invasion, and on 29th October Stevens received news that the Yakima, Cayuse, Walla Walla, Umatilla and Palouse Indians had risen against the settlers. The Nez Perce were restrained from joining the conflict by Lawyer and Old Joseph, though frequent outrages perpetrated by troops made up of Oregon volunteers increased support for the war faction under Old Looking Glass. At a second Walla Walla council in September 1856, Stevens found that although the Nez Perce were unwilling to fight, they were clearly divided, largely as a legacy of Spalding's days amongst them. Lawyer's Christian faction upheld the treaty, while Old Joseph denied that he had understood its tenets, and Old Looking Glass failed even to attend. In August 1858, Nez Perce scouts accompanied the punitive expedition of General George Wright, who ruthlessly subdued the tribes of the upper Columbia, hanging prisoners on the spot. As the influx of settlers continued, the Nez Perce now stood alone.

The 1855 treaty was finally ratified in 1859, with Old Joseph commenting: 'The line was made as I wanted it, not for me but my children that will follow me. There is where I live and there is where I want to leave my body'. Such aspirations were threatened in February the following year when one Elias Davidson Pierce discovered gold in the Clearwater. Within a year, 10,000 miners had flocked from the Walla Walla settlement on to the reservation, and Lawyer's followers readily signed an agreement exchanging mining rights north of the Clearwater for $50,000. A military post, Fort Lapwai, was established in 1862, when the Surveyors General Office reported 18,690 whites illegally encamped on the Nez Perce reservation.

In January 1863, Old Looking Glass died and was succeeded by a son of the same name, hanging his father's trade mirror, and his burdens, about his own neck. Old Joseph kept his people away from the miners, and mocked Lawyer as the annuities promised in 1855 failed to arrive. He warned: 'After a while they will claim that you accepted pay for your country'. On 28th April 1862, the *Oregon Statesman* reported:

If open hostilities have not commenced with the Nez Perce it is not because they have not been outraged to that degree when 'forbearance ceases to be a virtue.' In return for the continued friendship in times of want, and generous acts of hospitality always so readily extended towards the whites by these Indians, they now reap an abundant harvest of every species of villainy and insult.

The Thief Treaty

In response to growing friction between the Nez Perce and the miners, Superintendent of Indian Affairs Calvin Hale, escorted by six companies of troops, met with Lawyer's people at Lapwai. Opening the council on 25th May 1863, Hale made the incredible proposal that the Nez Perce sell 90% of their 10,000 square mile reservation, and retire to a 600 square mile area on the south fork of the Clearwater. The following day, the wily Lawyer gave his reply, expressing his people's wish:

To adhere to the (1855) treaty that has been made, and which we on our side have kept . . . you have broken the treaty not we . . . That engagement was made with us for 20 years . . . Here we are listening to what you say again, before the 20 years are ended. Perhaps by contemplating you will find something that is wrong in your proposition . . . Dig the gold and look at the country, but we cannot give you the country you ask for.

When the council re-convened on 3rd June, the arrival of the anti-treaty Nez Perce – led by Old Joseph and his son, Big Thunder, Eagle from the Light, Three Feathers, Red Owl and White Bird – had swelled the Indian ranks to 3000. Ignoring the newcomers, Hale coaxed Lawyer and his headmen over to his side by offering them personal guarantees and doubling the size of the proposed reservation. To protect the Lawyer faction, and his own interests, Hale then called up twenty cavalrymen under Captain George Currey. Arriving at 1 a.m., Currey found 53 Nez Perce chiefs gathered in one lodge. He witnessed a remarkable council and duly reported:

Nez Perce gauntlets of around 1890. The unusual altar design probably reflects the Christian church's powerful influence over the tribe.

Chiefs were debating the terms of the proposed treaty in an effort to reach some compromise, but neither group would yield. Finally convinced that there was no hope of agreement, they decided that the proper action was to disband the tribe, each chief becoming an independent leader of his own village . . . (and) declared the Nez Perce nation dissolved. . . . I withdrew my detachment having accomplished nothing but that of witnessing the extinguishment of the last council fires of the most powerful Indian nation on the sunset side of the Rocky Mountains.

Joseph and the other anti-treaty chiefs now struck their lodges and left the council grounds, believing that they had refuted Lawyer's right to speak for them. However, Hale proceeded regardless, and on 9th June 1863, he obtained fifty-two signatures for his treaty. All the signatories were Christians, many were minor headmen and all already lived within the new reservation – except Jason and Timothy, who received provision to live among the whites. Hale accumulated enough names to suggest tribal acceptance despite the absence of every anti-treaty chief. Even old Henry Spalding, who had returned to Lapwai in the spring, added his signature for good measure. Currey noted: 'Although the treaty goes out to the World as the concurrent agreement of the tribe, it is in reality nothing more than the agreement of Lawyer and his band, numbering in the aggregate not a third part of the Nez Perce tribe.'

In the Wallowa valley, Old Joseph tore in two the piece of paper he called the Thief Treaty. He cast aside his 'Book of Heaven', the Bible, and with it any pretence of Christianity. Drawing a map of his people's lands, he then hammered stakes around the Wallowa – creating a boundary that settlers called Old Joseph's Deadline – and made his declaration to his people, but also to his son:

Inside is the home of my people – the white man may take the land outside. Inside the

boundary all our people were born. It circles around the graves of our fathers, and we will never give up these graves to any man. When you go into council with the white man, always remember your country. Do not give it away. The white man will cheat you out of your home. I have taken no pay from the United States. I have never sold our land.

Young Joseph, soon to assume the burden of his father's chieftainship, also inherited his father's dignity and wisdom. He summarised the 1863 treaty eloquently:

If we ever owned the land, we own it still, for we never sold it. In the treaty councils the commissioners have claimed that our country has been sold to the government. Suppose a white man should come to me and say 'Joseph, I like your horses, and I want to buy them.' I say to him, 'No, my horses suit me. I will not sell them.' Then he goes to my neighbour and says to him: 'Joseph has some good horses. I want to buy them but he refuses to sell.' My neighbour answers, 'Pay me the money, and I will sell you Joseph's horses.' The white man returns to me and says, 'Joseph, I have bought your horses, and you must let me have them.' If we sold our lands to the Government, this is the way they were bought.

The treaty demanded that, within a year of its being ratified, the Nez Perce should abandon the Wallowa, Grande Ronde, Imnaha, Snake and Salmon valleys, and report on the Lapwai reservation. For this they would receive $315,000. They must have recalled the prophetic remarks in 1829 of the Nez Perce elder Speckled Snake: 'I have listened to many talks from the great father. But they always began and ended in this – Get a little further, you are too near me'.

Nez Perce warrior's sacred wing-bone whistle adorned with buckskin carrying-thong and eagle fluffies. Such whistles were blown only during war to offer the warrior supernatural protection.

Chief Joseph

Before his death at Lapwai in the summer of 1874, Henry Spalding led a Christian revival among the Nez Perce. He recorded over 200 baptisms, including those of Lawyer and Rotten Belly, though some whispered that due to his failing eyesight he baptised certain individuals more than once. The gaping division between the settled, Christian, treaty Nez Perce, and the 'heathen', non-treaty faction was further widened at this time by the appearance of the Dreamer religion, introduced by a hunch-backed Wanapum holy man named Smohalla. After a mysterious five-year absence from his tribe in the 1850s, Smohalla had returned preaching the Dreamer doctrine:

My young men shall never work. Men who work cannot dream; and wisdom comes to us in dreams.

You ask me to plough the ground. Shall I take a knife and tear my mother's breast? Then when I die she will not take me to her bosom to rest.

You ask me to dig for stone. Shall I dig under her skin for bones? Then when I die, I cannot enter her body to be born again.

You ask me to cut grass and make hay and sell it and be rich like white men. But how dare I cut off my mother's hair?

Joseph leads the Nez Perce warriors in hauling the women and children, clinging together, across the flooded Snake River, May 1877.

Like the Shawnee prophet Tenskwatawa in 1805, and the Paiute Ghost Dance shaman Wovoka in 1890, Smohalla predicted that a return to traditional life among the Indians would lead to the demise of the white men. This doctrine reflected the beliefs of Young Joseph, whose first wife gave birth to a daughter in 1865. Now twenty-five winters old, Joseph was a powerfully built, strikingly handsome man. Like all the Wallowa Nez Perce, he wore his hair long with a distinctive swept up fringe. This style was characteristic of the Dreamers, and Smohalla's doctrine became increasingly identified with the non-treaty bands.

While white society engulfed the Christian Nez Perce, the 200 or so people of Joseph's Wellamotkin band remained aloof in the Wallowa valley. They wintered in the lush lowlands of canyons on the Grande Ronde and Imnaha valleys, wandering up Joseph Creek in the spring to harvest kouse on the higher meadows. After gathering camas in July, they travelled to the shores of the crystal blue Wallowa Lake, where surrounding streams yielded fat salmon. Here in the Valley of Winding Waters, Joseph was at home. Meanwhile his brother Ollokot, of even larger build and with an unquenchable thirst for life, led buffalo-hunting expeditions to the far off Blackfoot lands. His stature as a war-chief grew in proportion to Joseph's stature as a civil leader. The Wellamotkin also journeyed to the reservation to sell cattle to the Christian Nez Perce. In autumn they hunted deer on Joseph Creek on their return.

Many Nez Perce warriors carried a sacred war-club like this, with a stone head encased in elk rawhide. The handle was wrapped with otter-skin and daubed with paint designs in order to offer the warrior the protection of his vision-spirits.

The Promise

Although over 500 settlers occupied the Grande Ronde valley, the Wallowa remained free from invasion until surveyors, those harbingers of doom among the Indians, arrived in 1866. Joseph's people pulled up the stakes that the surveyors planted, but after the ratification of the Thief Treaty the next year, they continued to arrive.

The first Wallowa settler, A.C. Smith, met the Nez Perce on friendly terms in 1868, returning permanently with cattle and comrades three years later. Old Joseph had by now grown so blind that he rode with a child in his lap to guide him, and so was spared the sight of this first intrusion. In October 1871, the proud old man called his son to his side:

I saw he was dying. I took his hand in mine. He said, 'My son, my body is returning to my mother earth, and my spirit is going very soon to see the Great Spirit. . . . When I am gone, think of your country. You are the chief of these people. They look to you to guide them. Always remember that your father never sold his country. You must stop your ears whenever you are asked to sign a treaty selling your home. A few years more and white men will be all around you. They have their eyes on this land. My son, never forget my dying words. This country holds your father's body. Never sell the bones of your father and your mother.' I pressed my father's hand and told him that I would protect his grave with my life.

(Joseph)

Having guaranteed his homeland's future, Old Joseph, Tuekakas, was

'We are going by you without fighting if you will let us, but we are going by you anyhow.' Joseph and Looking Glass guide their cavalcade high over Fort Fizzle into Montana, 28th July 1877.

buried in the Wallowa. His favourite horse was shot and draped over the grave and a dreamer bell was suspended over the chief's body, to ring in the wind until a white man stole it in 1874. Joseph rode away at the head of his people, seeking shelter from the winter snows, recalling of his father:

I buried him in that beautiful valley of winding waters. I love that land more than all the rest of the world. A man who would not love his father's grave is worse than a wild animal.

Valley of Winding Waters

Returning to the Wallowa in late spring 1872, Joseph found some sixty settlers living in cabins. He immediately made a formal protest and Agent Monteith was summoned to mediate. On 23rd August, at a council of thirty settlers and eighty Nez Perce, many with their faces painted, Joseph made the situation clear to Monteith:

I did not want to come to this council, but I came hoping that we could save blood. The white man has no right to come here and take our country. We have never accepted presents from the government. Neither Lawyer nor any other chief had authority to sell this land. It has always belonged to my people. It came unclouded to them from our fathers, and we will defend this land, as long as a drop of Indian blood warms the hearts of our men.

Monteith received Joseph's guarantee that the settlers would not be molested, but noted in his report:

It is a great pity that the valley was ever opened for settlement. It is so high and cold that they can raise nothing but the hardiest kind of vegetables . . . it is the only fishery the Nez Perces have and they go there from all directions. . . . If there is any way by which the Wallowa Valley could be kept for the Indians I would recommend that it be done.

In response to Monteith's report, the Secretary of the Interior dispatched T.B. Odeneal, Superintendent of Indian Affairs for Oregon, to meet Joseph on 27th March 1873. Odeneal was swayed by the eloquence and truth of Joseph's argument, and submitted a practical solution. He recommended that the 'upper' country, meaning the highlands east of and including Wallowa Lake, be granted to the Nez Perce; and the 'lower' country, meaning the westerly Grande Ronde valley where white settlers were concentrated, remain open to settlement.

In June, President Grant issued an executive order establishing a Wallowa Reservation 'for the roaming Nez Perce Indians', which bore no relation to Odeneal's recommendations. The Bureau of Indian Affairs, making no reference to the actual territory, had translated Odeneal's 'upper' as north, and 'lower' as south, and divided the land laterally instead of vertically. The Nez Perce received the settled lands to the north, while the settlers received the Wallowa Lake region so treasured and traversed by the Indians. The alarmed settlers immediately formed themselves into a blustering militia, and Lafayette F. Grover,

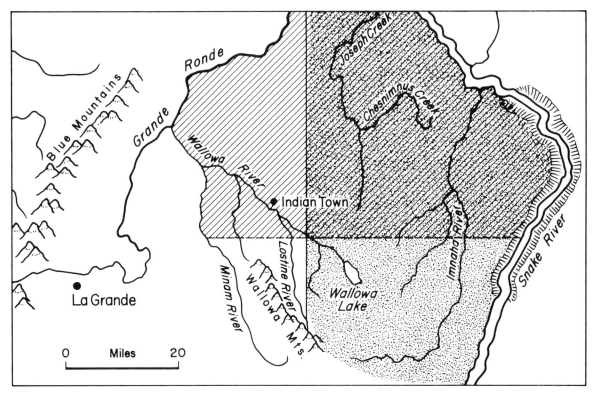

Wanted by the Wallowa Nez Perce

Wallowa Reservation as set up by the Commissioners in 1873

The part of the Wallowa Valley desired by the Nez Perce in 1873, and the completely contradictory area allocated them by the Indian Bureau. In fact, the Bureau translated 'upper' and 'lower' to mean north and south, and thus divided the land in ignorance of its true topography and contours.

Joseph's ceremonial robe and Winchester rifle, which are now in the Fort Benton Museum.

Governor of Oregon, successfully petitioned the Secretary of the Interior to re-examine the situation, declaring: 'Joseph's band do not desire Wallowa Valley for a reservation and for a home. This small band wish the possession of this large section of Oregon simply for room to gratify a wild, roaming disposition, and not for a home.'

At the beginning of August, Joseph was summoned to Lapwai by yet another commission desiring his settlement at an agency. He was asked if his people wanted schools: 'No, we do not want schools . . . they will teach us to have churches. : They [churches] will teach us to quarrel about God. We do not want to learn that. We may quarrel with men sometimes about things on this earth, but we never quarrel about God. We do not want to learn that'.

In September, Joseph requested permission to travel to Washington to correct the mistakes made in the recent settlement. Agent Monteith refused it, pressured by the settlers' supporters and frustrated by the Wallowa band's reluctance to farm. 'Nearly every year,' Joseph recalled, 'the agent came over from Lapwai and ordered us on to the reservation. We always replied that we were satisfied to live in Wallowa. We were careful to refuse the presents or annuities which he offered.'

On 18th May 1874, Commissioner of Indian Affairs E.P. Smith informed Oregon Senator James Kelly that 'the whole (Wallowa) valley is now open for settlement'. Two months later, there was an inconclusive exchange of shots between a Nez Perce and one of the settlers. Encouraged by Lawyer, Monteith responded by stationing troops on Weippe Prairie and on the Wallowa, where the Nez Perce and Umatilla fished for salmon. When the troops withdrew in October, the anti-treaty Nez Perce met in council at Tepahlewam (Split Rocks), an age-old meeting place on Camas Prairie. Representing their bands were Joseph and Ollokot from the Wallowa; Red Owl (Koolkool Snehee) and Looking Glass from the Middle Fork of the Clearwater; White Bird from the Salmon River; and a powerful warrior, holy man and orator named Toohoolhoolzote from the Snake River region. After addresses by Looking Glass, Red Owl and the renowned warriors Rainbow (Wahchumyus), Five Wounds (Pahkatos Owyeen) and Grizzly Bear Ferocious, the Nez Perce voted against war. The decision pleased Joseph, who later lamented:

Our young men were quick-tempered, and I have had great trouble in keeping them from doing rash things. I have carried a heavy load on my back ever since I was a boy. I learned then that we were but few, while the white men were many, and that we could not hold our own with them. We were like deer. They were like grizzly bears. We had a small country. Their country was large. We were contented to let things remain as the Great Spirit . . . made them. They were not, and would change the rivers and mountains if they did not suit them.

On 10th June 1875, President Grant rescinded his 1873 executive order, officially re-opening the entire Wallowa valley for settlement.

The Death of Wilhautyah

Leading a band of forty-five lodges up the Valley of Winding Waters in the summer of 1875, Joseph found two companies of cavalry under Captain Whipple stationed there as a peace-keeping force. The troops returned to Fort Walla Walla in September, but were recalled to the valley on New Year's Day by reports that Joseph's Nez Perce were murdering the settlers. After battling through four-feet snow drifts, the soldiers discovered that Joseph was, in fact, peacefully visiting the Lapwai agency, some 100 miles from the imagined outrages.

In January 1876, the one-armed General Oliver Otis Howard, Commander of the Department of the Columbia, received a commissioned report from Major H.C. Wood which concluded: 'The non-treaty Nez Perces cannot in law be regarded as bound by the treaty of 1863; and in so far as it attempts to deprive them of a right to occupancy on any land its provisions are null and void.'

The one-armed, 'Praying General' Oliver Otis Howard predicted of his campaign against the Nez Perce: 'Think we will make short work of it'. However, Howard's quarry, Chief Joseph, after frequently and comprehensively out-manoeuvring him, soon re-named him 'General Day After Tomorrow'.

However, such considerations were overshadowed by an incident five months later. A settler called A.B. Findley tracked five missing horses to the Chesnimnus region, where Wallowa Indians were gathering roots. He returned the following day, the 23rd June, with 21-year-old Wells McNall, a renowned Indian-hater, and confronted three Nez Perce. In the ensuing argument, McNall began to wrestle with a young Nez Perce named Wilhautyah (Wind Blowing) for possession of the Indian's gun. Weakening, McNall bellowed at Findley to open fire. Eventually he did, shooting Wilhautyah dead. The two white men fled back to the settlements.

When Wilhautyah's body was carried into his camp, Joseph urged restraint from his angry warriors. Hurrying to Lapwai, he received Monteith's assurance that the white men would be brought to justice before returning to his people. On 22nd July, Major Wood came to the Wallowa to investigate the killing, and reported Joseph as saying that 'the valley was more sacred to him than ever before, and he would and did claim it now as recompense for the life taken.' Despite Wood's assurances that Findley and McNall would be tried, they remained at large in the valley. Joseph complained: 'We had no friend who would plead our cause before the law councils'. The Nez Perces' patience wore thin.

On 1st September, Nez Perce warriors in ugly mood summoned the Wallowa settlers to a council the following day. When it convened, Joseph instructed the white men to leave the valley, and turn over Findley and McNall to the Nez Perce for trial. Leading sixty warriors stripped for battle to McNall's cabin, where several families had fortified themselves, Joseph repeated his warning.

The settlers dispatched messengers to warn their comrades and seek help. One of them, Gerard Cochran, boasted that he personally 'would kill Joseph and scalp him and wear his scalp as a bridle'. On 9th

September, Joseph led seventy painted warriors to Cochran's cabin, and holding a war-club over him, asked to hear the boast again. Other settlers intervened, insisting that Cochran would leave the Wallowa immediately; and Joseph rode away peacefully.

With a militia from Grande Ronde mustering, Lieutenant Forse arrived with a troop from Fort Walla Walla on 10th September. Approaching Wallowa Lake, he found the Nez Perce warriors mounted on an impregnable high bluff, and reported: 'Joseph could have fallen upon the settlers in detail, killing them and destroying their property. . . . An enemy could not approach him without being under his fire for the distance of more than a half-mile.'

Upon receiving Forse's promise that the murderers would be arrested, Joseph agreed to keep his warriors in the vicinity of Wallowa Lake.

Although Findley was charged with manslaughter four days later, McNall, who the Nez Perce held responsible, was not. The Indians refused to testify at Findley's trial, and he was freed.

The Last Councils

Summoned to meet another commission, Joseph and Ollokot led a delegation up the Snake River in November 1876. On 13th November, the Wallowa delegation entered the Lapwai mission church, already crowded with Nez Perce, to meet the commissioners. Joining General Howard and Major Wood were three easterners, described by Monteith's wife as, 'kings of finance but with not a speck of Indian sense, experience or knowledge'. Though Howard believed himself to be championing Joseph's cause, his solution to the problem was simply to compensate the Wellamotkin band for its removal to Lapwai. The bible-thumping 'Christian General' dismissed Joseph's intrinsic love for his land as a reflection of his 'pagan' Dreamer religion.

For two days, Joseph rejected the commissioners' overtures to buy his territory, explaining simply: 'We love the land. It is our home'. As Joseph led his people away to winter in the Imnaha canyons, however, all the commissioners except Wood signed a report recommending the suppression of all Dreamer shamans, military occupation of the Wallowa and removal 'by force' of all non-treaty bands.

Instructed on 6th January 1877 to bring the Nez Perce on to the reservation within 'a reasonable time', Monteith set an over-eager deadline of 1st April. He foolishly declared, 'They can come one time just as well as another, having nothing to hinder them in moving'. Monteith then dispatched a group of treaty Nez Perce to deliver the ultimatum, to which Joseph responded:

I have been talking to the whites many years about the lands in question, and it is strange they cannot understand me; the country they claim belonged to my father, and when he died it was given to me and my people, and I will not leave it until I am compelled to.

Joseph was alarmed by Monteith's message, and bewildered that he could have been so misunderstood at the previous council. Through the Cayuse headman, Young Chief, he arranged another meeting with Howard, at the Umatilla Agency on 1st April – Monteith's optimistic deadline. Joseph fell seriously ill at this time, and so Ollokot, accompanied by a few Wellamotkin warriors and an elderly holy man, represented the Wallowa band. Ollokot had expected to meet Howard and receive his permission to settle on the Umatilla Agency rather than Lapwai. Instead, he was confronted by Howard's aide-de-camp Lieutenant Boyle, who sharply refuted the suggestion. Stretching out his arm, and spreading his fingers like a snake's tongue, Ollokot asked:

Old-time Nez Perce shirt of the 1840s, short in length and fashioned according to the shape of the animal skin. It is decorated with pierced holes – a feature common on Blackfoot Indian shirts and possibly invoking sacred protection against bullets – and with the uncommon technique of wrapping horsehair in porcupine quills.

Nessameiek (liar), who are you? Where is General Howard? . . . I came a chief to talk to a chief. General Howard sends one of his boys to give orders to the Nez Perce!   General Howard talks with a forked tongue! He has lied to the Nez Perce. Was he ashamed to meet men to whom he talked two ways? . . . He has insulted me! Made me ashamed before my people!

The council dissolved in ill humour, but on 20th April, Ollokot met Howard at Walla Walla. Howard re-iterated his demands for the Nez Perce to settle at Lapwai, but said that they would be given hunting and fishing passes for the Imnaha valley. A final council was arranged for Lapwai twelve days later, and Ollokot returned to his sick brother at a camp near Asotin, saying: 'Government wants all Indians put in one place. If you say "Yes" I will bring in the stock and we will go there. If the white officers ask what you will do, you answer, "Nothing to talk about, Ollokot has settled everything".'

Joseph's path, though, was not to be taken for him, and he prepared to travel to Lapwai.

On 4th May 1877, the council convened in a Lapwai hospital tent, and Howard was confronted by the anti-treaty headmen. Looking Glass, a formidable warrior of forty-five winters, was still talking against war. White Bird, the septuagenarian Salmon River warrior and chief, was described by Howard as, 'A demure looking Indian . . . . His face assumed the condition of . . . rigid fixedness while in council . . . ; he kept his immense ceremonial hat on, and placed a large eagle's wing in front of his eyes and nose'.

The Nez Perce elected Toohoolhoolzote as their spokesman, the eloquent, uncompromising Dreamer Shaman who could reputedly carry a slain deer on each shoulder. Howard called him a 'cross-grained growler', and a 'large thick-necked, ugly, obstinate savage of the worst type'.

Of Joseph and Ollokot, the general noted differently that they:

presented the finest appearance of the invited chiefs. Alokut (*sic*), the younger of the two, was even taller than his brother, as graceful and supple as a cougar. Carefree and full of youthful enthusiasm, his happy disposition attracted whites and Indians alike. Clearly, he was the idol and leader of the young men.

Howard and Monteith argued their case against Toohoolhoolzote until the council was adjourned. As night fell, Howard ordered troops up to

Grande Ronde, Lewiston and Fort Walla Walla. When the two sides re-convened on 7th May, the non-treaty ranks had been swelled by the arrival of the Palouse under Hahtalekin and Husishusis Kute (Little Baldhead or Preacher), described by Howard as 'bright-eyed and oily', whose 'manner of extreme cunning inspired distrust'. Joseph arrived in sullen mood, having learnt that soldiers were marching through the Wallowa among his women and children. He confronted Howard:

The measure of the land and the measure of our bodies are the same. Say to us if you can say it, that you were sent by the Creative Power to talk to us. Perhaps you think the Creator sent you here to dispose of us as you see fit.

   If I thought you were sent by the Creator I might be induced to think you had a right to dispose of me. Do not misunderstand me, but understand me fully with reference to my affection for the land. I never said that land was mine to do as I chose. The one who has a right to dispose of it is the one who has created it. I claim a right to live on my land, and accord you the privilege to live on yours.

To Howard's stubborn insistence that the Nez Perce move immediately to the reservation, Toohoolhoolzote answered: 'The earth is part of our body, and we never gave up the earth'. Howard replied, 'We do not wish to interfere with your religion, but you must talk about practicable things. Twenty times over you repeat that the earth is your mother, and about chieftainship of the earth. Let us hear it no more.'

   Arguing from vastly different viewpoints, compromise proved impossible, until Toohoolhoolzote mumbled: 'What person pretends to divide the land and put me on it?'

   Losing his temper, Howard roared, 'I am that man. I stand here for the President, and there is no spirit good or bad who will hinder me. My orders are plain and will be executed.'

   The argument continued until Howard seized Toohoolhoolzote by the arm and marched him to the guardhouse, where he was locked away. 'If you do not mind me', the Christian General told the astonished headman, 'I will take my soldiers and drive you on the reservation!'

   With Toohoolhoolzote imprisoned, soldiers marching among their families, and Howard bellowing threats, the Nez Perce chiefs acquiesced. With heads bowed they agreed to tour the reservation, but Yellow Wolf recalled: 'In peace councils force must not be talked. It was the same as showing us the rifle . . . . That was not suited for the Indians. That was what brought war, the arrest of this chief, and showing us the rifle.'

   A week later, Howard released Toohoolhoolzote. Many years later, Joseph recalled Howard's words:

He informed us in a haughty spirit that he would give my people thirty days to go back home, collect all their stock, and move to the reservation, saying, 'If you are not here in that time, I shall consider that you want to fight, and will send my soldiers to drive you on'.

Joseph protested that he could not be ready to move in thirty days. His stock was scattered and the Snake River was very high. 'Let us wait until fall,' he asked Howard.

The one-armed general remained insistent though, supporting Monteith's opinion that if Joseph be 'allowed to have his own way at this time, it will only make him more stubborn in the future'.

Nez Perce gun case and saddle bag of about 1850. The buffalo and elk hide are decorated with red cloth and beads, sewn with a sinew.

Showing the Rifle

Joseph and Ollokot returned to their people on Joseph Creek, accompanied by Toohoolhoolzote. The shaman was still determined to resist and encouraged the growing unrest among the warriors. But Joseph was now resigned to moving to the reservation, saying: 'It required a strong heart to stand up against such talk, but I urged my people to be quiet, and not to begin a war.'

With unaccustomed haste, the Nez Perce herded up their scattered horses and cattle and at the end of May Joseph led his band and 6000 animals up the Imnaha valley. For two days they battled to cross the Snake River, swollen by winter's melted snows. The men, stripped to breech-cloths, plunged into the torrential waters on horseback, and hauled the women and children across on great buffalo-robe bundles filled with their belongings. Then the bellowing animals were driven into the torrent. Several hundred were swept downstream, and the settlers eagerly claimed those animals that refused to attempt the crossing.

Miraculously, the Nez Perce emerged without loss of life, and proceeded wearily and bitterly up Rocky Canyon. Leaving their cattle west of the Salmon, they crossed the river to join the other non-treaty bands at Tepahlewam. Here, 600 Nez Perce enjoyed their last days of freedom, digging the bountiful camas, dancing, gambling and racing their horses.

Battle of White Bird Canyon
After a week, Joseph, his daughter Hophoponmi (Sound of Running Feet), Ollokot, his wife Wetatonmi, and the half-man, half-woman Welweyas re-crossed the Salmon to butcher beef. Returning to camp several days later with twelve horses laden with meat, they were met by a warrior named Two Moons, who announced that the war had started.

In Joseph's absence, one of White Bird's young men, Wahlitits (Shore Crossing) – whose father, Eagle Robe, had been murdered by settlers two winters before – had trampled some drying kouse roots during a horseback parade. Yellow Grizzly Bear had rebuked him: 'Playing brave, you ride over my woman's hard-worked food! If you are so brave, why not go kill the white man who killed your father?'

Wahlitits, with his cousin Sarpsis Ilppilp (Red Moccasin Tops) and

nephew Swan Necklace, had set out to do just that. Unable to locate his father's murderers, he killed four other Salmon River settlers against whom the Nez Perce nursed particular grievances.

Joseph galloped into Tepahlewam to find the Indians fleeing. He urged them to stay, in the forlorn hope of restoring peace; but soon only his own followers' lodges remained. The other bands whispered that Joseph would now head for Lapwai, abandoning them as Lawyer had done.

The Wallowa headman remained at Tepahlewam through the night, and in this time of killing, his wife gave birth to their second daughter. In the morning, Joseph led his people sixteen miles to White Bird Creek, and into the war he had tried so hard to avoid. He joined Toohoolhlzote and White Bird, whose warriors had by now killed fourteen settlers on Salmon River. Looking Glass remained at peace, having returned to his village at Kooskia.

On 15th June, Howard sent 92 cavalrymen from Fort Lapwai under Captain Perry to pursue the Nez Perce, teasing his subordinate: 'You must not get whipped'. To this, Perry replied: 'There is no danger of that, sir'.

On 15th June 1877, a scout's coyote howl alerted the Nez Perce camp in White Bird Canyon to Perry's approach. His command had travelled seventy miles in thirty hours, and had been reinforced en route by eleven settlers under Arthur Chapman. At dawn, a six-man truce party under Vicious Weasel (Wettiwetti Howlis) rode forward with a white flag. Approaching the canyon's sloping mouth, the delegation met Perry's advance detachment under Lieutenant Theller. As Vicious Weasel cried, 'What do you people want?' Chapman opened fire. An old Nez Perce warrior named Fire Body responded, shooting Perry's lead bugler from his saddle.

As the soldiers deployed into a thin line across the canyon, sixteen warriors under Two Moons charged Chapman's volunteers on Perry's left. The civilians were routed, exposing the left flank of Theller's dismounted central line. Emerging from a concealing butte, Ollokot, wearing a sash and riding a magnificent cream-coloured mount, led fifty warriors in a frontal assault against Theller. On Ollokot's left, Wahlitits, Red Moccasin Tops and Strong Eagle (Tipyahlahnah Kapskaps), all wearing red blanket coats to flaunt their bravery, broke the soldier line. With both flanks exposed, Theller's troops took to their heels, and 'the panic became general'. Hanging beneath their horse's bellies, Nez Perce warriors swept through the fleeing soldiers, and opened fire in their rear. Eighteen men under Lieutenant Theller were cut off and slain.

The warriors pursued Perry to within four miles of Mount Idaho, before returning to gather sixty-three rifles from the battleground. Only three Nez Perce were wounded in the encounter, and Joseph accurately recalled:

Typical Nez Perce cradle-board, with buckskin-covered wooden board and geometric beadwork decoration (above). Comparison (below) of Nez Perce (left) and Crow (right) cradleboard designs, the shaded areas indicating the beaded or decorated areas.

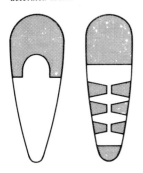

We numbered in that battle sixty men, and the soldiers a hundred. The fight lasted but a few minutes, when the soldiers retreated before us for twelve miles. They lost thirty-three killed and had seven wounded. When an Indian fights, he only shoots to kill; but soldiers shoot at random. None of the soldiers were scalped. We do not believe in scalping, nor in killing wounded men. Soldiers do not kill many Indians unless they are wounded. Then they kill Indians.

The following morning, the Nez Perce camp was further heartened by the return of the formidable warriors Five Wounds and Rainbow from buffalo-hunting in Montana. The headmen councilled, and on 19th June the Nez Perce re-crossed to the Salmon River's west bank. Thirty warriors remained behind as scouts.

Nez Perce bowcase, quiver and bandoleer of about 1870. The quiver and bowcase are made of buffalo hide covered with otter skins and adorned with beaded cuffs. From the top of the quiver and bowcase hang two elaborately decorated panels beaded in the style of the Crow, with pendants of fur and red cloth. The case and quiver were carried by means of the bandoleer which is decorated with red and dark blue stroud, otter fur and small triangles of beadwork. This excellent example was collected from a descendant of Ollokot.

The scouts flourished their red blankets to announce General Howard's approach several days later. Having left Fort Lapwai five days before with 227 regulars and 20 volunteers, Howard reached the Salmon at White Bird Canyon on 27th June having been reinforced en route to 400 soldiers plus 100 scouts and packers. The Nez Perce scouts taunted Howard from the far bank of the river. They were, according to Joseph, 'hoping General Howard would follow. We were not disappointed'.

While Howard gingerly tested the Salmon's swirling waters, the Nez Perce, on 1st July, quietly packed camp and withdrew north-west into the pine-covered mountains. Toohoolhoolzote, Rainbow and Five Wounds led the warriors, while Joseph guided the women, children and elderly through the treacherous but familiar terrain. Thirty-six hours later, the cavalcade re-crossed the Salmon at Craig's Ferry some twenty five miles to the north. They camped at a kouse ground called Aipadass, west of Camas Prairie, having severed Howard's supply line.

Howard spent the entire day crossing the Salmon, before blundering after his elusive quarry. Battling up slippery trails and losing several pack-mules in precipitous canyons, Howard finally reached Craig's Ferry four days later. Commandeering and demolishing a house belonging to a treaty Nez Perce, Luke Billy, the soldiers constructed a raft; then watched the boat, its occupants and Luke Billy's home career downstream for four miles. Defeated, Howard doubled back into the tortuous mountains, re-traced his arduous journey, and re-crossed the Salmon at White Bird Canyon. Outwitted and outmanoeuvred, he reached Grangeville on 8th July.

Looking Glass

Having received misleading reports that Looking Glass was planning mischief, Howard had, on 29th June, dispatched two cavalry companies under Captain Whipple to arrest the chief. Breakfasting in his lodge two days later, Looking Glass was alerted to the approach of Whipple's troops, with twenty Mount Idaho civilians led by D.B. Randall. Bird Alighting (Peopeo Tholekt) rode out to parley, but returned in consternation after one of the civilians repeatedly jabbed a rifle into his ribs.

The Nez Perce raised a white flag, and Bird Alighting, accompanied by an old man named Kalowet, rode out again to tell the soldiers: 'Leave us alone. We are living here peacefully and want no trouble'. Whipple insisted upon seeing Looking Glass, and as Bird Alighting returned to his chief's lodge, a civilian suddenly shot a watching Nez Perce to the ground. The firing became general and as Looking Glass's people scattered, a woman and her baby were drowned trying to cross the Clearwater. After destroying the abandoned village's crops and rounding up the Nez Perce cattle, Whipple's troops marched north-west to Cottonwood, having 'stirred up a new hornet's nest'.

On the morning of 3rd July, Charles Blewell, a civilian scouting for Whipple, was killed by one of Joseph's scouts. He alerted the Nez Perce camp at Aipadass, whereupon Rainbow and Five Wounds led a war-party to attack Cottonwood. They came instead upon another of Whipple's scouting parties, under Lieutenant S.M. Rains, and wiped out the entire twelve-man detachment. The Nez Perce attacked Cottonwood the following day, but reinforcements from Lapwai, under Perry, helped resist the assault.

On 5th July, Joseph and the older fighters shepherded their people east across the Camas Prairie towards Piswah Ilppilp Pah (Place of Red Rock), guarded by an advance screen of fourteen warriors. These warriors stumbled upon seventeen civilian volunteers under Randall, heading for Cottonwood from Mount Idaho. The volunteers made a desperate charge through the Nez Perce ranks towards Perry's position but were forced to make a stand against the warriors' close pursuit. Besieged from 11.00 a.m. to mid-afternoon, Randall and another civilian were killed and three others wounded, before Perry belatedly dispatched a relief force. An aged warrior named Wounded Mouth (Mimpow Owyeen) was also killed.

Pausing only to bury Wounded Mouth, the Nez Perce bands travelled on to the south fork of the Clearwater. There their numbers were swelled to 200 fighting men and 500 elders, women and children by the arrival of Looking Glass, who declared bitterly: 'Now, my people, as long as I live I will never make peace with the treacherous Americans. I am ready for war.'

Leaving the War in Idaho

Nez Perce moccasins of the late nineteenth century and decorated with 'scatter-beading'. This type of decoration, consisting of individually stitched beads, was found only among a few of the Plateau tribes.

Four days after the fight with Randall, the Nez Perce's Clearwater camp was alerted, on 9th July, to the presence of eighty Lewiston volunteers under Colonel G. McConville, dug in on Possossona Hill. For two days, Ollokot, Five Wounds and Rainbow led frequent attacks against the soldiers' position, which became aptly known as Misery Hill, and forty-eight horses stolen by Whipple from Looking Glass's village were re-captured.

Since scouts had reported no signs of Howard's anticipated arrival from the south-west, the Nez Perce remained contentedly on the Clearwater. Their calm, though, was shattered by the sudden explosion of a howitzer shell in the early afternoon of 11th July. The one-armed General, reinforced by Perry, had led 400 regulars and 150 volunteers across the Clearwater south of Joseph's camp. Proceeding north along a plateau high above the eastern bank of the river, he had stumbled upon the Nez Perce.

While Howard attempted to organise his straggling, two-mile-long column into a cohesive attacking force, he came under fire from twenty-four snipers organised by Toohoolhoolzote. Warriors including Ollokot meanwhile scampered up the slope and mounted a defensive fire into the soldiers' flanks from improvised rifle-pits. Joseph divided his time between fighting and councilling with the other headmen in a concealed 'smoking lodge'.

As sporadic fighting continued through the next day, many Nez Perce warriors became keen to withdraw. In mid-afternoon, Joseph rode down from the lines to organise the packing of the lodges, but, Yellow Wolf recalled: 'The women, not knowing the warriors were disagreeing, quitting the fight, had no time to pack the camp. Chief Joseph did not reach them soon enough.' As Perry's cavalry advanced, the warriors retreated, and the women were forced to abandon their camp. Only Perry's hesitancy permitted the Nez Perce to withdraw safely north up the Clearwater to Kamiah. Lodges, clothing and large amounts of flour were lost to the soldiers, and war correspondent Tom Sutherland reported his discovery of 'a much worn pair of small moccasins and an absurd little rag doll under a tree'.

The Nez Perce lost four warriors – Going Across (Wayakot), Grizzly Bear Blanket (Yoomtis Kunnin), Red Thunder (Heinmot Ilppilp) and

This war-shirt of around 1865 and accredited to Joseph, illustrates the close relationship between the costume of the Nez Perce and that of the Crow tribe of the Great Plains.

Whittling (Lelooskin) – while fifteen of Howard's troops were killed. Although the soldiers reported 'Joseph is in full flight', Howard foolishly delayed his pursuit until the sun rose the following day.

At dawn on 13th July, the Nez Perce scuttled across the Clearwater on their buffalo-bundle boats. As the last of their horses plunged across, Perry and Whipple's cavalry approached. They were scattered in panic by the Nez Perce warriors' fierce fire. According to Howard, the only damage inflicted, was, 'the shame to us and a fierce delight to the foe'.

'Plenty of Fighting'

The Nez Perce made camp on the Clearwater, which Howard dared not cross, then struck their lodges the following morning and headed for Weippe Prairie and the Lolo Trail east. A warrior named No Heart delayed the soldiers' pursuit, parleying across the river with Howard before promptly slapping his buttocks in derision and galloping away from the man the Nez Perce were now calling 'General Day After Tomorrow'.

At Weippe Prairie, the people's future was discussed by the headmen: Joseph, White Bird, Looking Glass, Toohoolhoolzote and Hahtalekin, who had recently brought sixteen Palouse warriors to join the cause. Joseph told them:

Some of you tried to say, once, that I was afraid of the whites. Stay here with me, and you shall have plenty of fighting. We will put our women behind us in the mountains, and die in our own land fighting for them. I would rather do that than run I know not where.

Looking Glass's voice, though, dominated the council, and it was agreed that he should lead the Nez Perce on the Lolo trail over the Bitterroots, to join the Crows in Montana, and perhaps on to the 'Old Woman's Country', Canada, where Sitting Bull had sought sanctuary after the Custer massacre. 'We intended to go peaceably to the buffalo country', Joseph noted, 'and leave the question of returning to our country to be settled afterward'.

Fort Fizzle

While the people followed the rugged Lolo Trail high into the mountains, to camp at Mussel Creek, five warriors left behind as scouts discovered Howard's advance party under Major E.C. Mason. The soldiers were being guided by treaty Nez Perce, who were ambushed on 17th July by Joseph's warriors. Scout John Levi's body was later found with forty-five bullet wounds, indicating the fugitive Nez Perces' anger toward their own people's treachery. Mason retreated to Howard on the Clearwater where the one-armed General idled for a fortnight, allowing the Nez Perce to trail out of his jurisdiction.

The tortuously narrow Lolo Trail, blocked by crags, trees and undergrowth, was quickly traversed by Joseph's uncomplaining cavalcade.

Howard later reported that the Nez Perce had 'jammed their ponies through, up the rocks . . . and among the fallen trees, without attempting to cut a limb, leaving blood to mark their path; and abandoned animals with broken legs . . . or stretched dead by the wayside.'

The Nez Perce then descended the eastern Bitterroots into Montana on 25th July to find their path blocked by a crude stockade, subsequently dubbed 'Fort Fizzle'. It was manned by thirty-five regulars under Captain C.C. Rawn summoned from Fort Missoula by Howard, plus 200 Montana volunteers and, to the Nez Perce's disgust, twenty Flathead Indians. Joseph, Looking Glass and White Bird calmly approached the defenders under a white flag. For three days they parleyed; Rawn demanding their surrender and the Nez Perce asking to be allowed into Montana in peace. 'We are going by you without fighting if you will let us', Joseph warned, 'but we are going by you anyhow'. Looking Glass chided Rawn: 'If the officer wishes to build corrals for the Nez Perce he may, but they will not hold us back. We are not horses.'

At 10.00 a.m. on 28th July, those of Rawn's men who hadn't by now deserted reported that they:

heard singing apparently above our heads. Upon looking up, we discovered the Indians passing along the side of the cliff, where we thought a goat could not pass, much less an entire tribe of Indians, with all their impedimenta. The entire band dropped into the valley beyond us, and then proceeded up the Bitterroot.

'No more fighting!' Yellow Wolf declared optimistically, 'We had left General Howard and his war in Idaho.'

Big Hole Battle

While the Nez Perce procession passed high above Fort Fizzle, a screening line of warriors exchanged shots briefly with the soldiers. Three civilian volunteers were captured, then quickly released with instructions to inform the Montana settlers of the Nez Perces' peaceful intentions.

Camping in the Bitterroot valley, the headmen councilled once more. Ignoring advice to head directly north to Canada, Looking Glass insisted upon travelling south to Crow country. Joseph complied, saying: 'I have no words. You know the country, I do not.'

For ten days the Nez Perce trailed slowly south, trading peacefully with settlements on the Bitterroot. Their caravan was joined by a small Nez Perce group resident in the valley, and by a half-blood called Lean Elk or Poker Joe. Looking Glass kept the warriors under close control, and offered horses as compensation when one of Toohoolhoolzote's followers stole some flour.

At the southern end of the valley, the band passed the revered

Medicine Tree, an ancient yellow pine in which a mountain sheep horn was embedded eight feet above the ground, considered a place of sanctuary and Wyakin powers. In subsequent camps, several men experienced visions of foreboding. Wahlitits prophesied his own death, and the warrior Lone Bird intoned: 'My shaking heart tells me trouble and death will overtake us if we make no hurry through this land!'

Looking Glass dismissed his people's fears and refused even to post scouts when the Nez Perce reached Iskumtselauk, Place of Ground Squirrels, by the Big Hole River, on 7th August. Pitching their eighty-nine lodges on the river's eastern bank, the people grazed their ponies in the westerly hills and cut new lodge poles which were to be dragged to the Crow country when seasoned.

At dawn on 9th August, Natalekin, a short-sighted old man, rode out towards the horse herds. Dimly making out figures, he leant forward on his mount, and a volley of fire tore him to the ground. A long line of soldiers splashed across the river and poured their fire into the silent lodges.

The soldiers, numbering 17 officers, 146 men, and 35 volunteers, were led by veteran Indian fighter Colonel John Gibbon, who had been wired by Howard on 25th July at Fort Shaw. They had approached the camp silently the previous night, while Howard, with 700 soldiers, emerged from an arduous crossing of the Lolo Trail.

Gibbon launched a three-pronged attack from the north, north-west and west, cutting the Indians down as they stumbled from their lodges. Some warriors desperately engaged the leading soldiers. Others fled among the riverside willows, and then circled around the soldiers' rear. The women and children rushed for the shelter of the riverbank. Rainbow, whose *Wyakin* served him only after sunrise, fell in the first attack when his rifle jammed. Five Wounds, in his grief, was killed making a lone charge. Captain Logan fulfilled Wahlitits' omen of death and then fell himself as Wahlitits' wife took up the warrior's rifle.

Joseph's lodge was at the north of the camp, and one of his wives was cut down by a bullet while carrying her daughter to safety. Joseph, bare-footed and wearing just a shirt and blanket, had led a charge across the river to rescue the horses. He returned to carry screaming children to safety, while White Bird and Looking Glass organised their warriors into sharp-shooting positions. 'Almost every time one of their rifles went off', Gibbon lamented, 'one of our party was sure to fall.'

After four hours of fighting, Gibbon, wounded in the thigh, ordered a retreat to a wooded plateau to the south-west. Digging in, the soldiers resisted a fierce onslaught from Ollokot's warriors. To the west, a group led by Bird Alighting seized Gibbon's pack-train, destroying a mountain howitzer and capturing 20,000 rounds of Springfield ammunition.

Joseph now urged his grieving people to strike their lodges. Gibbon had ordered his men to take no prisoners, and the Nez Perce women

Caught in the horse-herd, Joseph rescues his daughter from advancing troopers of the 2nd Cavalry, after General Miles' attack in a snowy hollow of the Bear Paws Mountains, 8.00 a.m., 30th September 1877.

were crying for the dead, the children screaming from their pain. Yellow Wolf told how he found one tipi containing two women shot dead, one still clasping her newborn baby with its head smashed as by a gun breech or boot heel. In another, he found two other children, both killed. 'Some soldiers acted with crazy minds,' he said later.

Despite possessing the advantage of numbers and surprise, Gibbon had lost twenty-nine men, including seven officers, and suffered forty wounded, two mortally. The Nez Perce reported the deaths of 'Fifty women and children and thirty fighting men', including such treasured warriors as Rainbow and Five Wounds. Leaving a dozen men under Ollokot to besiege Gibbon, Joseph led his people south at noon, hauling the wounded on travois and noting sadly: 'The Nez Perce never make war on women and children; we could have killed a great many women and children while the war lasted, but we would feel ashamed to do so cowardly an act.'

The Net Closes

The Nez Perce hurried south under the shadow of the Bitterroots, guided now by Poker Joe, since Looking Glass carried the burden of blame for the Big Hole disaster. Ollokot re-joined the camp at Lake Creek, where his wife Fair Land (Aihits Palojame) died from her wounds, leaving a baby named Tuekakas after its grandfather. Reaching Horse Prairie on 12th August, the chiefs could no longer restrain the warriors from killing five settlers in raids for fresh horses. At Junction, on the Lemhi River, the Nez Perce found the settlements fortified, and were warned off by Chief Tenday of the Lemhi Shoshoni. Heading south-east, some Nez Perce captured a wagon-train laden with whiskey, and in a drunken orgy killed five freighters and one of their own warriors, Kettalkpoosmin.

General Howard had meanwhile reached the Big Hole on 10th August and resumed his pursuit three days later, after watching his Bannock scouts mutilate the Nez Perce dead. On 17th August the Nez Perce camped at Beaver Creek. Howard, a day's march behind them, dispatched forty-three troopers under Lieutenant G. Bacon east to Targhee Pass to intercept the Nez Perce if they turned north for the Crow country.

Howard spent the night of 19th August at Camas Meadows, a few

U.S. army mountain howitzer and carriage, like that seized from General Gibbon by Peopeo Tholekt (Bird Alighting) at the Battle of the Big Hole.

A blanket wrapped about him against the cold, his bravest warriors at his flanks, Joseph rides out to make peace with Generals Miles and Howard, and their officers, in the Bear Paws Mountains, 5th October 1877.

miles south-east of the Nez Perce camp. Assured of success by the dream of a warrior called Black Hair, twenty-eight warriors, including Ollokot, Looking Glass, Toohoolhoolzote, Two Moons and Bird Alighting, stealthily entered Howard's camp at 3.30 a.m. to steal his horses. However, the premature report of one warrior's gun alerted the soldiers, and the raiders hurriedly stampeded 200 mules. Three cavalry companies gave pursuit, but were scattered when the warriors turned to defend a lava escarpment. Three soldiers were killed and six wounded, delaying Howard's pursuit for another day.

On 22nd August, the Nez Perce cavalcade trailed through Targhee Pass, recently vacated by Lieutenant Bacon in the belief that the Indians had already eluded him. Proceeding up Madison River, the fugitives entered what in 1872 had become Yellowstone National Park, and were guided east by a captured prospector, John Shively. Some warriors also seized nine bewildered tourists, wounding two of them before the chiefs interceded. One captive described Joseph as 'Sombre and silent, foreseeing in his gloomy meditations possibly the unhappy ending of his campaign . . . . Grave and dignified, he looked a chief.'

Joseph had reason for his concern, for Commanding General Sherman, currently visiting the park, had intensified his military campaign. To the north of Joseph, two companies of cavalry and one of Crow scouts waited at Mammoth Hot Springs; General George Crook had deployed five cavalry companies on Shoshoni River and ten 5th Cavalry companies on Wind River to the east and south-east respectively; Colonel Nelson 'Bearcoat' Miles lurked at Fort Keogh; and in the north-east Colonel S.D. Sturgis' six 7th Cavalry companies, accompanied by Crow scouts, waited on Clark's Fork. The *New North-west* reported:

General Sherman . . . has raised up an army on the four sides of Joseph just when it seemed most probable that he was about to escape. . . . We wait now hopefully for news that the Nez Perces have been struck hard and fatally.

As Poker Joe guided the people north-east, the warriors killed several white men attempting to carry messages between the soldiers. When they sighted Sturgis' command on 8th September, the Nez Perce suddenly turned south. Believing Clark's Fork Canyon to be impassable, and convinced that Joseph was escaping, Sturgis set off in pursuit. Out of sight, the Nez Perces milled their ponies to confuse their trail, then doubled north once more, concealed by the timbered mountain slopes. Passing close to, and parallel with, Sturgis' southbound command, the Nez Perce band silently traversed the now unguarded Clark's Fork Canyon, 'where rocks on either side came so near together that two horses abreast could hardly pass'. They emerged north of the Absaroke Mountains, having brilliantly outfoxed their pursuers once more. Sturgis re-entered Clark's Fork in Howard's rear on 11th September, much to the general's chagrin. Reaching the junction of the Yellowstone and Canyon Creek, Looking Glass rode ahead to council with the Crow chiefs on whom he had relied so heavily. He returned with his head bowed, saying that the Crows, his closest friends, would offer no help.

Death in the Bear Paws

On 13th September, the Nez Perce scouts flourished their red blankets to warn of the approach of Sturgis, who had marched sixty miles the previous day. As the warriors turned to fight, Joseph hurried the helpless ones towards the gorge into which Canyon Creek ran. Ollokot overtook them and joined a group of warriors in resisting Captain Benteen's attempt to outflank the fleeing families. As Sturgis frustrated his own attack by ordering his troopers to dismount, the Nez Perce secured the mouth of the narrow canyon. The band retreated safely, blocking pursuit with rocks and fallen trees.

Hastening north towards the Musselshell River early the next morning, the Nez Perce fought a fierce rearguard action against Sturgis' Bannock and Crow scouts which continued for two days and resulted in the deaths of one Nez Perce warrior and two old men, and the capture of forty horses. Sturgis suffered three dead and eleven wounded.

The Nez Perce crossed the Musselshell on 17th September and raided fresh horses from Crow chief Dumb Bull's camp. Crossing the Judith Mountains, Poker Joe set a hard pace, and the elderly and wounded silently drifted behind their people. The Nez Perce reached the Missouri on 23rd September, where they asked to trade with the fifteen soldiers at Cow Island Landing supply station. Insulted by Commander Moelchert's offer of a side of bacon and half a sack of hardtack, the warriors looted the station for flour, sugar, coffee, pots and pans. One of the soldiers wired Fort Benton:

The array of rifles employed by the Nez Perce on the Camas Meadows battlefield.

Chief Joseph is here, and says he will surrender for two hundred bags of sugar. I told him to surrender without the sugar. He took the sugar and will not surrender. What will I do?

Pushing north the following day, the Nez Perce looted a wagon-train, killing three teamsters, and skirmished briefly with soldiers from Fort Benton. Weary of the hurried march, the chiefs again placed themselves under Looking Glass's protection, though Poker Joe warned: 'All right, Looking Glass, you can lead. I am trying to save the people, doing my best to cross over into Canada before the soldiers find us. You can take command, but I think we will be caught and killed.'

For four days, Looking Glass led the band lazily north, and Joseph noted: 'We had heard nothing of General Howard, or Gibbon, or Sturgis. We had repulsed each in turn, and began to feel secure.' After visiting with Assiniboin Indians , the Nez Perce camped in the ravines on the east bank of Snake Creek between the Bear Paw Mountains and the Milk River. In a depression sheltered from the snow-laden winds, but open to attack on three sides, it was a good place to rest, but a poor place to fight. Toohoolhoolzote camped to the north, Looking Glass, White Bird, Husishusis Kute and Koolkool Snehee in the centre, and Joseph, Ollokot and Poker Joe to the south. The warrior Wottolen protested in vain to Looking Glass that he had seen a vision of disaster at this place.

At sunrise on 30th September, stampeding buffalo alerted the camp to approaching soldiers. As the women struck the lodges, a Nez Perce scout signalled: 'Enemies right on us! Soon the attack!' At 8.00 a.m. 383 men under General Miles – having made four days of forced marches from Fort Keogh – swarmed over the southern bluffs. The camp was thrown into turmoil, with warriors sprinting to natural rifle-pits, and the helpless ones taking flight north. Joseph's voice rose above the uproar, barking, 'Horses! Horses! Save the horses!', as the chief splashed across the creek to gather mounts for the fleeing families.

Miles attacked in two sweeping wings from south and east, the 7th Cavalry striking the south with their commander Captain Hale complaining, 'My God, have I got to go out and get killed in such cold weather!' The Nez Perce marksmen met his cavalry charge with a withering volley, reducing it to a bloody mêlée of screaming men and horses. Twenty-four soldiers, including Hale, fell dead, with forty-two wounded; and Lieutenant Erickson wheeled around to scream at Miles, 'I am the only damned man of the Seventh Cavalry who wears shoulder straps alive!'

Captain Tyler's 2nd Cavalry, with some Cheyenne scouts, circled west into the Nez Perce horse herd, separating Joseph and his warriors from the main camp.

We had no knowledge of General Miles' army until a short time before he made a charge upon us, cutting our camp in two, and capturing nearly all of the horses. About seventy men, myself among them, were cut off. My little daughter, twelve years of age, was with me. I gave her a rope, and told her to catch a horse and join the others who were cut off from the camp.

(Joseph)

Startled by the camp's ferocious defence, Miles mustered the 5th Infantry for a charge 'towards the village on foot, but the withering fire of the Indians soon proved too severe, and attempts to capture the village by such means had to be abandoned.' Reluctantly, Miles formed his men into a thin line around the village, and the assault degenerated into a siege.

In a fresh attack in the afternoon, the bluecoats penetrated the camp from the south-west:

The soldiers kept up a continuous fire. Six of my men were killed in one spot near me. Ten or twelve soldiers charged into our camp and got possession of two lodges, killing three Nez Perce and losing three of their men, who fell inside our lines. I called my men to drive them back. We fought at close range, not more than twenty steps apart, and drove the soldiers back upon their main lines, leaving their dead in our hands. We secured their ammunition. We lost, the first day and night, eighteen men and three women.

(Joseph)

Four of those killed, including Poker Joe, had been mistakenly shot by their own warriors. Toohoolhoolzote and Hahtelekin also lay dead, but the sadness in Joseph's heart was for Ollokot, who had tragically fallen in the thick of the early fighting.

The Boston Truce

Five inches of snow fell through the night. A woman of the band later recalled how the besieged Nez Perce dug shelter-pits for the helpless ones and rifle-pits for the warriors:

We digged the trenches with camas hooks and butcher knives. With pans we threw out the dirt . . . . Dried meat would be handed round. If not enough for all, it would be given to the children first. I was three days without food. Children cried with hunger and cold. Old people suffering in silence. Misery everywhere. Cold and dampness all around.

Six warriors escaped north to seek help from the 2000 Lakota living in Canada under Sitting Bull, but they were murdered by the same Assiniboin Indians who had been their hosts two days before.

When the report of Miles' Hotchkiss gun heralded morning, the Nez Perce were entrenched in a remarkable network of tunnels. The fighting was at stalemate until noon, when the soldiers raised a white flag, and a voice cried out in the Chinook jargon: 'Colonel Miles would like to see Chief Joseph'. The chiefs hurriedly councilled, and Joseph, less intransigent than some of the headmen, agreed to meet Miles. After sending a half-blood, Tom Hill, to arrange the parley, Joseph rode out with two warriors. Miles met them, and clasping Joseph's hand, said, 'Come; let us sit down by the fire and talk this matter over'.

This Nez Perce knife and sheath date from the late nineteenth century and are decorated with beadwork in designs that continue to demonstrate a strong Plains influence.

The parley was unproductive, with Miles demanding unconditional surrender of all arms and Joseph requesting that his people be allowed to return peaceably to the Wallowa, while retaining half their guns for hunting. In his frustration, Miles led Joseph back to his command tent, where, in flagrant violation of the flag of truce, he took the stoic chief prisoner. 'That', Lieutenant Jerome stated, 'was Miles' way'.

Fortunately for Joseph, Jerome misread the situation and rode into the Indian camp, where he himself was seized. Held through the night, he wrote the following morning: 'I am treated like I was at home. I hope you officers are treating Chief Joseph as I am treated.' According to Yellow Wolf, though, 'Joseph was bound hands and feet. They took a double blanket . . . rolled him in it like you roll a papoose on a cradle board . . . put where there were mules, not in soldier tent.'

When Yellow Bull visited his detained chief, Joseph told him, 'I do not know what they mean to do with me, but if they kill me, you must not kill the officer. It will do no good to avenge my death by killing him.' That afternoon, though, the two hostages were escorted to a buffalo robe spread between the lines, where, shaking hands, they were exchanged.

Sporadic firing and the misery of Joseph's people continued for the next two days. On 4th October, Miles' Napoleon cannon, raised like a mortar, inflicted the first Indian casualties since the opening battle: burying a girl, Atsipeeten, and her grandmother, Intetah, in their shelter. The people were divided about surrendering, and White Bird deferred to Joseph's judgement. The chief's despair was completed by the arrival that evening of General Howard with the vanguard of his army.

Towards noon on 5th October, Howard's treaty Nez Perce scouts Captain John and Old George carried a white flag to the fugitives' lines and asked them to make peace. Sending the messengers 'back where they belonged', Joseph consulted Looking Glass and White Bird. They both refused to surrender to a 'man of two faces', but Joseph said, 'Many of our people are out on the hills, naked and freezing. The women are suffering with cold, the children crying with the chilling dampness of the shelter pits. For myself I do not care. It is for them I am going to surrender.'

When Captain John and Old George returned to say that Miles wished to have no more war, and would return the Nez Perce to the reservation, Joseph became convinced that he was now being asked to negotiate not a surrender, but a peace.

As a tragic postscript, a mounted Indian approached the battleground that afternoon. Believing him to be one of Sitting Bull's warriors, Looking Glass leapt from his rifle-pit. The horseman was, in fact, one of Miles' Cheyenne scouts, and Looking Glass was cut down by a sharp-shooter's bullet; the only warrior to die after the opening battle.

'From Where the Sun Now Stands'

In a preliminary council, Joseph received Miles' assurance that his people could winter with Miles on the Yellowstone before returning to Lapwai. The Nez Perce were confident of a return to their homeland. 'Everybody', according to Howard's adjutant Lieutenant Wood, 'took this as an accepted fact'.

At 2.00 p.m. Joseph rode slowly from the southern end of the camp, with five warriors walking beside him and leaning against his horse's flanks. Joseph was shrouded beneath a grey, black-striped blanket, and rested his rifle across his saddle pommel. Bullets had scarred his wrists and forehead, and torn his shirt and leggings. The silent contingent approached a buffalo robe laid between the lines where Miles, Howard, Wood, two more officers, interpreter Arthur Chapman, an orderly and a mounted courier waited.

Dismounting, Joseph drew his blanket around him and, carrying his rifle in the crook of his arm, proudly offered it to Howard. The general deferred this honour to Miles, before Joseph stepped back to deliver his speech of surrender:

Tell General Howard I know his heart. What he told me before, I have in my heart, I am tired of fighting. Our chiefs are killed. Looking Glass is dead. Toohoolhoolzote is dead. The old men are all killed. It is the young men who say yes or no. He who led the young men[Ollokot] is dead.

An unusual photograph of Joseph presented to the U.S. National Archives by General Miles. Joseph wears a blanket, leggings and war-shirt with ermine drops. His hair is in braids, with a striking example of the raised Crow-style fringe characteristic of Joseph's band of the Nez Perce.

It is cold and we have no blankets. The little children are freezing to death. I want time to look for my children, and see how many of them I can find. Maybe I shall find them among the dead. Hear me, my chiefs. I am tired; my heart is sick and sad. From where the sun now stands, I will fight no more forever.

Then Joseph hid his head beneath his blanket, and with it the war.

Into Exile

The fight was the most fierce of any Indian engagement I have ever been in. . . . The whole Nez Perce movement is unequalled in the history of Indian warfare.

Such was Miles' view of the Nez Perces' epic struggle. They travelled 1,700 miles in eleven weeks, defied ten separate US commands, and capitulated only forty miles from the Canadian border. Of the 750 Nez Perce that had left Idaho, 120 had died, and 87 men, 184 women and 147 children surrendered under Joseph, with 1500 horses and 300 saddles; 180 whites had been killed in the campaign, with 150 wounded.

Joseph had been the guardian of the women and children throughout the long march, and though he conferred constantly with the other headmen, the whites regarded him as the figurehead of the Nez Perce resistance. After the surrender, reporter J.J. Healey wrote that Joseph was 'walking round about his people talking to the wounded and occasionally addressing the warriors by signs, and seemed quite unconcerned about his defeat.'

While most of the Nez Perce surrendered with Joseph, White Bird, with fourteen warriors and a similar number of women, escaped during the night. Yellow Wolf slipped away during a snowstorm the following morning, after Joseph had told him, 'You better go find your mother and my daughter. Bring them here!'

Joseph's 'old wife', Heyoom Yoyish (Bear Crossing) and daughter had fled during the opening battle, and were among some 230 Nez Perce who escaped from the Bear Paws to Sitting Bull's camp in Canada. From spring 1878 onwards, several small groups of these homesick exiles straggled back to the Lapwai Reservation.

On 8th October, Miles started his ragged caravan of troops and captives towards Fort Keogh, on the Tongue River. He arrived a week later, having developed a profound respect for the eloquent Joseph and his kinsmen. Commanding General Sherman, though, declared that the Nez Perce's confinement at the fort would prove too expensive. He instructed Miles instead to break his surrender terms, and herd the 432 prisoners 800 miles to Fort Lincoln, near Bismarck, North Dakota. Bearcoat complied reluctantly, ferrying the wounded up the Yellowstone and Missouri, and protesting the Nez Perce 'treatment unusually severe. Joseph can tell you his own story'.

In Bismarck, on 16th November, the ragged Nez Perce were received as heroes, reflecting the growing public sympathy for their plight. They received food in the town square while a band played the Star Spangled Banner, and Joseph received an invitation to a feast in his honour:

To Joseph, Head Chief of the Nez Perces. Sir: Desiring to show you our kind feeling and the admiration we have for your bravery and humanity, as exhibited in your recent conflict with the forces of the United States.

Amid the accolades, Joseph learnt that his people were to be sent as prisoners of war, by train, to Fort Leavenworth, eastern Kansas. He asked: 'When will the white man learn to tell the truth?'

Eeikish Pah – The Hot Place
On 27th November 1877, Joseph's people disembarked at Fort Leavenworth. They were ordered to camp in a swampy depression beside the Missouri which one observer suggested had been selected 'for the express purpose of putting an end to Chief Joseph and his band'. Malaria was rife and by the following July it had claimed twenty-one Nez Perce lives.

We had always lived in a healthy country, where the mountains were high and the water was cold and clear. Many of our people sickened and died, and we buried them in this strange land. I can not tell how much my heart suffered for my people while at Leavenworth. The Great Spirit . . . seemed to be looking some other way, and did not see what was being done to my people.

(Joseph)

A Nez Perce dress from about 1890. It is made from two bighorn or deer skins decorated with paint and beadwork, the untrimmed tails ornamenting the middle of the bodice. Even in exile, the traditional crafts survived.

A petition for a new home, submitted by Joseph in December 1877 and endorsed by Captain Randall at Fort Leavenworth, was disapproved by Sherman. In July 1878, though, the Bureau of Indian Affairs assumed responsibility for the Nez Perce, and transferred them south to the parched 7000-acre Quapaw Reservation in Kansas Territory. 'We were not asked if we were willing to go', Joseph recalled, 'We were ordered to get into the railroad cars. Three of my people died on the way'.

By October 1878, forty-seven more Nez Perce had died, in the land they hatefully called Eeikish Pah, The Hot Place. 'I think very little of this country', Joseph lamented, 'It is like a poor man; it amounts to nothing'. That month, Joseph's frequent complaints resulted in visits from Indian Commissioner E.A. Hayt and a congressional committee. Both parties concurred with the chief's protests, and Hayt accompanied Joseph and Husishusis Kute on a 250-mile tour of the southern plains. They selected a 90,710-acre area of the Ponca Reservation, Oklahoma as a possible new home for the Nez Perce, though it was little better.

When informed that his dream of a return to Idaho was out of the question, Joseph said:

This talk fell like a heavy stone upon my heart . . . . Other law chiefs came to see us and said they would help me to get a healthy country. I did not know who to believe. The white people have too many chiefs. They do not understand each other. They do not talk alike.

Pleas in Vain

Through the efforts of Indian Inspector General John O'Neill, Joseph was granted permission to visit Washington with Yellow Bull and veteran interpreter Arthur Chapman, to meet President Hayes. On 14th January 1879, the 38-year-old chief stirred an important Lincoln Hall audience with a moving address:

I have shaken hands with a great many friends, but there are some things I want to know which no-one seems able to explain. I can not understand how the Government sends a man out to fight us, as it did General Miles, and then breaks his word. Such a Government has something wrong about it. I can not understand why so many chiefs are allowed to talk so many different ways, and promise so many different things. . . .

I have heard talk and talk, but nothing is done. Good words do not last long until they amount to something. . . . Good words will not give me back my children. . . . Good words will not give my people good health and stop them from dying. Good words will not get my people a home where they can live in peace, and take care of themselves. I am tired of talk that comes to nothing. It makes my heart sick when I remember all the good words and all the broken promises. . . .

If the white man wants to live in peace with the Indian he can live in peace. There need be no trouble. Treat all men alike. Give them all an even chance to live and grow. . . . The earth is mother of all people, and all people should have equal rights upon it. You

Chief Joseph, wearing an embroidered cotton shirt and beaded sash. It is likely that he was photographed in 1887, shortly after the Nez Perce war, probably at Bismark.

might as well expect the rivers to run backward as that any man who was born a free man should be contented penned up and denied liberty to go where he pleases. . . .

I only ask of the Government to be treated as all other men are treated. If I can not go to my own home, let me have a home in some country where my people will not die so fast. I would like to go to Bitter Root Valley. There my people would be healthy. . . .

Let me be a free man – free to travel, free to stop, free to work, free to trade where I choose, free to choose my own teachers, free to follow the religion of my fathers, free to think and talk and act for myself – and I will obey every law or submit to the penalty. . . .

I have asked some of the great white chiefs where they get their authority to say to the Indian that he shall stay in one place, while he sees white men going where they please. They can not tell me.

Joseph's words fell on stony ground. In June 1879, Hayt compromised by transferring Joseph's 370 Nez Perce about 180 miles west to Oakland on the Ponca Reservation. The Lapwai Nez Perce opened a school there, but the children continued to die. A visiting doctor counted the graves of 100 infants including the daughter born to Joseph on the eve of the Nez Perce flight at Tepahlewam.

In July 1879, Joseph despairingly told a group of white visitors:

You come to see me as you would a man upon his death-bed. The Great Spirit above has left me and my people to their fate. The white men forget us and death comes almost every day for some of my people. He will come for all of us. A few months more, and we will be in the ground. We are a doomed people.

The Final Heartbreak

Joseph's cause was adopted by General Miles, by the Presbyterian Church, and by the Indian Rights Association, and became a national issue. In May 1883, the school of Oakland closed, and twenty-nine widows and orphans were permitted to accompany teacher James Reuben back to Lapwai. A year later, the arrival of fourteen petitions persuaded Congress to give Secretary of the Interior H.M. Teller discretion in the matter.

Teller decided to return the White Bird and Looking Glass bands to Lapwai, but directed that Joseph's people should go to the Colville Reservation, north-east Washington, because the Idaho settlers still nursed grievances towards them. To this, Joseph protested: 'If I could, I would take my heart out and hold it in my hand and let the Great Father and the white people see that there is nothing in it but kind feelings and love for him and them.'

On 1st June 1885, a group comprising 118 of the exiled Nez Perce arrived at Lapwai, while Joseph's 150 followers continued on to the Colville Reservation. Even here, troops were required to settle the band peaceably, amid opposition from Agent Gwydir, the resident Sans Poil Indian chief Skolaskin and suspicious white traders. In December, the band migrated fifty miles west to the more productive Nespelem valley.

Distinctive Nez Perce 'corn-husk' bags of the late nineteenth century. They were woven from hemp and embroidered with wool.

In 1889, all the members of the Nez Perce tribe were offered allotments of 160 acres on the Lapwai Reservation; the surplus to be sold to the highest bidder. Joseph visited the Allotting Agent, but refused, on principle, to take any land other than the Wallowa valley. One observer noted, 'It was good to see an unsubjugated Indian. One could not help respecting the man who still stood firmly for his rights, after having fought and suffered and been defeated in the struggle for their maintenance.'

Joseph visited Lapwai with increasing frequency, and even participated in the old-time procession of warriors at the raucous 4th July celebrations. Missionary Kate McBeth wrote: 'For a few years at first Joseph was afraid to come down upon the Nez Perce reserve – afraid of the surrounding whites and because of the many indictments against him – but this fear wore off. Then he visited his friends – too often for their good for he held to his heathenism with all the tenacity with which he had clung to his beloved Wallowa Valley.'

When white squatters again threatened his lands in 1897, Joseph travelled to Washington to petition President McKinley. He paraded with Generals Howard and Miles in New York during the dedication of Grant's Tomb, and appealed once more to be returned to his Wallowa home.

In August 1899, Joseph revisited his Valley of Winding Waters for the first time in twenty-two years. He was treated kindly, but found no land available to his people. Joseph returned in June, the following year, with Indian Inspector James McLaughlin. While Joseph tearfully attended his father's grave, and gazed into the reflections of Wallowa Lake, McLaughlin reported that the Nez Perce's return there would be impractical. Joseph met President Roosevelt in 1903, and visited the Carlisle Indian School, Pennsylvania on his journey home, where he graciously met General Howard. The following year he sadly addressed a Seattle audience:

Today my heart is far away from here. I would like to be in my old home in the Wallowa country. The white father promised long ago that I could go back to my home, but the white men are big liars. That is all.

On 21st September 1904, the great Nez Perce headman suffered a heart attack while sitting beside the fire in the tipi at Nespelem that he still preferred to the white man's house. He was buried at Nespelem, where a monument now stands. Dr Edwin Latham suggested that Joseph 'died of a broken heart'. Four years before his death, Chief Joseph had expressed the lifelong wish for which he had fought so persistently and waited so patiently:

My heart is in the Wallowa Valley, and I want to go back there to live. My father and mother are buried there. If the government would only give me a small piece of land for my people in the Wallowa Valley, with a teacher, that is all I would ask.

Chronology of Events

1805	Lewis and Clark discover the Nez Perce.
1807	Nez Perce enter the fur trade at Canadian North West Company's Kootenae House.
1831	Nez Perce delegation travels to St. Louis seeking religion.
1835	Samuel Parker meets Nez Perce chiefs.
1836	Henry Spalding establishes mission at Lapwai.
1840	Young Joseph is born.
1847	The Whitman Massacre precipitates Cayuse War.
1855	Nez Perce sign the Walla Walla Treaty (ratified 1859).
1860	Gold discovered in the Clearwater.
1863	Old Looking Glass dies.
1863	Lawyer's people sign the Thief Treaty.
1868	First settler arrives in the Wallowa Valley.
1871	Old Joseph dies.
1873	Wallowa reservation established (dissolved 1875).
1874	Nez Perce council at Tepahlewam.
1876	Wilhautyah murdered by Findley and McNall.
1876	Joseph and General Howard council at Lapwai.
1877	6 JANUARY Nez Perce ordered to attend Lapwai Reservation.
1877	1 APRIL Ollokot and Lt. Boyle council at Umatilla.
1877	20 APRIL Ollokot and General Howard council at Walla Walla.
1877	7 MAY Howard arrests Toohoolhoolzote at the final Lapwai council.
1877	14 JUNE Wahlitits kills four Salmon River settlers; beginning of Joseph's War.
	15 JUNE Howard sends Capt. Perry's troops after Nez Perce.
	17 JUNE Battle of White Bird Canyon.
	1–8 JULY Nez Perce evade Howard's troops on west bank of Salmon River.

	1 JULY Attack on Looking Glass's village.
	3 JULY Massacre of Lt. Rains' party.
	4 JULY Nez Perce attack Cottonwood.
	5 JULY Nez Perce fight Randall's militia on Camas Prairie.
	9–10 JULY Siege of Misery Hill.
	11–12 JULY Battle of the Clearwater.
	16–27 JULY Nez Perce cross the Lolo Trail.
	17 JULY Joseph's warriors ambush Howard's treaty-Nez Perce scouts.
	28 JULY 'Battle' of Fort Fizzle.
	9 AUGUST Battle of the Big Hole.
	20 AUGUST Nez Perce raid Howard's camp at Camas Meadows.
	23 AUGUST–6 SEPTEMBER Nez Perce traverse Yellowstone National Park.
	8 SEPTEMBER Nez Perce elude Col. Sturgis at Clark's Fork Canyon.
	13 SEPTEMBER Canyon Creek skirmish.
	23 SEPTEMBER Nez Perce cross the Missouri and raid Cow Island station.
	30 SEPTEMBER–5 OCTOBER Battle of the Bear Paws.
	5 OCTOBER Joseph's surrender ends his war and the flight of the Nez Perce.
1877	27 NOVEMBER Joseph's Nez Perce settled at Fort Leavenworth, Kansas.
1878	Nez Perce are transferred to Eeikish Pah.
1879	Joseph visits Washington.
1879	Joseph's people are transferred to Oakland.
1885	Some 118 exiled Nez Perce return to Lapwai; Joseph's people settled at Colville Reservation.
1899	Joseph revisits the Wallowa.
1904	Death of Chief Joseph.

Bibliography

In addition to the books listed below, a number of articles in periodicals are worthy of attention including 'Chief Joseph's Own Story' in the *North American Review* of April 1879, 'Chief Joseph' in the *National Geographic Magazine* of March 1977, and 'From Where the Sun Now Stands' by Bruce Wilson in the 1960 edition of *Omak*.

Beal, M.D. *'I Will Fight No More Forever'* University of Washington, 1963.

Brown, D. *Bury My Heart at Wounded Knee* Barrie & Jenkins/ Pan, 1970.

Capps, B. *The Great Chiefs* Time Life, 1975.

Catlin, G. *North American Indians* Dover, 1973.

Gay, E.J. *With the Nez Perces* University of Nebraska, 1981.

Gidley, M. *With One Sky Above Us* Webb & Bower, 1979.

Gulick, B. *Chief Joseph Country* Caxton, 1916.

Holloway, D. *Lewis & Clark* Weidenfeld & Nicolson, 1974.

Josephy, A.M. *The Patriot Chiefs* Viking, 1961.

Josephy, A.M. *The Nez Perce Indians & Opening of the Northwest* Yale, 1971.

McLuhan, T.C. *Touch the Earth* Abacus, 1973.

McWhorter, L.V. *Yellow Wolf* Caxton, 1940.

Swanton, J.R. *Indian Tribes of North America*, Smithsonian Institution 1952.

Utley, R.M. *Bluecoats and Redskins* Purnell, 1973.

608
GERONIMO APACHE CHIEF

Geronimo

LAST RENEGADE OF THE APACHE

The area of the South-west prowled and raided by Geronimo. Also shown is the route of the Warm Springs Apache to San Carlos after Geronimo's arrest at the hands of John Clum in 1877; and the route taken by Geronimo's raiders when they drove Loco's Mimbreño away from the agency in 1882.

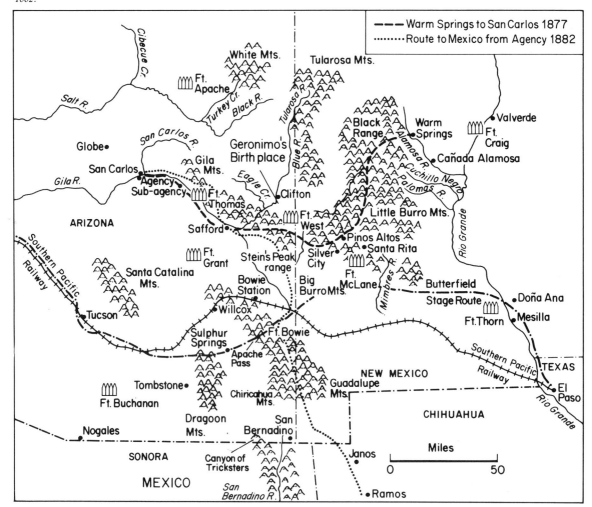

– – – Warm Springs to San Carlos 1877
.... Route to Mexico from Agency 1882

Cibecue Cr.

Salt R.

White Mts.

Tularosa Mts.

Ft. Apache

Turkey Cr.

Black R.

Tularosa R.

Black Range

Warm Springs

Valverde

Ft. Craig

Globe

San Carlos R.

Geronimo's Birth place

Alamosa R.

Cuchillo Negro

Cañada Alamosa

Gila Mts.

San Carlos

Eagle Cr.

Blue R.

Palomas R.

Agency Sub-agency

Ft. Thomas

Clifton

Little Burro Mts.

Gila R.

ARIZONA

Safford

Ft. West

Pinos Altos

Santa Rita

Rio Grande

Ft. Grant

Stein's Peak range

Silver City

Ft. McLane

Mimbres R.

Butterfield

Doña Ana

Southern Pacific Railway

Santa Catalina Mts.

Bowie Station

Big Burro Mts.

Stage Route

Ft. Thorn

Mesilla

Tucson

Willcox

NEW MEXICO

Southern Pacific Railway

TEXAS

Sulphur Springs

Apache Pass

Ft. Bowie

Guadalupe Mts.

El Paso

Tombstone

Chiricahua Mts.

CHIHUAHUA

Ft. Buchanan

Rio Grande

Dragoon Mts.

San Bernadino

Nogales

Miles

SONORA

Canyon of Tricksters

Janos

0   50

MEXICO

San Bernadino R.

Ramos

144

One of the brightest, most resolute, determined looking men I have ever encountered . . . . Every movement indicated power, energy and determination. In everything he did, he had a purpose.

(General Nelson 'Bearcoat' Miles)

Supreme and Implacable

An unlovely character, a cross-grained, mean, selfish old curmudgeon of whom . . . I never heard recounted a kindly or generous deed.

Such was the view of Geronimo taken by Colonel H.L. Scott, in common with most of the white officers tormented by him. Yet Geronimo's treacheries were nothing more than a reflection of the treacheries suffered by him and his people. Just as the Apaches lifted scalps only in imitation of the Spanish, Geronimo attacked the Mexicans only after they had massacred his family, and turned on the Americans only when they drove him from his home.

Among his own people, Geronimo became an influential leader without ever really being considered a true chief; but a war chief's attributes were certainly Geronimo's. His cousin, Jason Betzinez, noted that Geronimo maintained a true identity while other chiefs:

The Southwest culture region

by smooth talking and keeping their gambling and drinking secret, made a better impression on the whites than Geronimo . . . the latter, who was perfectly open with his roistering, was actually a better man. Certainly he had been a much braver warrior and abler leader than the rest of them.

Geronimo was, essentially, uncompromising. Therefore she posed a terrifying threat to the whites.

His popular image persists:

A thoroughly vicious, intractable, and treacherous man. His only redeeming traits were courage and determination. His word, no matter how earnestly pledged, was worthless. His history . . . was a series of broken pledges and incitements to outbreaks.

(Lieutenant Britton Davis)

Geronimo's prolonged and bloody wars were among the most frustrating in America's history. Few in number, but masters of their daunting mountain homeland, the Apaches were the ultimate guerrilla fighters, with Geronimo supreme among them. His last campaign, in which, with only twenty warriors, he ran ragged a pursuit force of 5000 troops demonstrated one officer's wonderful observation that chasing the Apache was like 'chasing deer with a brass band'.

The Apache

'Apache' probably originates in the traditional Zuni name for the Navajo, *Ápachu*, 'the enemy'. The Apache referred to themselves as *Ndé*, 'the People'. They comprised seven tribal groups: the Navajo, Kiowa-Apache, Jicarilla, Lipan, Mescalero, Western Apache and Chiricahua.

The Navajo were considered a distinct people because of their unique culture, and the Kiowa-Apache, Jicarilla and Lipan groups were more closely associated with the Plains Indians than the other Apache. The Mescalero Apache lived in the lands encompassed by the Sacramento, Guadalupe and Davis Mountains of south-east New Mexico and western Texas, and centred on the 12,000-foot Sierra Blanca. The Western Apache roamed across Arizona and were also known as Coyoteros, though Geronimo referred to them contemptuously as *Bi-ni-e-diné*, 'brainless ones'. They were divided into five groups: the White Mountain Apache (divided into eastern and western bands and sometimes designated specifically as Coyoteros); the San Carlos Apache (including the San Carlos, Apache Peaks, Pinal and Arivaipa bands); the Cibecue Apache; the Northern Tonto; and the Southern Tonto.

Geronimo's people were the Chiricahua, who were divided into three sub-tribes. The first were the Chokonen, also called the Central or True Chiricahua, or the Cochise Chiricahua after their famous chief. Their domain stretched into Mexico and New Mexico from south-east Arizona's Chiricahua Mountains. South of the Cochise Chiricahua were the second sub-tribe, the Southern Chiricahua or Nednhi. The third were the Eastern Chiricahua, the Cihene or 'Red Paint People', whom the Spanish called Gila Apache or Gileños. They roamed south-west New Mexico and south-east Arizona, and contained two divisions. The Mimbre or Mimbreño roamed the Mimbres Mountains and contained the Coppermine and Warm Springs (Ojo Caliente) bands. The Mogollon Apache lived in the mountains of the same name, and contained Geronimo's people, the Bedonkohé.

A Warrior People

The Chiricahua were marvellously adapted to life in their part of *Apacheria*, a land of extremes in temperature, climate and terrain. They knew every trail and landmark of their forbidding domain of mesas and precipices, canyons and deserts. They drew a sacred power from the ground itself, and believed: 'There is food everywhere if one only knows how to find it'. The men hunted deer, antelope and bighorn using stealthy pursuit, animal head masks and, after adopting the Spanish bounty of the horse around 1630, in mounted relays. The women gathered a bountiful harvest of wild plants, nuts and seeds. The most important staple foods were the spike-leaved mescal, which were prised from the ground each July, roasted in pits, sun-dried and hauled back to

Unusually shaped Apache bow, with traditional stone-headed arrows.

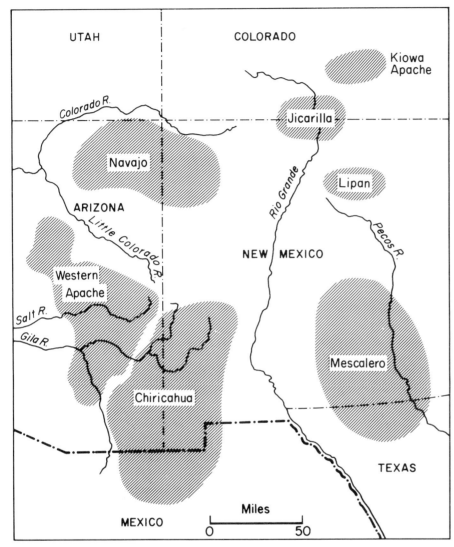

UTAH | COLORADO

Kiowa Apache

Colorado R.

Jicarilla

Navajo

Rio Grande

Lipan

ARIZONA

Little Colorado R.

Pecos R.

NEW MEXICO

Western Apache

Salt R.

Gila R.

Mescalero

Chiricahua

TEXAS

Miles

MEXICO

0   50

camp in pack-trains to provide a long-lasting, nutritious food.

The Apache displayed prodigious skills in war. When they attacked towns or camps they struck swiftly and ferociously, before recoiling into their mountain fortresses. The fate of captives depended largely on their age, and the warriors' motivation for attack; some prisoners were adopted into the tribe and treated with kindness whereas some suffered a grisly death. The Apache were the supreme thieves, and although they usually shunned flamboyance or risk at war because their numbers were so precious, Lieutenant Davis noted:

The most striking characteristic of the Apache was his utter disregard of consequences when excited or enraged. This trait of character was doubtless what made him such a desperate fighter when cornered. When at war with his enemies, the Apache took no unnecessary chances. His long suits were ambuscade, sudden attacks on the defenseless, and flight from superior numbers. Corner him and he was madness personified.

Approximate locations of the seven Apache groups before the government's concentration policies forced them together on the reservations.

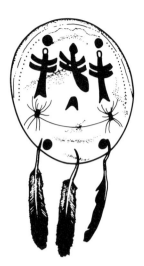

Apache raw-hide shield, decorated with sacred paint designs and pendant eagle feathers.

Trappings of Battle

The Apache fought with medicine shields, using bows of mulberry and arrows fletched with eagle or turkey feathers in quivers and cases often of mountain lion skin. They carried lances, war-clubs and knives, often blackened for camouflage – with guns and cartridge belts.

Warriors travelled light, wearing:

Scarcely any clothing save a pair of buckskin moccasins reaching to mid-thigh and held to the waist by a string of the same material; a piece of muslin encircling the loins and dangling down behind about to the calves of the legs, a war-cap of buckskin surmounted by hawk and eagle plumage, a rifle (the necessary ammunition in belt) or a bow with a quiver filled with arrows reputed to be poisonous, a blanket thrown over the shoulders, a water-tight wicker jug to serve as a canteen, and perhaps a small amount of 'jerked' meat or else of *pinole* or parched cornmeal.

(Lieutenant John G. Bourke)

The warrior's war paint and regalia had a special significance. It signified his 'Enemies Against' power, the sacred guidance an Apache warrior received from his supreme being *Usen* or 'Life Giver'. This was obtained through a vision-spirit or indirectly from a war shaman and was invoked directly by the paint and regalia. Before battle he would most likely don an impressive outfit:

Sacred cords of buckskin and shells, sacred sashes ornamented with the figures of the powers . . . a sacred shirt . . . medicine arrows, pieces of crystal, petrified wood, little bags of the sacred meal called 'hoddentin' [cattail pollen], fragments of wood which had been struck by lightning . . . and the cross, the medals, the Agnus Dei or the rosary of the Mexican victims whom his rifle or arrow had deprived of life.

(Lieutenant John G. Bourke)

Strategy of the Land

The Apache were renowned for their cunning defence strategies. When their camp was threatened or closely pursued, they would scatter, 'like a flock of frightened quail' (Davis). They would then leave a myriad of diverging trails, 'most of which disappeared in the rocks anyway', before re-convening at a distant and pre-arranged rendezvous. There they would make a false camp of raging fires and worn-out horses to deceive their pursuers, before resting safely some distance away. Water-holes, of which the Apache had unequalled knowledge, were visited only at night. If pressed, the Apache might kill their horses and clamber up sheer rock walls 'like deer'. 'No serpent can surpass him in cunning', Bourke observed. 'He will dodge and twist and bend in all directions . . . doubling like a fox, scattering his party the moment a piece of rocky ground is reached.'

The Apache warrior, by alternating between a walk and dog-trot could cover over 70 miles a day, and Lieutenant Davis noted 'The thought of attempting to catch one of them in the mountains gave me a queer feeling of helplessness'. By inserting a pebble in his mouth an Apache could quench his thirst and could 'go without water for as long a

Chiricahua sacred, four-strand medicine cord, of a date before 1891. It is adorned with feathers, beads, turquoise, and a wooden cross to guide its wearer. Such cords were considered very powerful medicine and were worn by many warriors to invoke 'enemies against' power.

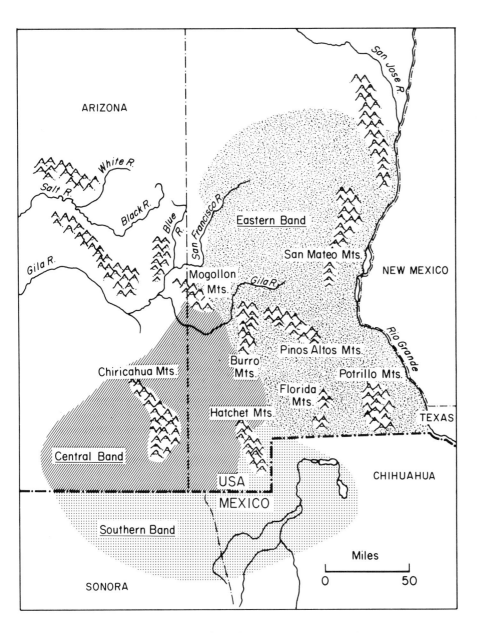

time almost as a camel.' He found water not beneath cottonwoods, where it lay too deep, but by burrowing in seemingly parched rock basins.

A Mescalero named Quick Killer demonstrated the art of concealment to John C. Cremony. While Cremony took ten steps away from a small bush, 'hardly sufficient to hide a hare', Quick Killer vanished:

I returned to the bush, went around it three or four times, looked in every direction . . . the prairie was smooth and unbroken and it seemed as if the earth had opened and swallowed up the man. Being unable to discover him, I called and bade him come forth, where to my extreme surprise, he arose laughing . . . within two feet of the position I

Approximate territories of the three Chiricahua bands, and the mountain ranges within the tribe's domain.

149

then occupied. With incredible activity and skill he had completely buried himself under the thick grama grass within six feet of the bush, and had covered himself with such dexterity that one might have trodden upon him without discovering his person.

Such a foe could not be conquered by the US army until they employed Apache scouts, who possessed similar skills in tracking, able to 'follow through grass, over sand or rock, or through the chapparal of scrub oak, up and down the flanks of the steepest ridges, traces so faint that to the keen-eyed American they do not appear at all.' Only by turning Apache against Apache did the Americans bring Geronimo within their reach.

War with the Spaniards

When Francisco Vasquez de Coronado led the brutal Spanish *conquistadores* beyond Mexico in 1540 to plunder treasure and heathen souls, the Chiricahua were probably already ranging their traditional territory. Certainly, they soon witnessed the barbaric nature of the Spanish, who eagerly ensnared the Indians of the south-west for sale in the thriving slave market. Many Apache were captured for this vile trade while visiting the subdued Pueblo Indians, but unlike the sedentary Pueblo, the Apaches were able to mount swift counter-attacks before recoiling from the power of the Spanish army, and vanishing into the mountains.

The Apache, not least of all Geronimo, were adept card players, using rawhide cards derived from Spanish examples. The four suits of clubs, cups, coins and swords (top to bottom) each run from two to seven with picture cards representing a page, mounted knight, king and ace, depicted in red, yellow and black paint.

By 1630, Spanish horses had been adopted by many of the southern tribes, but the Chiricahua, whose terrain was not entirely suited to a mounted culture, had received a different legacy from the conquerors of Mexico: their entire economy had become adjusted to accommodate frequent raiding of Mexican settlements. As this pattern of life escalated, large war-parties were required to attack the towns, and because families could not be left unguarded for fear of Spanish reprisal, the entire band participated in raids. This resulted in the disruption of the old plant-gathering economy, which was compensated for by the abundant booty available in the settlements. The Spanish grew crops and raised live-stock, and the Apache duly carried them away to the mountains, like distant overlords exacting tribute. The Mexicans pursued with varied success, and treaties were usually unreliable:

The Indians would frequently enter the Mexican towns, declare an armistice, and go on a high old drunk with the citizens to celebrate it. A month later they might be at war with that town and at peace with another not twenty miles away.

(Lieutenant Davis)

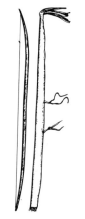

Typical Apache bow, with only a slight curve in the wood, made from elmwood with a bowstring of sinew; the fringed bowcase is of deerskin.

Dependent on raiding, the Apache adopted the Spanish lance, shield, horse-gear, cloth and firearms. Being keen gamblers, they also adopted Spanish playing cards.

For ten years after 1777, Juan Bautista de Anza, Governor of Mexico, organised many offensives into the depths of the Chiricahua's labyrinthine strongholds. Then Viceroy Bernardo de Gálvez implemented a new policy and attempted, through turning the tribes against each other and encouraging their dependence on Spanish rations and alcohol, to settle them on reservations known as '*Establicimiento de paz*'.

Some Chiricahua settled near Bacoachi, and the scheme enjoyed some success until the Apache sensed the decline in strength of their Spanish neighbours after the 1821 declaration of Mexican Independence.

One Who Yawns

Geronimo was born among the forbidding mountains clustered about the Gila River, near present-day Clifton, Arizona. He placed his date of birth in June 1829, though it is possible that he was born several years earlier. Safely secured in his Apache cradle or *tsoch*, the sleepy baby was given the name Goyahkla, meaning 'One Who Yawns'.

Goyahkla's family lived among the Bedonkohé band of Apache who inhabited the Mogollon range of mountains. His father was called Taklishim, The Gray One, and his mother Juana. Goyahkla's grandfather, Mahko, had been a famous chief of the Bedonkohé, and Goyahkla grew up listening to the stories of this noted warrior who had successfully raised corn and horses, traded with the Mexicans, and brought great security to his people.

Although Mahko had died before his grandson's birth, Goyahkla grew up under the peace that he had created. 'During my minority,' he later recalled, 'we had never seen a missionary or a priest. We had never seen a white man. Thus, quietly lived the Bedonkohé Apaches.'

As he grew older, Goyahkla learnt the legends of his people, recounted by his mother, while his father told him stories of war. When old enough, he assisted in working the small plots of corn, beans and pumpkins that the Apache farmed to supplement their land's natural harvest. Goyahkla also participated in making *tizwin*, a beer of crushed and fermented corn which would play an important part in the troubles of his later life. He accompanied expeditions to gather wild plants, and learnt the Apache art of utilising every aspect of their apparently sparse homeland. 'For each tribe of men Usen created He also made a home,' Geronimo explained later. 'In the land created for any particular tribe, He placed whatever would be best for the welfare of that tribe.'

When he was about ten, Goyahkla joined the men in hunting, and remembered fondly: 'To me this was never work.' Small game like rabbits were hunted by the young boys, and provided an important meat supply. Deer were considered the most important prey, and also the most difficult to stalk. Their hides were used to construct the tipis in which the Apache often lived before constant warfare with the whites

Rawhide sling, and typical Apache lance, some nine feet in length and adorned with cloth and two feathers at the blade. Lance-heads were crafted from sabres, knives and bayonets obtained or captured in battle from the whites. In the hands of a skilled Apache, the diamond-shaped sling needed only one swing in order to launch a stone a distance of up to 150 yards.

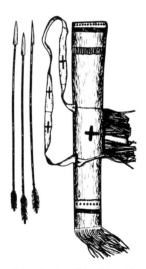

Fringed quiver of deerskin with iron-tipped hardwood arrows. The fringed and decorated central panel is typical of the Apache.

Traditional Apache dwelling, the wickiup, *a low-domed shelter of poles lashed together with yucca fibre and covered with bear-grass and brush.*

Apache tsoch *or cradle, 1885–1895, with willow frame and yucca backboard. Typical is the large sunshade from which hang bead and shell amulets to ward off evil spirits from the child.*

forced them to adopt the more mobile *wickiup*. Despite the importance of game, not every animal was considered good to eat. Snakes and fish were regarded as embodiments of evil spirits, and taboos also existed against the coyote, bear and turkey – although Geronimo listed the last two as good for food. He also noted that having hunted alone and killed large game, a boy claimed the right to smoke the tobacco that grew wild in the Apache lands.

The Young Warrior

Goyahkla was, like all Apache males, trained for warfare from boyhood. He learnt to identify every rock and crevice of his sacred homeland, and participated in mock, but very rough, battles with others of his own age. Apache youths plunged each morning into the nearest creek, even if it meant breaking the ice to do so. They also raced up the mountainside and back with mouthfuls of water, spitting it out at the finish to demonstrate that they were breathing correctly through the nose.

Because of the Bedonkohé isolation during this period, Goyahkla saw little of real warfare as he grew up. While he was in his teens, though, his family was visited by a group of Nednhi Apache, including a chief's son named Juh (Whoa). The Nednhi, whose name means 'Enemy people', were Southern Chiricahua from the Sierra Madre and their prime purpose was the constant raiding of Mexican settlements. Their warriors were drawn from many different bands and included Navajo and captured Mexicans; even among the war-like Apache the Nednhi were regarded as outlaws.

Juh was a robust and mischievous boy, who enjoyed stealing the baskets of acorns painstakingly gathered by Goyahkla's cousin Ishton. Under instructions from his grandmother, Mahko's formidable widow, Goyahkla put a stop to this by raising a band of friends and giving Juh a sound beating. A lasting friendship nevertheless developed between the two, and Goyahkla came to regard Juh as a brother. Goyahkla was undoubtedly influenced by the Nednhi's war-like ways, while Juh returned some years later to take Ishton as his wife.

As Goyahkla approached adulthood, his father Taklishim sickened and died. Goyahkla watched in sadness as Taklishim, dressed in his finery, and wrapped in a rich blanket, his face fresh-painted, was buried in a cave in the mountains. His favourite horse was shot, his belongings destroyed, and his name never spoken thereafter.

Goyahkla now assumed responsibility for his mother, and they sought to escape their grief by travelling to the Sierra Madre to meet with Juh and their relatives among the Nednhi. The journey was perilous, for they had little knowledge of where to find water in the mountains of Old Mexico. Even when they approached the location of Juh's stronghold, it took Goyahkla several days to find the camp, since the Nednhi expertly concealed their trails and tethered their livestock a safe distance from their homes.

Renewing his friendship with Juh, Goyahkla soon followed the difficult path towards becoming a warrior. The apprenticeship in war was considered a sacred undertaking, and Goyahkla ritually assumed the role of the culture hero Child of the Water for his first four raids. As such, he performed menial tasks for the mature warriors, wore a special war-cap, drank only through a tube, and used a scratcher embellished with lightning designs whenever he wished to scratch himself. Having completed the four novice raids, Goyahkla was 'admitted to the council of warriors', which, according to his recollections, he achieved at the age of seventeen.

As an accepted warrior, the One Who Yawns was permitted to take the Nednhi girl he had been courting as a wife. Her name was Alope, and Goyakhla determinedly met the high price of ponies that her father asked for her:

She was a good wife, but she was never strong. We followed the traditions of our fathers and were happy. Three children came to us – children that played, loitered and worked as I had done.

(Geronimo)

The Melting Pot

While the Bedonkohé remained relatively isolated, their Eastern Chiricahua cousins to the south-west, the Mimbreño, came in close contact with the Mexicans and, with increasing frequency, the Americans. Mexico's new-found independence, and subsequent instability, resulted in a lapse in the raids against the Apache made so frequently by the Spanish. The Mexicans made conciliatory gestures towards the Mimbreño, but the impossibility of united action by either the Mexican states or the scattered Apache bands prevented any effective truce.

In 1822, the leading Mimbreño chief, Juan José Compá, permitted the

Buckskin awl-case (lower) with beadwork, tin cones and red flannel; and buckskin tobacco pouch with beadwork, tin cones and painted designs. Such items were commonly carried in a warrior's belt, and these particular ones probably belonged to Juh, whom Geronimo regarded almost as his brother.

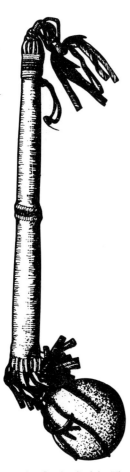

Apache 'flop-head' club. The stone head is encased in hide and connected to the beaded handle by twisted strips of rawhide, making it flexible and preventing the head from breaking off upon impact.

Mexicans to resume copper mining at Santa Rita del Cobre. Half of the Mimbreño resented this decision and migrated under chief Cuchillo Negro to Ojo Caliente (Warm Springs), dividing the Mimbreño into the Coppermine and Warm Springs bands. In 1825, Juan José leased the mines to American trappers.

Two years after Goyahkla's birth, the Coppermine Apache negotiated a peace treaty with the commander of Chihuahua. However, the rations promised to the Apache under this treaty failed to materialise, and as the weakness of the Mexican regime became apparent, the Apache resumed raiding with renewed fury and confidence. As Goyahkla grew up, the Mexican states abandoned the *Establicimiento de paz* system, and resurrected a policy of extermination.

A bounty of 100 pesos (about $100) was introduced by Sonora in 1835 for the scalp of any Apache warrior over fourteen years of age. Two years later, Chihuahua adopted a similar policy, with the barbaric addition of 50 peso and 25 peso bounties respectively for the scalps of Apache women and children. The bounties attracted various scalp-hunters, most notably the notorious 'King of New Mexico', James (Don Santiago) Kirker.

In April 1837, Juan José and several hundred Mimbreño attended a feast given by an American trader called James Johnson, whom the chief believed to be his trusted friend. As the Indians ate and drank, Johnson discharged a concealed howitzer into their midst, and his associates completed their dark work with guns, knives and clubs. Johnson carried the scalps of Juan José and many others back to Sonora, where he had a signed contract waiting.

Red Sleeves

In the aftermath of this atrocity, the Coppermine, Warm Springs and Bedonkohé Apache were united under the leadership of the 50-year-old Mangas Coloradas (Red Sleeves):

a large athletic man considerably over six feet in height, with a large broad head covered with a tremendously heavy growth of long hair that reached to his waist. His shoulders were broad and his chest full, and muscular . . . and altogether he presented quite a model of physical manhood.

Mangas Coloradas and his Mimbreño warriors waylaid the *conducta* which carried supplies to the fort at Santa Rita and when the miners were forced to abandon the settlement, the Apache chief, in his fury, ensured that none escaped.

When war broke out between the United States and Mexico in 1846, Mangas Coloradas welcomed the invading force of General Stephen Watts Kearney, and pledged Mimbreño support against the Mexicans. Under the 1848 Treaty of Guadalupe, however, in which the United States acquired most of present-day Arizona and New Mexico, the Americans agreed to prevent the Apache raiding across the border into

Mexico. Putting this into practice was a different matter, for the Apache could not comprehend the States' objections to their continuing a pattern of raiding that had existed for centuries.

While Apache hostility towards the Mexicans was by this time innate, their distrust of the Americans was engendered by another incident at Santa Rita. In the wake of the 1851 Boundaries Commission, the copper mines were re-opened, and gold discovered at nearby Pinos Altos. Mangas Coloradas visited the miners and offered to lead them to larger gold deposits. However, fearing a trap, the miners seized the great chief, bound him to a tree, and lashed him mercilessly with bull-whips. Mangas Coloradas slunk away to nurse his wounds and his pride at Ojo Caliente, and silently planned revenge for this humiliation.

Geronimo!

By the time of the 1853 Gadsen Purchase, which brought all the Chiricahua lands under US control, Goyahkla had attained a fearsome reputation for raiding in Sonora. In his twenties, he had developed the fierce countenance that was to scowl from so many photographs in the 1880s. About five-feet-eight-inches tall, he was barrel-chested, with a hawk's-beak nose, jutting cheekbones and an uncompromising slit of a mouth; and according to one observer his eyes resembled 'two bits of obsidian with lights behind them'. His descent from Mahko accorded him a certain status, and by this time Goyahkla had attained sufficient rank to have warned Mangas Coloradas against his ill-fated visit to the Santa Rita miners.

In the summer of 1858, according to the recollections of Geronimo and his cousin Jason Betzinez, a large band of Chiricahua, including Goyahkla and his family, journeyed to Janos, where they had recently accepted rations. The band camped outside the town, and for two days the warriors rode into Janos to trade and drink whiskey, leaving a small group behind to guard their families. While the Apache celebrated, two troops of Mexican cavalry under General Carrasco, Commander of Sonora, with whom the Chiricahua were in open conflict, made forced marches west across the state border towards Janos. Carrasco had clear intentions:

Not being able to comprehend the virtue of a policy which feeds Indians in one State that they might prey upon and destroy the citizens of another, I concluded that my duty was to destroy the enemy wherever I could find him.

Massacre

Returning to camp after the third day of revelry, the Apache warriors were met by a small group of women and children, who told them that

Another type of Apache 'flop-head', war-club encased in raw-hide, with twisted rawhide flexible neck and horsehair pendant.

their camp had been destroyed. Following the traditional pattern, the warriors scattered, meeting at a pre-arranged rendezvous after nightfall. There, they heard the full horror of the story from the few survivors. Carrasco's men had surrounded the camp, shot the few sentries, then fallen upon the families with bayonets. Carrasco claimed 130 killed and 90 captured, principally women and children.

Goyahkla learned that among the dead were his mother, his wife and his three children. He attended the council of warriors without a word, hardly hearing Mangas Coloradas advise the depleted Chiricahua to head back to Arizona. Geronimo said later:

> I stood until all had passed hardly knowing what I would do – I had no weapon, nor did I hardly wish to fight, neither did I contemplate recovering the bodies of my loved ones, for that was forbidden. I did not pray, nor did I resolve to do anything in particular, for I had no purpose left. I finally followed the tribe silently, keeping just within hearing distance of the soft noise of the retreating Apaches.

Returning to his people's settlement on the Gila River, Goyahkla, according to Apache custom, burnt his family's tipis, and all their possessions, including the children's toys. He vowed vengeance against the Mexicans, lamenting: 'None had lost as I had, for I had lost all'.

The Ramos Incident

Some authorities place the massacre of Geronimo's family as early as 1850, quoting Jason Betzinez as a source. However, according to Betzinez, there was an entirely separate incident in that year, which occurred at Ramos. Warm Springs Apache invited to the town were seduced with copious quantities of liquor. While they slept off the effects of the alcohol during the night, the Mexicans entered their camp, clubbed and stabbed the unconscious Apache to death, then lifted their scalps. According to Betzinez, the Apache exacted their revenge against Ramos 'in the greatest and bloodiest conflict in which Apaches were ever involved'. It was apparently in this battle that Goyahkla built much of his reputation as a warrior. Geronimo's own chronology in *His Own Story*, told to S.M. Barrett, is also questionable. The dating of certain events is confusing, and may be several years late. So, the massacre of his family may have taken place in the early rather than late 1850s.

Named in Revenge

As the Eastern Chiricahua recovered from the treachery of Janos, Mangas Coloradas called a council of war, which resolved to organise a large, old-time war-party against the Mexicans. Goyahkla was dispatched to secure the support of the Central Chiricahua, led by the famed chief, Cochise. Cochise, whose wife Dos-teh-seh was the daughter of Mangas Coloradas, was later described by Captain J.G. Bourke:

> A fine-looking Indian, straight as a rush – six feet in stature, deep-chested and roman-nosed. A kindly and even somewhat melancholy expression tempers the determined

look of his countenance. There was neither in speech or action any of the bluster characteristic of his race.

The Central Chiricahua having agreed to join the war, Goyahkla went on to the Sierra Madre, where Juh pledged the support of the Nednhi.

In the summer of 1859, according to Geronimo's recollections, the great war-party, having hidden their families in natural mountain fortresses, traversed the Sierra Madre and emerged across the Sonora River from the town of Arispe. Eight Mexicans who rode out to meet them under a flag of truce were killed by the Chiricahua, and their scalps lifted in full view of the town walls. The following day, two troops of infantry marched from the town. Skirmishes continued until dusk, when the Apache captured the Mexicans' supply train, forcing them to withdraw

Two companies of cavalry and two of infantry rode out from Arispe at 10 a.m. of the third day, just as the Apache completed their medicine preparations and prayers. As the Mexican horses, their silver trappings jangling, forded the river into a timbered hollow, Goyahkla led the Chiricahua charge. Two hours of fierce, confused fighting ensued. Venting his grief, Goyahkla felled a number of the troopers, believing them to be the same soldiers that had murdered his family. Each time he charged, the Mexicans screamed, *Geronimo!* – which is the Spanish equivalent for the name of Jerome – appealing to their patron saint. Goyahkla's companions took up the cry, and so the Bedonkohé warrior found his adult name of Geronimo.

Finally, together with three companions, their weapons lost, he stood among the dead, confronted by two armed soldiers. Two of the Apache were shot down, the third fell to a sabre blow, and only Geronimo escaped to his own warriors' lines. Seizing a lance, Geronimo turned and impaled the leading soldier. He then snatched up the trooper's sabre and grappled with the second Mexican, until, drawing his knife, he completed his morning's bloody revenge.

Raiding Old Mexico

Having avenged the death of his family, Geronimo returned to live among the Bedonkohé. He soon took a new wife, 'a very handsome woman' named Chee-hash-kish, who produced a son Chappo, and a daughter Dohn-say (Tozey), also known as Lulu. Later he took a second wife, a Bedonkohé named Nana-tha-thtith, who also gave him a child.

Though the other Chiricahua were satisfied with the revenge at Arispe, Geronimo's obsessive hatred of the Mexicans endured. Several months after the battle, he persuaded two warriors to join him in raiding a small village in Sonora. However, the raiders were discovered stealing horses, and Geronimo's two friends were killed. For two days, the Mexicans pursued Geronimo. Alone, hungry and exhausted, he employed all the skills of flight and concealment he had been taught through his childhood and, after shooting two Mexicans, eventually escaped to his Arizona homeland.

> Some of the Apaches blamed me for the evil result of the expedition, but I said nothing. Having failed it was only proper that I should remain silent. But my feeling towards the Mexicans did not change – I still hated them and longed for revenge. I never ceased to plan their punishment, but it was hard to get other warriors to listen to my proposed raids.

> (Geronimo)

A war-chief was only as influential as his last battle.

Bullet Proof

Some months later, and with two more colleagues, Geronimo attempted a raid beyond the Sierra Madre. But their night camp was discovered by Mexican troops who, having killed one of the Apache, then pressed on to the Bedonkohé stronghold in Arizona.

Overtaking them, Geronimo joined his people's defence which resulted in eight Mexicans being killed, while the Bedonkohé lost three boys and two warriors. The following summer, Geronimo led twenty-five raiders in ambushing a Mexican cavalry company in a mountain pass. The troopers defended themselves strongly and, leading a charge against them, Geronimo was felled with a rifle butt, scarring him for life.

He was wounded once more the following year, when a bullet grazed his face below his left eye, as troops again pursued him to the Chiricahua camp.

While Geronimo's continued raiding won him renown as a warrior, his violent nature won him enemies even among his own people; and the lack of success of his war-parties earned him few friends: 'Again I was blamed by our people, and again I had no reply.'

While Geronimo's wounds healed, his camp was once more caught unawares by Mexican troops. Again, many women and children were killed, among them Nana-tha-thtith and her child. Geronimo sought his revenge the next summer, capturing a Mexican and an American mule-train. Then when a punitive expedition arrived from Mexico, Geronimo and Mangas Coloradas routed the troops, killing ten for the loss of one warrior. The next year Geronimo undertook 'perhaps the most successful raid ever made by us into Mexican territory,' driving out the inhabitants of a Mexican village and leading their laden livestock back to Arizona.

When Geronimo's raiders terrorised Sonora the following year, they plundered a mule-train loaded with the liquor *mescal*. Although he became as intoxicated as his companions, he played the role of peace-maker in the drunken orgy of violence that followed.

This pattern of raiding the Mexican settlements continued to dominate Geronimo's life, and his reputation grew with each success. On one

The earliest known photograph of Geronimo, posed with a Springfield rifle, in a studio portrait by A. Frank Randall in the spring of 1884.

occasion, the Mexicans mounted a reprisal raid, running off the Bedonk-ohé horses. Geronimo gave pursuit, recovered the horses, and when nine vaqueros gave chase, doubled back to steal their mounts for good measure. 'It was a long time,' Geronimo said, 'before we again went into Mexico or were disturbed by Mexicans.'

Geronimo believed his success in war lay in a vision he had experienced shortly after the massacre at Janos. A voice had called him four times, the sacred number, and said: 'No gun can ever kill you. I will take the bullets from the guns of the Mexicans, so they will have nothing but powder.'

In 1898, at Fort Sill, he showed the artist E.A. Burbank his upper torso, placing a small pebble in the many bullet-holes that peppered his body, while making the sound of a gun, 'Crack!' and warning, 'Bullets cannot kill me!'

Cochise's War

White settlers travelling along the California Trail had caused considerable discomfort to the Mimbreño during the 1850s, and infiltrated the lands of the Central Chiricahua. In 1858, a delegation led by Dr Michael Steck, who had recently established reservations for certain of the disrupted Mimbreño bands, met with Cochise at Apache Pass in southeast Arizona. He asked the great chief's permission to construct a stage station for the Butterfield Overland Mail at the spring at Apache Pass. Cochise consented, agreeing to safeguard the passage of the mail-coaches for three years, and even negotiated a contract to chop firewood for the mail employees in 1860. Geronimo had recently married a relative of Cochise, and claimed to have been present at the Central Chiricahua meeting with Steck.

The Bascom Affair

The peace was shattered in late January 1861, when Second Lieutenant George N. Bascom, with fifty-four men of the 7th Infantry, rode up to the Apache Pass station and summoned Cochise to his tent. Not expecting any trouble, Cochise arrived with his wife and child, brother, and two nephews. After a brief exchange of pleasantries, Bascom abruptly accused Cochise of having stolen stock and kidnapped a boy from the ranch of John Ward, near Sonoita. The boy, Ward's son, was to grow up to be called Mickey Free, once described as 'Half-Irish, half-Mexican and whole son-of-a-bitch.'

The astonished Cochise denied knowledge of the boy – who had, in fact, been kidnapped by a Western Apache Coyotero band – but offered to inquire about his whereabouts. The impetuous Bascom, however, summoned troops to arrest the chief, and ransom him for the boy.

In a wooded hollow on the bank of the Sonora River, near Arispe, in the summer of 1859, Goyahkla avenges the massacre of his family – the battle in which he earned the name Geronimo.

Before the soldiers could enter, Cochise had drawn his knife, slashed the tent, and vanished. His family, though, were seized.

Gathering his warriors, including Geronimo, Cochise attacked the Butterfield Station. Despite Bascom's intervention, one of the stagecoach employees was killed, one wounded, and a third, J.F. Wallace, seized by Cochise as a hostage. The Chiricahua then effectively sealed off the Butterfield Trail, and ambushed a small wagon-train. Two Americans were captured, and, according to some accounts, eight Mexican teamsters were lashed to the wagon wheels and the wagons set aflame. That same evening, Cochise escorted Wallace to the station, and left a note for Bascom reading: 'Treat my people well and I will do the same by yours, of whom I have three'.

The following day, Cochise parleyed with Bascom, and offered to exchange hostages. But Bascom persisted in his demands for the Ward boy to be produced, and Cochise skulked away once more, leading Wallace by a lariat. The next evening, the Chiricahua attacked two stages, which only found the safety of the station after desperate flight. Cochise's warriors then drove off Bascom's mules as they were watered, rewarding the astute chief's original insistence that the Butterfield Station be constructed some distance from the Apache Pass spring.

With the arrival in early February of two companies of dragoons from Fort Breckinridge under Lieutenant I.N. Moore, Cochise became convinced that Bascom had no intention of releasing his family. So, he led his warriors away, having executed his own hostages in a manner learnt from the Spanish. The method of their death was discovered by Moore's dragoons when they scouted the country for Cochise:

We came upon three bodies, one of which, upon examination, I knew to be that of Wallace by the gold filling of some of his teeth, and the other two could be no others than his fellow prisoners. They had been tortured to death. All the bodies were littered with lance holes.

The Americans promptly responded by hanging Cochise's brother and two nephews, along with three captive Coyotero warriors. Cochise's wife and son (probably Naiche who was later to become a close associate of Geronimo) – were subsequently released at Fort Buchanan. Bascom was promoted to captain for his part in an affair which transformed a highly influential and capable chief from friend to embittered enemy.

From his stronghold in the Dragoon Mountains, Cochise, ably assisted by Mangas Coloradas and Geronimo, mounted an unprecedented campaign against the Americans, which was rumoured to have accounted for 150 lives within two months. Geronimo noted with characteristic understatement: 'After this trouble all of the Indians agreed not to be friendly with the white men any more.'

Greatest of Wrongs

Cochise's war coincided with the sudden withdrawal of troops from the

A variation of the Apache 'flop-head' club with wooden handle and stone head encased in buckskin and decorated with leather fringes, beadwork and tin cones.

With his San Carlos Apache police, Agent John Clum affects the delicate arrest of Geronimo and his warriors, on the morning of 21st April 1877, at Cañada Alamosa parade ground.

The cross and crescent emblems embellishing these three Western Apache buckskin medicine caps may relate to the early twentieth century daagodigha religious movement of the prophet Daslahdu. It was a movement which ended when his followers cut off his head and his proclaimed resurrection failed to occur. The caps are adorned with beadwork, eagle feathers and silver buttons hammered from U.S. coins.

Chiricahua lands as the Americans became pre-occupied with their own internal and far bloodier conflict (Civil War 1861–65).

When, in 1862, General James Carleton's California Volunteers re-possessed New Mexico and Arizona from the Confederates for the Union, Cochise summoned Mangas Coloradas, and the two great chiefs joined forces against the invading Bluecoats.

Carleton dispatched Captain T.L. Roberts east, through the Chiricahua Mountains, to establish a station on the now obsolete Butterfield Trail. With him were 114 infantry, with seven cavalrymen to escort the wagon-train, and two mountain howitzers. When his advance party entered Apache Pass on 15th July 1862, Cochise, Mangas Coloradas, Geronimo and over 400 warriors were watching them. Roberts' approach to the old Butterfield Station was abruptly halted by the concerted crack of the Apache rifles. Cochise's men were concealed behind crude breastworks thrown up on the crags overlooking the station. The soldiers withdrew in disorder but then rallied and reached the station. However, the Apache's heavy fire kept them from the precious Apache Pass spring, and Roberts noted: 'They seemed very loath to let me have water'. Then Roberts ordered up his howitzers. They bellowed smoke, 12-pound cannister exploded over the Apache breastworks, and Cochise's warriors where thrown into retreat.

When Roberts dispatched six cavalrymen back to warn his approaching wagon-train, fifty warriors under Mangas Coloradas set off in pursuit. One of the riders, Private Teal, fell behind and was surrounded by the Chiricahua, who circled Teal. He put up a rapid fire with his carbine until the largest of the warriors fell in his sights. A shot struck Mangas Coloradas in the chest, and as the Apache rushed to their wounded chief, Teal made a miraculous escape.

Cochise led a second attack against the Apache Pass station when the wagon-train was escorted in, but was again repulsed by the howitzers. With the subsequent arrival of troops under Carleton, work began on the construction of Fort Bowie, while the Chiricahua were left complaining: 'We would have done well enough if you had not fired wagons at us'.

The wounded Mangas Coloradas was carried to Janos, where stern Mimbreño, burnishing their knives, told the Mexican doctor that he would do well to cure their chief. Mangas was soon well again.

In January 1863, Mangas Coloradas and a band of followers, weary of war, sought to make peace with the miners at Pinos Altos. Geronimo protested and refused to accompany them, but his people offered the followers of Mangas most of their arms and ammunition. On 17th January, when Mangas Coloradas approached Pinos Altos under a flag of truce he was abruptly seized by miners and California Volunteers under Captain E.D. Shirland. The huge chief was taken to Fort McLane where Brigadier General J.R. West, Carleton's second-in-command, purportedly told his soldiers: 'Men, that old murderer has got away from every soldier command and has left a trail of blood for 5,000 miles on the old stage line. I want him dead or alive tomorrow morning, do you understand, I want him dead.'

That night, a miner watched the soldiers guarding the chief, 'Heating their bayonets in the fire and burning his feet and legs. Mangas rose upon his left elbow, angrily protesting that he was no child to be played with.' The sentries then shot Mangas Coloradas four times. They scalped then decapitated him, and boiled his head in a big black pot, to be sent east as a phrenologist's exhibit. This murder, said Geronimo, was 'Perhaps the greatest wrong ever done to the Indians'.

Vengeance

The avenging Chiricahua now, 'went to war in earnest', whilst Carleton pursued a policy of extermination against them. After the murder of Mangas Coloradas, West's soldiers assailed the nearby camp of the chief's immediate followers, decorating the bridles of their horses with the scalps of his family.

Hearing no word of Mangas Coloradas' fate, Geronimo led his poorly armed band towards Cochise's stronghold once more. After stealing some cattle and killing four drovers, however, the Bedonkohé were surprised by US troops, and lost seven of their number. Having thrown his spear and exhausted his supply of arrows, Geronimo escaped by dodging from side to side of his horse.

Geronimo's band were attacked twice more in a fortnight, and were reduced to fighting with clubs and rocks before the US troops abandoned their pursuit.

After frequent expeditions against the Eastern Chiricahua, by May 1865 Carleton felt secure in sending Captain N.H. Davis to instruct the hostile bands to settle at Bosque Redondo. Many Navajo and Mescalero tribesmen – traditional enemies of one another – had already been concentrated at this barren and unsuitable tract, and Victorio, Mangas Coloradas' successor among the Mimbreño, arranged a meeting with Davis to tour the hated site. When Victorio failed to show up, Davis characteristically wrote, 'Death to the Apache, and peace and prosperity to this land'.

Victorio soon resumed raiding, while Geronimo recommenced his much-loved tormenting of Mexico. He later recounted the injuries he suffered in his long-running feud with the Mexicans:

I received seven wounds, as follows: shot in the right leg above the knee, and still carry the bullet; shot through the left forearm; wounded in the right leg below the knee with a sabre; wounded on top of the head with the butt of a musket; shot just below the outer corner of the left eye; shot in left side; shot in the back. I have killed many Mexicans; I do not know how many, for frequently I did not count them. Some of them were not worth counting.

Buckskin war-cap (upper) adorned with eagle feathers, silver buttons, and tacks, all invoking the wearer's sacred power during war. The medicine cap (lower) is furnished with eagle 'fluffies' and faint paintings of humming-birds, which would have been believed to act as messengers from the earth to the holy powers of the sky.

Geronimo also joined Cochise's Chiricahua in their wars. Cochise's raids had assumed new venom since the death of Mangas Coloradas – and in 1870, General Sherman noted wryly:

We had one war with Mexico to take Arizona, and we should have another to make her take it back.

Peace at Warm Springs

By 1869, a large number of Mimbreño under Victorio had settled peacefully at Cañada Alamosa Agency, near Warm Springs. The itinerant Geronimo subsequently joined them there:

We had heard that Chief Victorio . . . was holding a council with the white men near Hot Springs in New Mexico, and that he had plenty of provisions. We had always been on friendly terms with this tribe, and Victorio was especially kind to my people.

The 'council' took place in October 1870, when Indian Agent William Arny parleyed with twenty-two chiefs, including Victorio, Nana and Loco of the Mimbreño, Cochise, and probably Geronimo. Victorio was satisfied that Arny promised him the Cañada Alamosa Agency forever. Cochise expressed his desire for peace, but refused to become settled, and rode off south-west into his Chiricahua Mountain stronghold once more. Geronimo feasted and danced with the Mimbreño before striking out alone once again.

Coming of the Generals
Under President Grant's Peace Policy of 1869, three new influences entered the life of the Chiricahua. After successfully subduing the Paiute in Oregon, General George Crook – the 'Gray Wolf' who 'Knew the Indian better than the Indian did' – assumed command of the Department of Arizona. Vincent Colyer (Vincent the Good) and the pious 'Praying General' Oliver Otis Howard were, meantime, dispatched to supervise the establishment of a reservation system for the Apache. Colyer's immediate contribution was to instruct the removal of Victorio's band west from Warm Springs to the unsuitable Tularosa Valley. While Victorio reluctantly attended the Tularosa Reservation, over 1000 Apache fled from Warm Springs in 1871 in preference to the removal.

The next year, Howard was led to Cochise's stronghold by the red-bearded Thomas Jeffords. A remarkable man, Jeffords had, in the mid-1860s, as superintendent of US Mails, ventured alone into Cochise's camp, handed his gun-belt to a Chiricahua woman, and sat down beside the astonished chief. He had asked that the Apache cease their attacks on his mail-trains and, in honour of Jeffords' bravery, Cochise had com-

plied. Afterwards Jeffords returned frequently to drink *tizwin* with the chief.

In the autumn of 1872, Jeffords and two Chiricahua, Ponce and Chie, escorted Howard into the fastness of the Dragoon Mountains. Having been shadowed by Chiricahua warriors for some 100 miles, they eventually reached Cochise's imposing stronghold. The next morning the famed chief rode up, embraced Jeffords, and bid General Howard: 'Buenas dias señor.'

For eleven days the men met in council. Howard urged Cochise to settle at Cañada Alamosa, but was beguiled by the Chiricahua leader's pleas for his people to remain in their homeland:

I was forced to abandon the Alamosa scheme, and to give them, as Cochise had suggested, a reservation embracing a part of the Chiricahua Mountains and of the valley adjoining on the west, which included the Big Sulphur Spring and Rodgers' Ranch.

Cochise accepted peace at this Fort Bowie Reservation, and Jeffords was appointed his agent.

Geronimo claimed to have subsequently met Howard: 'When I went to Apache Pass (Fort Bowie) I found General Howard in command, and made a treaty with him.' Certainly Geronimo was among the Apache responsible for the reservation's failure. Like disillusioned Coyotero from San Carlos and Mimbreño from Tularosa, he visited Fort Bowie

The only known photograph of the Mimbreño leader Victorio, who advocated peace with the whites – until his removal, along with Geronimo, from Warm Springs to barren San Carlos in 1877, precipitated his bloody, three-year war.

165

and depleted its rations. Because the reservation was on the Mexican border, Cochise's men were blamed for these other bands' raids. Credence was lent to this claim by Juh's Nednhi – still roaming the Sierra Madre – selling their stolen goods to the agency Chiricahua.

In 1874, the Indian Bureau admitted the failure of the Tularosa Agency, and shunted the Mimbreño back to Cañada Alamosa, where they had found them. Cochise was also instructed to go, but said of his people: 'The Government had not enough troops to move them, as they would rather die here than move there.' In mid-June Cochise died, and his body was painted yellow, black and vermillion and sealed in an unknown cave. The Chiricahua mourning was terrible: 'As the howling from one rancheria would lag, it would be renewed with vigor in another.'

Concentration

In 1875, General Cook was transferred away to fight the Sioux, and the Indian Bureau launched a disastrous policy of 'concentration', intended to settle all the disparate Apache bands on the hated San Carlos Reservation. Bourke wrote: 'It was an outrageous proceeding, one for which I should still blush, had I not long since gotten over blushing for anything the United States Government did in Indian matters.' An excuse for dissolving the Fort Bowie Reservation was found when two drunken Chiricahua warriors, Skinya and Pionsenay, killed a trader named Rogers, who had sold them whiskey and then refused them more.

In June 1876, John Clum, San Carlos agent, arrived at Apache Pass guarded by fifty-four of the Apache Indian police force he had formed to govern his reservation. Cochise's sons, Taza and Naiche, consented to go to San Carlos, and killed five members of a faction led by Poinsenay who physically opposed them, including Skinya. When Clum commenced his march back to San Carlos, though, he escorted only 42 Chiricahua men and 280 women and children; Victorio's Mimbreño had fled back to their haven at Ojo Caliente and Geronimo had obtained a four-day pass and fled with Nednhi led by Juh and Nolgee to Mexico. There Geronimo resumed his raiding, coming north again the following spring with many stolen horses to establish a hideout near his friend Victorio at Cañada Alamosa.

Hell's Forty Acres

On 17th March 1877, Geronimo drove a large herd of stolen livestock into Warm Springs, then complained bitterly that he could not draw rations for the days he had been absent. A visiting lieutenant, Austin Henely, witnessed the event, and his report of Geronimo's presence eventually found its way to Clum. With two companies of Apache police, Clum made the 400-mile journey from San Carlos to Warm Springs Agency on foot. He arrived with an advance of twenty-two police on 20th April to learn that his military escort under Major Wade would not arrive for two days.

Early on 21st April, Geronimo received word that Clum wished to see him, later writing: 'The messengers did not say what they wanted with us, but as they seemed friendly we thought they wanted a council, and rode in to meet the officers.' Heavily armed and painted for war, Geronimo, Ponce and several warriors entered the parade ground, leaving the remainder of their band on its periphery.

Clum was sitting on the porch of the main agency building to the west, eleven of his Apache police lined up to the north, eleven to the south above the commissary building. As Geronimo approached, Clum warned: 'No harm will come to you if you listen with good ears.' Geronimo, contemptuous of the agent's small force, replied: 'Speak with discretion, and no harm will come to *you*.'

Clum then accused Geronimo of breaking his promises of peace, and said that he had come to take him to San Carlos. Clasping his rifle, Geronimo snarled back his response:

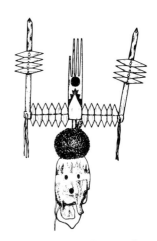

'Gan' mask, with painted buckskin hood topped with turkey feathers and painted wooden horns, with four-pronged centre-piece typical of the Chiricahua. Apache gan or crown dancers impersonated the Mountain Spirits in the most dramatic ceremony of a girl's puberty rite; to don the gan mask was a sacred and dangerous undertaking.

We are not going to San Carlos with you, and unless you are very careful, you and your Apache police will not go back to San Carlos either. Your bodies will stay here at Ojo Caliente to make feed for coyotes.

Now, Clum pointedly touched his hat-brim. The commissary doors suddenly swung open, and eighty Apache police raced across the parade ground to surround the renegades. They had been called up by Clum the previous night, under cover of darkness. Geronimo eased his thumb back against the hammer of his Springfield rifle; Clum touched the butt of his Colt 45; and the Apache police raised their rifles in unison.

Suddenly, a shrill scream shattered the tense silence, as a Chiricahua woman leapt upon the chief-of-police Clay Beauford. As Beauford brushed her aside, Clum stepped forward and took Geronimo's gun, catching the look of hatred in the Apache's eyes.

The other leaders were disarmed, and led onto the porch to council with Clum. When he informed them that they were to be held as prisoners, the renegades leapt to their feet, and Geronimo reached hesitantly for his knife. One of the Apache police stepped in and snatched the blade, and the others raised their rifles once more. Defeated, Geronimo conceded – *In-gew*, 'All right'.

Geronimo, Ponce and six others were shackled in leg-irons, and confined in the corral, since there was no guardhouse. Victorio came into the agency the following day, and consented reluctantly and bitterly to Clum's orders that the Warm Springs Apache also travel to San Carlos. The shackled prisoners were hauled to the reservation, while Victorio

167

followed with their people, plagued with an outbreak of smallpox.

San Carlos seethed with tribal conflict, administrative corruption, and the Apaches' resentment towards overcrowding, poor rations, and the arid lands. Lieutenant Britton Davis subsequently christened it 'Hell's Forty Acres' and Owen Wister wrote:

> The Creator did not make San Carlos. It is older than He. When He got around to it after dressing up Paradise with fruit trees, He just left it as he found it . . . He did not do any work around there at all. Take stones and ashes and thorns, with some scorpions and rattlesnakes thrown in, dump the outfit on stones, heat the stones red hot, set the United States Army after the Apaches, and you have San Carlos.

Resentful of military interference, Clum resigned in July 1877. Geronimo recalled how Clum's proclaimed plans to hang him were curtailed by his successor:

> I was kept a prisoner for four months, during which time I was transferred to San Carlos. Then I think I had another trial, although I was not present. In fact I do not know that I had another trial, but I was told that I had, and at any rate, I was released.

Escape

By September 1877, Geronimo was regarded as settled enough to be made 'captain' of the Warm Springs Apache that remained at San Carlos. The following spring, though, he engaged in a heavy *tizwin* drinking bout with his nephew, whom he then scolded bitterly. The nephew, intoxicated and aggrieved, subsequently took his own life. Geronimo took up with his old ally Juh, and fled to the Sierra Madre. Heading for the border they intercepted a wagon-train, killing its drivers and stealing its cargo of food. Although intercepted by US troops just north of Mexico, they melted away into the mountains after some brief skirmishes. The winter of hardship that followed, persuaded Geronimo and Juh to surrender with 105 followers. They returned to San Carlos in January 1880.

Victorio's War

A more serious outbreak had occurred on 2nd September 1877 when the frequently wronged Victorio, with Loco and over 300 Mimbreño fled from San Carlos. Eleven days later they surrendered at Fort Wingate, New Mexico, and were permitted by the officers there to settle peacefully at Warm Springs. However, a year later when the Mimbreño learnt that they were to be driven back to San Carlos once more, Victorio and eighty followers scattered into the mountains. In February 1879, Victorio and twenty-two remaining comrades surrendered at the Mescalero Reservation. Yet while the Indian Bureau was finally coming round to the idea of returning Victorio to Warm Springs, Grant County issued indictments against him for murder and horse-theft. Alarmed by the appearance of dignitaries – including a judge – who were in fact on a fishing trip, Victorio and his band fled again in August 1879. His patience exhausted, Victorio embarked on the bloodiest of wars, his warriors killing as many as 175 whites before being driven south into the wastes of Mexico. From there they continued to make lightning strikes across the border before vanishing into the mountains once more. Teamsters were discovered suspended by their feet over burning wagons, and during Geronimo's absence from San Carlos it became unclear which band was responsible for which outrages.

In May 1880, Victorio's warriors even raided San Carlos, but failed to persuade Geronimo's followers to join the war. Finally, on 15th October, Victorio was cornered by Mexican troops under veteran Indian fighter Colonel Joaquis Terrazas at Tres Castillos, three low peaks between Chihuahua and El Paso. Seventy-eight Apache were killed, and it is believed that Victorio stabbed himself in preference to being captured.

His war was adopted by the wrinkled, rheumatic little 70-year-old Nana. Victorio's death had created a new fury among the renegades and Nana's warriors set the pattern of the coming years by hacking to pieces a Mexican sergeant discovered riding in Victorio's saddle, a month after the great chief's death.

Nana, who despite his age and infirmity, assumed leadership of the hostile Mimbreño after Victorio's death in 1880. He conducted a terrifying campaign against the whites before he joined Geronimo's cause.

Holding Back The Daylight

At San Carlos, a restless Geronimo was digging ditches and growing water-melons, as he recalled:

We were treated very badly by the Agents here . . . and that made us want to leave. We were given rations but not all that we should have had . . . They gave us a little manta and cloth . . . not enough to make a breechcloth. On account of these things we were dissatisfied.

Miners invaded profitable parts of San Carlos, while Mormon farmers diverted the Gila River waters away from the Apaches' plots to their own. Beef contractors drove their thirsty cattle through that same river on ration day before weighing them, so that the Apaches were 'Paying for half a barrel of Gila River water delivered with each beef'. Corruption was rife and reached as far as the Indian Commissioner E.A. Hayt and the newly arrived agent J.C. Tiffany.

Shaman's Dance

As with so many other tribes, the Apache found hope in a new revivalist religion and its prophet, in this case a Coyotero shaman named Nocadelklinny. He augured the return of dead Apache warriors when the whites had been driven from the country, and his ritual dances on Cibecue Creek, 40 miles from Fort Apache, attracted large crowds in the summer of 1881. Formerly hostile bands camped there together, and Apache police sent to investigate returned without their weapons, and in a daze.

When Nocadelklinny ignored summonses to San Carlos Agency, and to Fort Apache, Agent Tiffany dispatched Fort Apache commander Colonel Eugene A. Carr to arrest him. On 30th August, Carr, with over eighty cavalrymen and twenty-four Apache scouts, rode to Cibecue Creek feeling 'rather ashamed to come out with all this force to arrest one poor little Indian'.

After seizing the diminutive preacher, Carr's command was assailed by Nocadelklinny's restless disciples, and in a confused mêlée the White Mountain Apache scouts mutinied. A number of Indians and troopers, including Captain E.C. Hentig, were killed, and Nocadelklinny was shot several times while crawling away from the scene, before being finished off with a sergeant's axe. Carr escaped during the night to Fort Carr, which the rampaging Apache besieged briefly before dispersing.

The Renegades

In response to the Cibecue outbreak, General Willcox, Commander of Arizona, rushed twenty-two companies of troops to San Carlos, much to the alarm of Geronimo. On ration day, 30th September 1881, a group of White Mountain Apache under Chief George, who had been paroled after admitting their part in the Nocadelklinny fighting, were attacked

Chiricahua medicine cap adorned with the horns and fur of a pronghorned deer, sacred paint designs, and locks of horsehair. Such medicine hats were worn by shamans during the medicine ceremonies. In addition, they were worn by warriors to invoke supernatural power against their enemies.

by troops and fled to Geronimo's Chiricahua band. Fearing for their own lives, Geronimo, Juh, Naiche and some seventy Chiricahua followers bolted from the reservation. After killing thirteen whites and fighting a rearguard action against four cavalry troops under Captain R.E.Bernard, they crossed into Mexico. In the Sierra Madre, the fugitive Chiricahua were re-united with Nana's small Mimbreño band, who that summer had won eight pitched battles, killed over fifty men, and eluded 1,400 troops in a remarkable 1,000-mile trek along the border.

At dawn, 18th April 1882, those Mimbreño who had remained in peace at San Carlos under Loco saw a silhouetted line of Apache warriors advancing from the west of their camp, with others crossing the river on horseback or clinging to floating logs. Their leader was beckoning: 'Take them all! No-one is to be left in the camp. Shoot down anyone who refuses to go with us!' The sixty audacious invaders were Geronimo's Chiricahua, who drove Loco's several hundred unarmed Mimbreño along the Gila River and away from their captivity at San Carlos, 'conscripting' them into the renegades' war. The chief of Indian police, Albert Sterling, with fifteen scouts, attempted to intercede, and was shot from his saddle. One of the raiders carried away his boots and, according to one questionable account, other warriors played football with Sterling's severed head.

After rustling several hundred sheep to feed their wards, and skirmishing briefly with troops from Fort Thomas under Colonel George W. Schofield, the Apache headed south for the safety of the Chiricahua Mountains. In the Steins Peak Range, though, six companies of cavalry under Lieutenant Colonel George A. Forsyth, guided by Indian scouts, stumbled upon the renegades. Hiding away the women and children of Loco's band in the highlands, the Chiricahua fought a brilliant retreat along Horseshoe Canyon. After a day's fighting, Forsyth withdrew; he had killed only one of the Apache and had lost seven of his men and a number of horses.

The Apache hurried south through the night, with Geronimo singing a medicine song to hold back the daylight. One of the Chiricahua recalled that he 'sang, and the night remained for two or three hours longer. I saw this myself.'

The Apache cavalcade covered 70 miles in the next two days, only relaxing their vigilance when they crossed the Mexican border into territory they considered their own. They camped some 25 miles north of Janos, unaware that two 6th Cavalry companies under Captain Tupper had maintained their pursuit in violation of the border agreement with Mexico. Tupper's forces struck the camp at dawn on 28th April, and after mounting a fierce defence, the Apache scattered. Tupper fought the Chiricahua rearguard, including Geronimo, all day, but as night fell the Chiricahua straggled south once more.

Fleeing from the attack, the renegades had become strung out over

Chiricahua warrior of about the 1880s. Like almost all of Geronimo's men, everything, from his armament, costume and appearance reflects the mixture of styles which resulted from the long history of Apache raiding on settled peoples of whatever origin.

some distance by the following day. An advance party, including Naiche, Chato and the Mimbreño Kaetennae, rested short of the Sierra Madre foothills to smoke tobacco. Loco's Warm Springs band of women and children, catching the scent of roasting coffee and believing it came from Naiche's party, pressed on and stumbled into the midst of Colonel Lorenzo Garcia's Mexican 6th Infantry.

Garcia's men, relishing their good fortune, fell upon the women and children without mercy. Many were shot while fleeing for the mountains. Geronimo and the warrior Chihuahua, who had been forming a rearguard against Tupper, rushed forward with thirty-two warriors to a deep arroyo, where their women were frantically scraping out rifle-pits. From here the Chiricahua turned the first Mexican charge. When a mule carrying 500 rounds of ammunition was downed 50 feet from the Apache's position, an old woman scrambled out towards it. Amid the flying bullets, she cut the ammunition free, and, too frail to carry it, dragged the precious sack back to the arroyo.

Taunting in Spanish, 'Geronimo! This is your last day!', the Mexicans charged again. Covered by the Chiricahua, Geronimo's cousin Fun, 'the bravest of all the band', leapt from the gully and, displaying his power to dodge bullets, turned the Mexican assault. At noon, an Apache woman called from her perch on a mesquite tree that the Mexicans had gone, but Geronimo, not recognising her voice, kept his warriors entrenched.

Garcia returned in the afternoon, but his repeated attempts to dislodge the Chiricahua were futile. As evening approached, the Mexicans resorted to setting fire to the grass, at which point Geronimo reportedly called: 'If we leave the women and children, we can escape'. Fun responded, 'Say that again and I'll shoot,' and proceeded to pin the Mexicans down while the women, amid the smoke and creeping darkness, carried their children to safety.

On 30th April, Forsyth and Tupper met the Mexicans. With the bodies of the seventy-eight Chiricahua dead at their feet, eleven of them warriors, Garcia handed Forsyth a formal protest for crossing his borderline, and told him to leave Mexico.

Gray Wolf In The Sierra Madre
General George Crook, 'The Gray Wolf', was restored as commander of the disorderly Department of Arizona in September 1882. He immediately re-organised San Carlos, declaring an amnesty for those involved in the Cibecue outbreak, evicting the white squatters, and permitting the various Apache bands to settle anywhere on the reservation they chose. He also re-introduced identification tags and revived Clum's Apache police and courts.

Stationing a cavalry unit at San Carlos to prevent Geronimo making a second raid, Crook then re-organised his system of mobile pack-trains and enlisted five companies of White Mountain Apache scouts. He signed on 'the wildest I could get,' noting of the hostiles, 'Nothing breaks them up like turning their own people against them'. The Gray Wolf's appetite had been sharpened by the 'hot pursuit' agreement of 29th July 1882, which permitted American troops to cross the Mexican border when chasing Indians.

The Chiricahua's capture of Loco's people had cost the lives of twenty-six warriors, but the largest number of renegades for some years was now camped with the Nednhi under Juh and Geronimo. Soon after the fight with Garcia, these two led their bands to trade at Casas Grandes with the Mexicans. But the Apache succumbed again to their weakness for alcohol, as Geronimo recalled:

We began to trade, and the Mexicans gave us mescal. Soon nearly all the Indians were drunk. While they were drunk, two companies of Mexican troops, from another town attacked us, killed twenty Indians, and captured many more. We fled in all directions.

Among those captured was Geronimo's wife Chee-hash-kish, and he subsequently resumed his raiding of Sonora with all his old spite.

Pursuit of Chato

By March 1883, the raiders had grown short of ammunition for their Springfield and Winchester rifles; so while Geronimo raided Sonora for livestock, Chato, Chihuahua and Bonito led 26 warriors to steel bullets from the United States. Terrorizing Arizona and New Mexico in six days of lightning raids, Chato's raiders killed 26 people, including Judge H.C. McComas. One warrior, Beneactiney, was killed in the raids, and his closest friend, the White Mountain Apache Tzoe deserted and sought refuge at San Carlos

On 1st May, Crook crossed the border in pursuit of Chato. With him were five officers, 42 men of the 6th Cavalry, a train of 260 mules, and 193 eager Apache scouts, under Captain Emmet Crawford. 'To polish a diamond,' Crook remarked, 'there is nothing like its own dust.' At Crook's side was his trump card, Tzoe, whom the soldiers had christened Peaches because of his smooth, pinkish complexion.

Peaches guided Crook into the 'knife-edge mountains' and through the labyrinthine canyons of the Sierra Madre, where the scouts soon outpaced the white soldiers. At the top of a tortuous climb, on 15th May, the scouts discovered Chato's camp and, ignoring Crook's orders, opened fire. Nine of the renegades were killed, including the mother of Speedy, who in his fury split little Charlie McComas' skull with a rock. Bonito's daughter was captured, and Crook sent her to seek the surrender of the Apache. Bewildered to find the Gray Wolf prowling their own lair, and dismayed to see their own people as his mercenaries, the Chiricahua bands, one by one, came in. By 20th May, 121 renegades had surrendered.

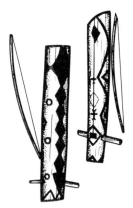

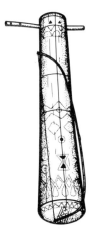

Large, two-string Apache fiddle and smaller, one-string fiddles. They are crafted from plugged and painted agave stalks strung with horsehair, and fitted with tuning pegs. The bows are of curved sumac strung with horsehair. Probably adapted from European influences, the fiddles were played at social occasions, an Apache practice which probably continued even in captivity.

Geronimo's Power

Three days earlier Geronimo was 120 miles to the east of Sonora, where his raiders had captured six Mexican women on the road from Galeana. Jason Betzinez recalled that Geronimo, squatting by a fire, suddenly announced: 'Men, our people whom we left at our base camp are now in the hands of US troops! What shall we do?' Confident of Geronimo's power to know what was occurring in another place, the warriors voted to hurry back to their families. Two days into the journey, Geronimo made a declaration:

Tomorrow afternoon as we march along the north side of the mountains we will see a man standing on a hill to our left. He will howl to us and tell us that the troops have captured our base camp.

The incident occurred as he had predicted, 'true as steel,' and Geronimo's band now knew that their people were indeed in Crook's hands.

On 20th May 1883, Geronimo advanced warily into the Gray Wolf's camp, and Captain Bourke said of him: 'He and his warriors were certainly as fine-looking a lot of pirates as ever cut a throat or scuttled a ship.' In the first of three long parleys, Crook told Geronimo, 'I am not taking your arms from you, because I am not afraid of you'. He warned that Mexican troops were approaching and expressed indifference towards Geronimo's surrender.

On 28th May, Crook started for San Carlos with 52 men and 273 women and children captives, including Nana, Loco and Bonito. Remarkably, though, the Gray Wolf let Geronimo, Naiche and Chato remain behind, accepting Geronimo's word that he would head for San Carlos in two months after he had 'Gathered up every last man, woman and child of the Chiricahua'.

As Geronimo's deadline came and went, and Arizona citizens blustered against the Apache, Crook dispatched a company of scouts to the border under Lieutenant Britton Davis to escort any returning renegades to San Carlos. By November 1883, Naiche, Chihuahua and Mangas – the son of Mangas Coloradas – had surrendered their people. On 7th February 1884, Chato gave himself up to Davis.

Finally, in March, a Yavapai shaman pronounced that Geronimo would arrive in three days on a white mule. Sure enough, the defiant Chiricahua rode up on a snow-white pony some days later. At his heels was a billowing dust-cloud, stirred by the hooves of 350 cattle that he had brought with him as his 'trust fund'. Barging his horse against Davis' mount, Geronimo expressed his distaste at being given a military escort.

Davis made slow progress to San Carlos with the cattle in tow, and at Sulphur Springs Geronimo insisted on halting to graze the beasts. Confronted here with a sub-poena for Geronimo's arrest from an Arizona marshall, Davis and the Chiricahua leader somehow drove the cattle off in silence during the night, and reached San Carlos unchallenged. Davis noted: 'If any people knows how to be quiet, it is the Apache.'

On the reservation, the stolen cattle were confiscated, despite Geronimo's protests that 'These were not white men's cattle, but belonged to us, for we had taken them from the Mexicans during our wars'. Geronimo could not understand this affront, and nurtured his resentment in the coming year.

The *tizwin* Breakout

Crook's campaign – 'one of the boldest and most successful strokes ever achieved by an officer of the United States Army', according to Bourke – had settled the bands of every Apache headman at San Carlos. Even the irreconcilable Juh had been silenced in the autumn of 1883; having become drunk once more at Casas Grandes, he had fallen from his horse into a river and drowned ignominiously.

Geronimo and the other leaders subdued by Crook selected Turkey Creek, 17 miles south-east of Fort Apache for their new home, under the supervision of Lieutenant Britton Davis. Although the land was more suited to stock-raising, as were the Indians, the Indian Bureau decreed that all Apaches must farm, and issued the Chiricahua with the appropriate equipment. Davis reported:

Some of them tried out their new plows in the San Carlos river bottom. The ponies, unaccustomed to a slow gait, preferred to trot or gallop, and the plow-points were oftener above ground than in it. Now and then a point would strike a hidden root or stump; then the plowman would execute a somersault over the plow handles, to the great delight of his friends.

For a year, Crook could boast that no 'depredation of any kind' was committed by the Apache, and Geronimo was noted as amongst the best farmers in his group – though his wives did most of the work. Beneath the surface, however, tensions at San Carlos were growing. Davis had made Chato first sergeant of scouts, and was on good terms with Benito, Loco and Geronimo's son Chappo. But Geronimo, Naiche, Chihuahua, Nana and young Kaetennae remained aloof and surly. Then the beating of wives and cutting the tip off the nose of an unfaithful bride had been forbidden. The drinking of *tizwin* had also been banned and the Chiricahua considered such prohibitions as intrusions on their traditional way of life.

In June 1884, Davis was climbing a ridge, when, hearing a turkey gobble, he turned and shot it. That night, one of the women he paid to spy on his wards cast a stone against Davis' tent, and whispered that if he had reached the top of the ridge he would have been shot by Kaetennae, who was drunk on *tizwin*. Regretting having eaten the 'gobbler' that saved his life, Davis effected the delicate arrest of Kaetennae without incident. He was later tried and sent to Alcatraz. Many of the Chiricahua

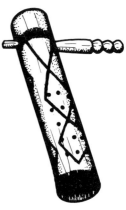

Another type of Apache fiddle (lower), and a flute crafted from a giant reed, pierced with sound-holes partially covered by a buckskin tie. The flutes were very often played by young men courting, and designs such as a butterfly were cut and burned into the reed to lure the young women.

resented this, feeling the charges had been fabricated by Mickey Free, Peaches and Chato, Kaetennae's rival to inherit Nana's chieftainship.

Rebellion and Flight

Since July 1883, Crook had assumed full military control at San Carlos, carried out with great success by Captain Crawford, whom the Apache trusted implicitly. When a new agent, C.D. Ford, arrived in December, however, friction between the military and civil authorities grew. Its immediate consequence was the failure of the Turkey Creek Chiricahua's clothing ration to arrive during the severe winter. Crawford subsequently resigned from his post and re-joined his regiment in disgust. Geronimo, perceiving the breakdown in authority, asked continually if the Gray Wolf had also left.

Through the night of 14th May 1884, Geronimo and the other Chiricahua leaders held a *tizwin*-drinking session. Still under the influence, they confronted Davis at dawn, demanding the suspension of the laws against alcohol and wife-beating. Chihuahua, 'palpably drunk,' challenged the lieutenant: 'We all drank *tizwin* last night, all of us in the tent outside, except the scouts; and many more. What are you going to do about it? Are you going to put us all in jail? You have no jail big enough even if you could put us all in jail.'

Davis told the chiefs that such a serious matter would have to be referred to Crook, and sent a telegram to Crawford's replacement, Captain Pierce, to be forwarded. The inexperienced Pierce, on the advice of his hungover chief of scouts Al Seiber, filed the telegram. With every day that Crook failed to appear, the Apache grew more nervous until on 17th May, Geronimo, Mangas, Naiche, Chihuahua and Nana, with thirty-eight warriors and ninety-two women and children, fled once more from San Carlos. Geronimo had apparently instigated the outbreak by telling Chihuahua and Naiche that he had killed Davis and Chato.

Sometime before I left, an Indian named Wadiskay had a talk with me. He said, 'They are going to arrest you,' but I paid no attention to him, knowing that I had done no wrong; and the wife of Mangas, Huera, told me that they were going to seize me and put me and Mangas in the guardhouse, and I learned from the American and Apache soldiers, from Chato and Mickey Free, that the Americans were going to arrest me and hang me, and so I left.

(Geronimo)

As the Chiricahua fled, the wily Nana cut the telegraph lines where they passed through the notch of a tree and then hid the sabotage by tying the wires together with rawhide. The fugitive Apaches then hurried south for 120 miles before making camp.

Learning of the outbreak later that day, Davis, after trying to alert the cavalry at San Carlos on the broken telegraph, summoned his scouts. When he ordered the scouts to ground arms, Chappo, Perico and one other, abandoning a plan hatched by Geronimo to kill Davis, suddenly

A Chiricahua brandishes murdered Chief of Indian police Albert Sterling's boots, as Geronimo 'press-gangs' Loco's Mimbreño into his cause, driving them away from San Carlos Reservation, at dawn, 18th April 1882.

fled. With troops from Fort Apache, and his loyal scouts, Davis set off in pursuit of Geronimo's band, but abandoned the chase when he saw their dust cloud some 20 miles distant the following morning.

Travelling south, Chihuahua and Naiche had discovered Geronimo's treachery in telling them of Davis' death, and threatened to murder the deceitful Bedonkohé. The feuding bands now scattered. Mangas and Geronimo continued towards Mexico by separate routes, while the betrayed Chihuahua and Naiche turned north-east into the Mogollons, to consider an immediate return to San Carlos.

Ten days later, Lieutenant Davis' scouts made up Chihuahua's mind for him when they discovered his camp and opened fire. Chihuahua's band resumed their flight to Mexico, leaving a bloody trail, and covering 90 miles without halt. Davis continued his pursuit, finding two new-born Apache babies dead on the trail. Just short of the border, the Apache killed three troopers of the 4th Cavalry in Skeleton Canyon.

Naiche and his wife. After the deaths of Cochise in 1874 and of Naiche's elder brother Taza in 1876, Naiche succeeded to the hereditary chieftanship of the Chiricahua; but he never displayed the statesmanlike authority of his father. He supervised the peaceful removal of his people from Fort Bowie to San Carlos in 1876, but was persuaded to join Geronimo in his subsequent outbreaks.

Beneath a flour-sack truce-flag, Lt. Gatewood and troopers, with Apache scouts Martine and Ki-eta, interpreters Horn and Maria, receives Geronimo's final surrender, near Fronteras, 24th August 1886.

Some seventeen civilians were killed during Chihuahua's flight; but the Arizona newspapers blamed all atrocities upon Geronimo, whose ghoulish legend they had helped to create. A posse from Silver City reported finding a rancher named Phillips dead, along with his wife and infant, and his 5-year-old daughter hanging alive from a meat-hook. In all, the outbreak claimed the lives of thirty-nine whites in New Mexico and thirty-four in Arizona.

The Chiricahua bands met up together in the Sierra Madre, where Geronimo assumed the leadership rôle once held by Juh. They began raiding in even smaller groups than before, and citizens on both sides of the border lived in constant fear of their appearance.

Crook had meantime placed a troop of cavalry at every water-hole on the border, knowing that the renegades must raid the United States for ammunition. On 11th June, Captain Crawford entered the Sierra Madre with one troop of 6th Cavalry and Lieutenant Davis' Apache scouts.

Twelve days later, scouts led by Chato killed one of Chihuahua's women, and captured fifteen. Captain Wirt Davis entered the eastern side of the Sierra Madre with two 4th Cavalry troops and Lieutenant Gatewood's White Mountain scouts. This force struck Geronimo's camp on 7th August, capturing a third of his band's women and children. Once again Geronimo saw his family, including his two wives, carried away by his enemies.

The Chiricahua struck back across the border in the autumn of 1885. With only four companions, Geronimo ghosted into Fort Apache on 22nd September, re-captured his wife and child, and vanished into Mexico beyond pursuit of the San Carlos scouts.

The most spectacular raid was mounted by Chihuahua's brother Ulzana, who with ten warriors plundered 1,200 miles of the south-west in a month, killing 38 people and capturing 250 horses.

On 23rd November, Ulzana struck Fort Apache, killing twelve of the reservation Indians in vengeance against the San Carlos scouts hunting their own people. The White Mountain Apache killed one of the raiders, proudly cutting off his head.

The Canyon of Tricksters
With the expiry of his Apache scouts' six-month enlistment, Crook withdrew Crawford and Davis in November. At San Carlos there was great excitement and ceremony among the medicine men, as the commands were re-equipped and a fresh draft of scouts recruited. In December, Crawford and Lieutenant Maus re-entered Mexico with only pack-trains and Apache scouts under Tom Horn, abandoning the cavalry that had hindered the Apache scouts in the previous campaign. On the Rio Aros, in the heart of Juh's old domain, Crawford's scouts scented the hostiles' trail, and pursued it in an unbroken eighteen-hour march. At dawn on 11th January 1886, they struck the renegades' rancheria,

driving them from the camp, and seizing all their ponies and possessions. The Chiricahua, demoralised to find the Bluecoats and their own relatives still hounding them, sent Victorio's sister, the noted woman warrior and shaman Lozen, to negotiate a parley for the next morning.

At daybreak on 12th January, as Geronimo, Naiche and Chihuahua prepared to council with the trusted Crawford, a body of Mexican irregulars, who had also been trailing the hostiles, suddenly appeared. Mistaking the American scouts for the renegades, they opened fire. As Crawford mounted a boulder to identify his men, he was shot through the head. The scouts, screaming for vengeance, then felled the Mexican commander and as many as a dozen of his troops, as Geronimo's bemused Chiricahua looked on. Lieutenant Maus eventually restored order and in the next council with Geronimo took nine hostages, including old Nana and one of Geronimo's wives, as guarantee that the renegades would bring their people in to council with Crook on the border in 'two moons'.

The Chiricahua gathered for the parley in the aptly named Cañon de los Embudos, the Canyon of Tricksters, 84 miles south of Fort Bowie. They visited the camp of Maus only in small groups, keeping their camp 500 yards away on a hill skirted by ravines, 'in such a position that a thousand men could not have surrounded them with any possibility of capturing them'. Crook arrived on 25th March, respecting the hostiles' request not to bring troops. Among his small party were the reformed Kaetennae, Nana, Alchise – son of Cochise and a dependable scout – and 'a couple of old Chiricahua squaws sent down with all the latest gossip from the women prisoners at Bowie'. In a preliminary council Crook found the Apache 'very independent and as fierce as so many tigers; knowing what pitiless brutes they are themselves they mistrust everyone else'.

Apache scouts under Lieutenant Maus in 1886. Maus assumed command of the scouts when Captain Crawford was killed by Mexicans. Parleying with Geronimo on 15 January 1886, he persuaded the Chiricahua to emerge from the Sierra Madre and meet with General Crook in March.

Chihuahua, Naiche and a third chief 'Catle' met Crook's delegation the following day, with Geronimo – perspiring and nervously toying with a rawhide thong – as their spokesman. Telling Crook, 'The Sun, the darkness, the winds are all listening to what we now say,' Geronimo listed his grievances at San Carlos. When Crook suggested that Geronimo had lied in the Sierra Madre about wanting peace, Geronimo countered: 'Then how do you want me to talk to you? I have but one mouth; I can't talk with my ears'. 'Your mouth talks too many ways,' Crook snapped. 'If you think I am not telling the truth,' Geronimo answered, 'then I don't think you came down here in good faith.'

The renegades' leaders councilled for a day, before Chihuahua and Naiche, soothed by the unexpected presence of Kaetennae, agreed to surrender on condition that they be exiled to the east for not more than two years, and that their families could join them there. Nana 'toddled after them, but he was so old and feeble that we did not count him,' wrote Bourke. Geronimo too conceded:

> What the others say, I say also. I give myself up to you. Do with me what you please. I surrender. Once I moved about like the wind. Now I surrender to you and that is all.'

Bearcoat and Long Nose

The Chiricahua celebrated the end of their war with copious quantities of *mescal* liquor purchased from an unscrupulous trader named Tribolet near San Bernardino Springs. Bourke, on the morning of 28th March, found Naiche unable to stand up, and Geronimo and four warriors 'riding on two mules, drunk as lords'. Tribolet completed his work by informing the Chiricahua that they would all soon be hanged. That night, Geronimo and Naiche fled into a drizzling rain with twenty warriors, including Fun, Chappo and Geronimo's cousin Perico, thirteen women and six children.

Crook, who had hurried on to Fort Bowie, leaving his captives under Maus' supervision, was informed by General Sheridan that his surrender terms were unacceptable, and only unconditional surrender of the Chiricahua would satisfy President Cleveland. Learning of the fresh outbreak, Sheridan implicated Crook's scouts, and on 1st April 1886 the Gray Wolf resigned.

The seventy-seven Chiricahua who had surrendered under Chihuahua were shipped to Fort Marion, Florida on 13th April, the day after the arrival of Crook's vainglorious successor General Nelson 'Bearcoat' Miles. Miles immediately disbanded Crook's brilliant scout units, and flooded the field with 5,000 soldiers, a quarter of the entire army. They were co-ordinated by the flashing mirrors of thirty heliograph stations; Geronimo avoided their mountain-top sites, as bad medicine.

Miles assigned a principal pursuit force of 100 hardy troopers and a dozen Apache 'trailers' to Captain H.W. Lawton, relentlessly to scour the Sierra Madre. Their horses broke down within a week, and in four

months of arduous campaigning the unit succeeded only in once capturing the hostiles' ponies and equipment. Lawton noted:

During this short campaign, the suffering was intense. The country was indescribably rough and the weather swelteringly hot, with heavy rains day and night. The endurance of the men was tried to the utmost limit. Disabilities resulting from excessive fatigue reduced the infantry to fourteen men, and they were worn out and without shoes.

After eluding Lieutenant Maus' scouts, Geronimo's desperate band had fled to the vicinity of Casas Grandes, where a forlorn negotiation for peace resulted in another whiskey-sodden murder of one of the Chiricahua warriors by the Mexicans. At the end of April, the Apache raided throughout Arizona. At Peck's Ranch, they murdered Mrs Peck, her 13-year-old child and a ranchhand, and captured a ten-year-old girl. They spared Peck himself when he started ranting, and stole his boots instead.

After killing two citizens of Nogales in Arizona, Geronimo was pursued by troops under Captain Hatfield. Hatfield struck on 15th May, capturing the Chiricahua ponies and equipment; but lost it all again, along with his cook and blacksmith, when ambushed by Geronimo on his homeward march. One warrior, Kieta, wounded in Hatfield's attack, now deserted and surrendered at Fort Apache.

Geronimo also continued his personal war with Mexico, recalling: 'We attacked every Mexican found, even if for no other reason than to kill. We believed they had asked the United States troops to come down

Western Apache rawhide medicine shields, painted with sacred designs in order to protect their carrier in battle. The smaller shield (twentieth century) is painted with simple designs relating to the four directions and trimmed with red cloth and eagle feathers. The larger shield (nineteenth century) is hung with a large number of eagle feathers. It includes, among its complex paint designs, a depiction of Slayer of Monsters; this was the Apache culture hero, to whom the vital 'enemies against' power was ultimately traced. Such shields could only be safely made by those with the medicine to control their great power, and were purchased only by wealthy warriors.

to Mexico to fight us . . . We were reckless of our lives, because we felt that every man's hand was against us.' Mexican troops surprised Geronimo's camp in June, re-capturing the girl kidnapped at Peck's ranch, and in July the Chiricahua renegades withdrew into the Sierra Madre to draw breath.

Fourteen US citizens had been killed in Geronimo's latest campaign when, on 1st July, Miles made an inspection of Fort Apache. There he learnt from Kieta, the deserter of Geronimo's cause, that many of the hostile band were keen to surrender. In a move more reminiscent of Crook, Bearcoat dispatched Kieta and a Nednhi named Martine to induce the renegades to surrender. The 'cool, quiet, courageous' Lieutenant Charles B. Gatewood, who had won Geronimo's trust while stationed at Fort Apache under Crook, was summoned, despite ill health, to accompany them.

Gatewood and his envoys joined Lawton's command on Aros River, 200 miles south of the border, where in mid-August they received word of Geronimo's presence in Fronteras, only 30 miles below the border. Here the Chiricahua were feigning peace to obtain *mescal*, while the Mexicans returned the compliment, hoping to trap and slaughter the Apache.

Borrowing six troops and interpreters Tom Horn and José Maria from the command of Lieutenant W. Wilder near Fronteras, Gatewood located the trail of the two Chiricahua women who had been obtaining the *mescal* for Geronimo. Raising a piece of flour sack as a flag of truce, Gatewood followed their tracks, sending Martine and Kieta in advance. After three days they discovered the Apache camp; Kieta was held hostage and Martine released to inform Gatewood that Geronimo was willing to council.

On the morning of 24th August, Gatewood, whom the Chiricahua knew as Long Nose, approached the council site on the bank of the Bavispe. He had been reinforced by thirty troops from Lawton's unit, but three painted Chiricahua warriors suddenly appeared and ushered them away. Then, Gatewood recounted:

By squads the hostiles came in, unsaddled and turned out their ponies to graze. Among the last to arrive was Geronimo. He laid his rifle down twenty feet away and came and shook hands, remarking my apparent bad health and asking what was the matter. . . .

Gatewood then passed on Bearcoat's message.

Surrender, and you will be sent *with your families* to Florida, there to await the decision of the President as to your final disposition. Accept these terms or fight it out to the bitter end.

At first Geronimo insisted that his band should be allowed to return to San Carlos; but Long Nose revealed that Miles had already removed the other hostile Chiricahua to Florida. At this, Naiche became concerned for the welfare of his family, and the following day Geronimo – being

advised by Gatewood to 'Trust General Miles and surrender to him' – agreed to accompany Lawton's troops to the border, providing Long Nose remained with the Chiricahua.

Evading a Mexican ambush and quelling plans by Lawton's men to slaughter the Chiricahua, Gatewood coaxed Geronimo to Skeleton Canyon in the Peloncillo Mountains. Here they waited for nine days while Bearcoat Miles avoided the council, meeting a dinner appointment in Tucson, and flashing messages over his heliograph inquiring as to the possibility of Lawton trapping and murdering the Apache!

Finally, after Geronimo had sent Perico as an emissary to Fort Bowie, the reluctant general arrived in a cavalcade of wagons on 3rd September. He found that Geronimo made a profound impression:

One of the brightest, most resolute, determined looking men that I have ever encountered. He had the clearest, sharpest dark eye I think I have ever seen, unless it was that of General Sherman when he was at the prime of life . . . Every movement indicated power, energy and determination. In everything he did, he had a purpose.

(General Miles)

Geronimo's hostile band of warriors, posed for one of a remarkable series of photographs taken in the Canyon of Tricksters by Camillus S. Fly, 25–27 March 1886, preceding their surrender to General Crook. Fly, 'cooley asked Geronimo and the warriors with him to change positions, and turn their heads or faces, to improve the negative', and obtained the only photographs taken inside a hostile Indian camp. Geronimo stands in the middle, wearing a spotted bandana, with Naiche to the far right in heavy coat, slouch hat, and a spy-glass case attached to his belt.

Surrender

Miles reiterated Gatewood's assurance that Geronimo would be reunited with his family, and promised him a spacious reservation in Florida. On 4th September 1886, Geronimo surrendered for the last time:

We placed a large stone on the blanket before us. Our treaty was made by this stone, and it was to last until the stone should crumble into dust; so we made the treaty, and bound each other with an oath. I do not believe that I have ever violated that treaty; but General Miles never fulfilled his promises.

Three warriors escaped during the march back to Fort Bowie, and created an enduring legacy of fresh raids from the Sierra Madre. Geronimo lined up with his people on Fort Bowie parade ground on 8th September, while the grinning soldier band struck up with Auld Lang Syne. The last Apache renegades were disarmed and hauled in wagons to

Bowie station. There Geronimo traded his moccasins for a pair of boots before boarding the train. Martine and Kieta were thrown in with the hostiles they had helped to catch, and at 2.55 in the afternoon the train jolted away, carrying Geronimo to further treachery.

Broken Promises

I hope nothing will be done with Geronimo which will prevent our treating him as a prisoner of war, if we cannot hang him, which I would much prefer.

With this opinion, President Cleveland sent word for Geronimo's train to be halted at San Antonio, Texas, and demanded to know why Miles had neither imprisoned the Chiricahua at Fort Bowie nor obtained their unconditional surrender as ordered. Bearcoat, touring Arizona as the conqueror of Geronimo, evaded questions of exactly what terms he had offered the hostiles, while they languished in Texas.

In flagrant violation of Gatewood and Miles' terms, Geronimo and his warriors were then diverted to the 'dungeons of Old Fort Pickens', on Santa Rosa Island, Pensacola Bay, Florida. They arrived on 25th October 1886, and were later joined by Mangas' captured band.

Cleveland, unaware of the distinction between hostile and settled Apache from his distant desk, and swayed by Miles' advice, had ordered the brutal removal of even the peaceful San Carlos Chiricahua in September. A group of 381 of them joined Chihuahua's band at Fort Marion in Florida on 20th September, one warrior named Massai having jumped from the train and escaped. A further thirteen, including Chato and Kaetennae, were diverted there while returning from a trip to Washington. A subsequent confidential report revealed that sixty-five of the eighty-two warriors held at Fort Marion had served loyally as scouts against Geronimo.

There is no more disgraceful page in the history of our relations with the American Indians than that which conceals the treachery visited upon the Chiricahuas who remained faithful in their allegiance to our people.

(Bourke)

The women and children of Geronimo's band were also sent to Fort Marion, and for two years Geronimo was denied the promised reunion with his family.

While Geronimo proved a popular tourist attraction, prowling the fortifications at Fort Pickens, his relatives at overcrowded, swampy Fort Marion succumbed in great numbers to malaria. Their children were snatched away to be scrubbed, shorn and schooled at Carlisle Indian School, where one quarter died from tuberculosis.

Largely due to the efforts of Crook and Mr Herbert Welsh of the

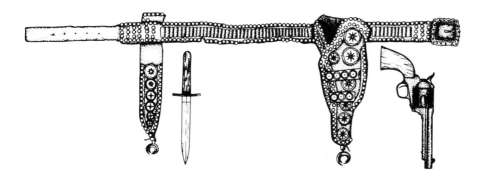

Indian Rights Association, the Fort Marion Chiricahua were removed in April 1887, only to be 'dumped' at the little better Mount Vernon Barracks, Alabama. The families of Geronimo's band were now allowed to join them at Fort Pickens, where one observer noted of Geronimo: 'He is a terrible old villain, yet he seemed quiet enough today, nursing a baby'.

All the Fort Pickens prisoners were transferred to Mount Vernon Barracks on 13th May 1888, joyfully re-joining their tribe. Here, though, Geronimo observed: 'We had no property, and I looked in vain for General Miles to send me to that land of which we had spoken'.

'They Sicken and Die'

When the Gray Wolf visited the Chiricahua in January 1890, he found them 'broken in spirit and humbled to the dust'. He rebuffed Geronimo as a liar, but councilled with the other headmen, and advocated the Apaches' removal to Fort Sill, Indian Territory, Oklahoma. This was eventually achieved in October 1894, and the Apache women wept joyfully on the journey when they heard the familiar sound of coyotes howling once more.

At Fort Sill, the Chiricahua were divided into villages, rather like their old bands, each under a headman – including Geronimo – who received the uniform and pay of an army scout. They farmed and raised cattle with some success, but their death-rate remained mysteriously high. When the Apache are taken away from their sacred homeland, Geronimo explained, 'they sicken and die'. Infant mortality remained high, and after the death of his own grandson Geronimo organised an old-time ceremony to discover if an old man was 'witching' the children, killing them to prolong his own life. The presiding shaman sang four songs before rounding on Geronimo and screaming: 'You did it! So you could live on.'

The Last Renegade

The aging Geronimo raised a considerable amount of money at Fort Sill by manufacturing bows and arrows and selling everything from autographed photographs of himself to his own buttons. Invented stories such as that of his coat of ninety-nine scalps increased Geronimo's legendary status, and the American public lionised him when he was 'exhibited' in a Cadillac at Roosevelt's inaugural procession and in the 1904 St Louis exposition. He became a studied observer of white society and exacted excellent appearance fees, investing his money with a frugality not generally associated with the Indians. However, in his heart, he yearned for his homeland, as he told a newspaper reporter in 1908:

I want to go back to my old home before I die. Tired of fight and want to rest. Want to go back to the mountains again. I asked the Great White Father to allow me to go back, but he said no.

Geronimo's love of liquor had endured and in February 1909, in his eighties, he drank his fill of whiskey in Lawton town. Riding unsteadily back to Fort Sill, he slipped from his horse, and spent the night sprawled in some damp weeds. He contracted pneumonia and on the 17th February Geronimo died.

The enduring symbol of Indian ferocity and implacable resistance to the white man, Geronimo was still officially a prisoner of war at his death. In 1913 his people finally were released from this status; on 4th April, 187 of the Chiricahua returned to Apacheria at last to live quietly with the Mescalero in New Mexico.

Deerskin quiver ornamented with typical beaded and fringed panels, and possibly made for sale by Geronimo while he was imprisoned.

So the last renegade was dead; the most determined foe of the US government was gone, his struggle finally over; the last handful of his people had gone home. It was the end of an era, the closing chapter to one of the most violent periods in America's formative years.

Chronology of Events

1540	Coronado explores the Southwest.
1821	Mexico wins independence from Spain.
1829	JUNE Geronimo born Goyahkla, the 'One Who Yawns'.
1835	Sonora offers bounties for Apache scalps.
1837	Mimbreño chief Juan José killed by James Johnson; succeeded by Mangas Coloradas.
1846–8	Mexico and USA at war.
1850	Chiricahua massacre Mexicans at Ramos.
1858	Geronimo's family massacred by Mexican troops at Janos.
1859	Geronimo leads massacre of Mexicans at Arispe.
1861	The Bascom Affair.
1861–5	The Civil War.
1862	Apache Pass battle.
1863	Mangas Coloradas murdered.
1869	President Grant issues Peace Policy.
1871	General George Crook becomes Commander of Department of Arizona.
1871	Victorio's Mimbreño removed from Warm Springs to Tularosa.
1872	Cochise accepts Fort Bowie Chiricahua Reservation.
1874	Victorio's Mimbreño removed back to Cañada Alamosa Agency, Warm Springs.
1874	Cochise dies.
1875	Indian Bureau launches Apache 'concentration' policy.
1876	Agent Clum removes Fort Bowie Chiricahua to San Carlos Reservation; Geronimo flees.
1877	Clum arrests Geronimo at Warm Springs; his and Victorio's people removed to San Carlos.
1878–80	Geronimo flees reservation to raid Mexico with Juh.
1877–80	Victorio's War.
1877	Victorio flees San Carlos for Warm Springs.
1879	Victorio surrenders at Mescalero Reservation.
1880	Victorio killed at Mexican ambush; Nana continues Victorio's war.

1881	Cibecue Outbreak; Nocadelklinny killed; San Carlos scouts mutiny; Geronimo flees.
1882	Geronimo's renegades 'kidnap' Loco's Mimbreño from San Carlos.
1883	MAY Geronimo surrenders to Crook in the Sierra Madre.
1884	MARCH Geronimo respects his surrender, coming in to San Carlos.
1885	17 MAY Geronimo flees San Carlos after drinking *tizwin*.
1886	12 JANUARY Captain Crawford killed by Mexicans while parleying with Geronimo.
1886	27 MARCH Geronimo surrenders to Crook in the Canyon of Tricksters.
1886	28 MARCH Geronimo gets drunk and flees once more.
1886	1 APRIL Crook resigns.
1886	13 APRIL Surrendered Chiricahua shipped to Fort Marion, Florida.
1886	25 AUGUST Geronimo surrenders to Lieutenant Gatewood.
1886	4 SEPTEMBER Geronimo makes his formal, and last, surrender to General Miles.
1886	SEPTEMBER Some 394 peaceful Chiricahua shipped from San Carlos to Fort Marion.
1886	OCTOBER Geronimo and his warriors sent to Fort Pickens, Florida; their families go to Fort Marion.
1887	APRIL Fort Marion Chiricahua removed to Mount Vernon Barracks, Alabama; Geronimo's family join him at Fort Pickens.
1888	MAY Fort Pickens Chiricahua join their people at Mount Vernon Barracks.
1894	OCTOBER Chiricahua removed to Fort Sill, Oklahoma.
1909	17 FEBRUARY Death of Geronimo.
1913	4 APRIL Of remaining Chiricahua, 187 move to the Mescalero Reservation; 84 choose to remain at Fort Sill.

Bibliography

Adams, A.B. *Geronimo* New English Library, 1975.

Ball, E. *In the Days of Victorio* Corgi, 1970.

Barrett, S.M. *Geronimo. His Own Story* Abacus, 1974.

Betzinez, J. *I Fought With Geronimo* University of Nebraska, 1959.

Bourke, J.G. *On the Border With Crook* Time Life, 1980.

Brown, D. *Bury My Heart at Wounded Knee* Barrie & Jenkins Pan, 1970.

Capps, B. *The Great Chiefs* Time Life, 1975.

Cremony, J.C. *Life Among the Apaches* University of Nebraska, 1868.

Davis, B. *The Truth About Geronimo* Yale University, 1929.

Debo, A. *Geronimo* University of Oklahoma, 1890.

Forbes, J.D. *Apaches, Navajo and Spaniard* University of Oklahoma, 1960.

Hook, J. *The Apaches* Osprey, 1987.

Mails, T.C. *The People Called Apache* Promontory, 1974.

May, R. *Indians* Bison, 1982.

Opler, M.E. *Southwest Handbook of N.A. Indians* Smithsonian Institution, 1983.

Utley, R.M. *History of the Indian Wars* Mitchell Beazley, 1977.

Worcester, D.E. *Apaches. Eagles of the Southwest* University of Oklahoma, 1915.

Index

Page numbers in *italics* refer to illustrations; text references may occur on the same page.

191

Illustrations
Colour plates by Richard Hook
Line illustrations and maps by Chartwell Illustrators
Photographs and other illustrations courtesy of: Arizona Historical Society (pages 142, 159, 165, 169 and 177); Arizona State Museum (pages 150, 179 and 183); Bernisches Historisches Museum (pages 29, 64, 68, 69 and 88); Field Museum of Natural History (page 39); Idaho Historical Society (pages 109, 115, 121 and 131); Library of Congress (page 43); Museum of the American Indian, Heye Foundation (pages 4, 6, 16, 31, 33, 35, 46, 47, 73 and 105); Nebraska State Historical Society (pages 80, 85, 86, 89, 91 and 92); Royal Ontario Museum (page 101); Smithsonian Institution National Anthropological Archives (pages 50, 88, 96, 98, 135 and 138) and National Portrait Gallery (pages 13, 23 and 193); Trustees of the British Museum (page 45); Ulster Museum, Belfast (page 9)